RHOSSILI: THE LAND, LANDSCAPE AND PEOPLE

RHOSSILI:
THE LAND, LANDSCAPE AND PEOPLE

Leonard Beynon

West Glamorgan
Archive Service
Gwasanaeth
Archifau
Gorllewin Morgannwg

2008

First publication – December 2008

Copyright © Leonard Beynon and West Glamorgan Archive Service, 2008

Published by
West Glamorgan Archive Service, Swansea

ISBN 978 0 9551703 2 4

Printed in Wales by
Gwasg Dinefwr Press, Llandybie, Carmarthenshire

Typeset in 12pt Helvetica

Foreword

I believe that people of my generation have a duty to record a way of life in the Gower Peninsula, which has now largely disappeared.

To be able to add his record, as Len Beynon has so ably done, and bring alive the history of the people who lived in Rhossili from medieval times to today is a fine achievement.

Rhossili is a very special place and, having lived in Gower for most of my life, Len's skilled narrative brought back some vivid memories.

I grew up in Porteynon and Horton and in many respects we were great rivals with Rhossili from 'wrecking' to hockey, from competitions at the Gower Show to the best village pub. We were, of course, all great friends living in rural and seaside village communities, many speaking a South Gower dialect, which is hardly ever heard today.

I went to Porteynon village school in 1940. It was a bit different to today's primary schools and the evacuees made for an interesting exercise in integration!

The way people lived and worked are skilfully highlighted in this book and bring a most important addition to our knowledge of the history and people of West Gower and Rhossili.

Len has increased our understanding of a wonderful part of our beautiful peninsula and I congratulate him on the success of his research.

Sir Robert Hastie
KCVO, CBE, KStJ, RD*, JP

Editor's Preface

This latest publication by the West Glamorgan Archive Service brings to the attention of a wider audience a work which has has been a labour of love for many years by the author, a native of the village of Rhossili. Leonard Beynon spent much of his working life away from the land, landscape and people which shaped his formative years but Rhossili has happily been the place of his retirement, during which time he has amassed a wealth of information on the history of the parish, using primary sources in the National Archives at Kew, the National Library of Wales in Aberystwyth and the West Glamorgan Archive Service in Swansea.

This is a work with a huge timespan, from prehistory to the present, but with a focus on elements which make the landscape of Rhossili distinctive. One of these is the Vile, a rare survivor of the medieval system of strip farming. Other landscape elements explained in the book are also seen across Gower and similar parts of coastal Wales, such as the prehistoric cliff forts, quarries, limekilns and relics of World War II which dot the parish. A unique feature, however, which has shaped the history of Rhossili over the centuries is the dramatic coastline contained within the parish, the broad sweep of Rhossili Bay ending in the long peninsula of Worms Head. This landscape forms a magnificent backdrop to the story which unfolds in the following pages, a story of the dozen or so families – the Stotes, the Bydders, the Beynons, the Bevans and others – who made up a good part of the isolated community of Rhossili between the sixteenth and nineteenth centuries, until the village was transformed, like so many others, by the advent of the motor car and the modern world.

Kim Collis
West Glamorgan Archive Service

Acknowledgements

In preparing this book, I have received help, encouragement and information from many people, in Rhossili and elsewhere, too numerous to mention.

I am particularly grateful to Mrs Doreen Leighton (*née* Richards); to my daughter Mrs Caroline Beynon for her help with the typescript; to Dr John Alban for guidance on the scope of the book; and to Mr Kim Collis, West Glamorgan County Archivist, for assistance in editing and proof-reading the text.

I am grateful to the Royal Commission on the Ancient and Historical Monuments of Wales for permission to use their excellent aerial views of archaeological sites in Rhossili, and also to the West Glamorgan Archive Service and Swansea Museum for use of images from their collections.

This book would not have been published without the support of the West Glamorgan Archives Committee and I would like to record my thanks to the Committee and particularly to its former chairman, Sir Robert Hastie, who has very kindly written a foreword to the text.

Leonard Beynon
Rhossili
August 2008

Contents

Rhossili: the Land, Landscape and People

Rhossili is a village at the south-western tip of the Gower peninsula. Gower was the first area in the country to be scheduled under the National Parks and Access to the Countryside Act 1949 when it was designated as an Area of Outstanding Natural Beauty in 1956. As such it is visited by many thousands of people who enjoy the spectacular scenery of the limestone cliffs which at Rhossili, as elsewhere on the southern coast of Gower, are two hundred feet high. The geological significance of a feature such as Worm's Head is perhaps of less importance than the majesty of its appearance; the bone caves in the limestone cliffs may have less appeal than the bays beneath them. Yet, as David Rees points out in his role as editor of *A Gower Anthology:* *'Throughout most of Gower the visitor becomes aware of a remarkably powerful sense of the past, of a continuity which stretches back to the beginnings of human life.'*

Nowhere is this truer than at Rhossili, and the feeling of timelessness makes itself known to those born and bred in the parish, as well as to the visitor. Standing on Rhossili beach in the early morning of a late September day when the tide is going out and there is no one else to be seen on the growing extent of sand, there is the obvious sense of loneliness. But there is at the same time a growing awareness that the scene you are enjoying has been largely unchanged for thousands of years. The only sound is that of the waves, the landmarks are the familiar ones of Worm's Head and Burry Holms. An evocative description by W.G. Hoskins in *The Making of the English Landscape* comes to mind:

> *Nothing has changed. We are seeing the natural world through the eyes of men who died three or four thousand years ago, and for a moment or two we succeed in entering the minds of the dead . . . It is easy, too, to feel this kinship while watching the summer morning waves falling with a meditative indifference on beach still untrodden by the human race. There are many such timeless scenes.*

It is a little uncanny to see in print the thoughts that have gone through your mind many years before reading them in what has been rightly called one of the greatest history books ever written.

The boundaries of the parish of Rhossili eventually became fixed in June 1984 when minor modifications were made in its boundary with the neighbouring parishes of Llandewi and Llangennith. The boundary between Rhossili and Llangennith is denoted by a river – Diles Lake – about two-thirds of the way along the three mile stretch of Rhossili Bay. The course of the boundary along Rhossili Down was never so clearly defined, a particular problem being found at Sluxton at the time of the Tithe Commutation Survey in 1845 in deciding which tithes belonged to which parish. A similar awkwardness meant that the fringes of Llandewi intruded on the parish of Rhossili at another point where Pilton Green inhabitants were attached to this village while their neighbours were in Rhossili. The third parish adjacent to Rhossili was Porteynon.

It might be thought that these brief points would clarify the settlement of Rhossili – the two parts of Rhossili and Pitton being separated for many years before, gradually, Middleton filled up the area between them. This would, however, ignore the fact that two parts of the parish of Rhossili as it is today were originally included in two other parishes – Penmaen and Penrice. It seems strange to find Paviland as part of the parish of Penmaen, with the tithe map noting *'This Hamlet is 7 miles from the Parish Church'*. Similarly, Pilton was included with Penrice parish and it was not until 1880 that the 'tidy' civil parish of Rhossili was created in the form we take for granted today. By Local Government Board Order No. 10,666 dated 3 June 1880, a detached part of Penmaen known as *Paviland* comprising 3 houses and 15 persons in 1881 and a detached part of Penrice known as *Pillon* [Pilton], comprising 5 houses and 23 persons in 1881, were transferred to *Rhoscilly*. The result of these changes was to increase the population of Rhossili to 68 inhabited houses and 332 people. The number of people was below this figure for nearly the next century, reaching 335 in 1961 and 333 in 1971.

Two notable local historians have commented on the uncertainty with which the name Rhossili is written throughout recent times. Stephen Lee in an article on the population of *Rhossili* in 1951 commented: *'It is amusing to find that the census reporters seem to have been as uncertain how to spell the name of the parish as people are today. In 1801 it is Rosilly, in 1811 Ros-sily, in 1821 and 1831 it appears as Roscily, and then it is steady at Rhoscilly from 1841 to 1881. In 1891 it becomes Rhossilly, the present Post Office spelling and from 1911 it is Rhossili which is the spelling now used by the County Council on the signposts.'* These variable explanations were summed up by the late Robert Lucas in his booklet on Rhossili: *'There are fifteen ways of spelling Rhossili; none of them much use in deciding what the name means.'* We will have to use the modern conventional spelling of Rhossili except where it appears in an alternative form in old documents. In the *Taxatio Ecclesiastica* of 1291 it is *Russely* or the alternative *Rosseby*. The name *Rossulby* in 1319 is followed by *Russely* in 1353. The list seems endless!

A definitive history of the parish of Rhossili has still to be written. Although aspects of its contribution to the rich tapestry of the history of Gower are clear, or even vivid, at times, others are vague and misty. We know very little of the religious settlement centred round a monastery at Rhossili which is identified in charters from the sixth to ninth centuries. In medieval times we are aware of the existence of the manor of Rhossili, with sub-manors of Fernhill, or *Vernhill*, and Pilton *alias* Pitton, but it has not been possible to clearly identify *Forshulle* which was held by the same lord in the early fourteenth century. The deserted medieval settlement in an area called the Warren at Rhossili also creates speculation that it was abandoned in the twelfth or thirteenth centuries with the Norman doorway in the present church at Rhossili being brought up to the new site of the village. The fact that the initial settlement of Rhossili – a little hamlet at the furthest extremities of the Gower peninsula – is invariably linked with the manor of Landimore throughout the centuries does not help to make its contribution distinct. This large manor, geographically distant from Rhossili, was the sun, with the planet of Rhossili orbiting around it. Sometimes they come closer together, but even then parts of the planet are in shadow.

The village of Rhossili has been the focus of a number of studies by historical geographers, most notably Dr Margaret Davies and Frank V. Emery. The use of estate maps, tithe maps, probate records and manorial records enabled them to throw light on the distinctive open-field feature at Rhossili called the *Vile*. Theses such as that of Doreen Richards (now Mrs Doreen Leighton) have contributed to the knowledge of the agricultural history of Gower, including Rhossili, in the last one hundred and fifty years. *An Agricultural and Social Study of Rhossili* was the title of her dissertation which gave so many helpful leads to the present study. More recently, Robert Lucas produced two narratives: *A Gower Family* and *Rhossili: A Village Background.* The deliberately broader canvas of the background booklet on Rhossili highlights themes of shipwrecks and smuggling, quarries and kilns, church and chapel. To these narrative sources must be added the *History of West Gower* by the Reverend J.D. Davies, which contains so much original source material.

It will be recognised that these secondary sources have been used, with many others, to provide very necessary detail of the background to the history of Rhossili. This synthesis of documentation on Rhossili has been coupled with the use of manorial records, hearth tax returns, land tax assessments, tithe maps, surveys, and census enumerators' returns to provide an original – and it is hoped, interesting – narrative of the history of Rhossili. It could be argued that it is overly ambitious to describe the history of the parish of Rhossili in terms of the land, landscape and people but these are the main threads which link the story in a way which is not too chronologically biased. If the end result does not match the ambition then it will be necessary to use the plea contained in *A Breviat of Glamorgan* by Rice Lewis, written between 1596 and 1600:

> *Gentle Reader no doubt but thou wilt laugh me to scorne, for bindinge up these bundell of papers, wherein thou shalt have occasions enough so to doe. But yet sith they were gathered out of many old peeces of paper, and with paines sought for of me in so many odd places. I hope thou wilt beare some thinge the more with me because I looke for no gaine but thy gentle takeing and be silent, and this hand ready to amend all faultes . . .*

The inspiration for this study of Rhossili came from a growing awareness that not only was it part of the exceptional scenery of the Gower peninsula but it had also what can be claimed to be the unique juxta-position of other landscape features. Rhossili Bay – with Burry Holms and Worm's Head at either end – is overlooked by Rhossili Down with its legacy of cairns, chambered tombs and common land. The limestone cliffs, rising to two hundred feet at the Rhossili end of the bay, are topped by a plateau which contains an open-field system dating to the Middle Ages. Along the cliffs, other promontory forts and bone caves confirm early settlement by man, with the *Red Lady of Paviland* putting Rhossili on the map following Dean Buckland's unique discovery in 1823. The motivation for the necessary research was the desire, as a native of the parish, to know more of its fascinating past. The intention was to try to make some parts of the history of this Gower village intelligible to others – to those born and bred in Rhossili, to those who have come to live here, and to the many thousands who visit Rhossili every year and would like to know more about what they see. Above all, there is the wish to record for posterity the story of a village community whose life over many centuries must have remained basic and remote, but is now altering substantially in the twenty-first century.

Prehistory

The diary of Lewis Weston Dillwyn in 1822 records that on December 23rd of that year, with Miss Jane Talbot of Penrice, he paid his first visit to Paviland Cave. Early the next year, on 21st January 1823, with Miss Talbot and John Traherne, he again visited the cave in the company of the Reverend William Buckland, Professor of Geology at Oxford. Dean Buckland, as he was sometimes called, had the intention of excavating the principal cave – Goat's Hole – following reports that two brothers named Davies of Reynoldston had found bones there, including teeth and part of the tusk of a mammoth as well. The cave has taken its name from the nearby Paviland Farm or Paviland Manor and so the discoveries Buckland made are associated with Paviland Cave. It is reached by a footpath from Pilton Green which arrives at the cliffland at the head of a ravine or valley which has a dry stone wall running down its centre to the edge of the sea. Paviland Cave is set in the base of the promontory called Yellow Top on the west of the valley, and is accessible at low tide near a full or new moon, when the waters retreat just a little bit further.

The initial excavation by William Buckland was followed by a more systematic and rigorous one ninety years later in 1912 by W.J. Sollas, also Professor of Geology in the University of Oxford, with the assistance of Abbé Breuil. His description of the cave highlights its use as a home for hunter-gatherers many thousands of years ago:

> As a temporary habitation it would be difficult to find a more excellent cave than Paviland; situated in the face of the steep limestone cliffs of Gower, it looks out over the changeful waters of the Bristol Channel; behind it is fertile land which must have provided a rich hunting ground in early times; it is roomy, well lighted and dry – with a natural chimney to promote ventilation – serving also to carry off the smoke of a fire kindled beneath; in front of the entrance is a rocky platform with natural seats where the hunter can sun himself in the open air. Add to these that it is concealed from the land-ward view and difficult of access to those unfamiliar with the way. Evidently in every respect a highly desirable hunting lodge! How its advantages appealed to the Palaeolithic man of Glamorgan during the Aurignacian age is shown by the great kitchen midden which forms its floor. Here, it is plain, he fabricated his implements and weapons, here he roasted his meat, flesh of the horse, the bison, the mammoth and the bear, and here on one solemn occasion he entombed his dead.

The exploitation of animals for food was evident from the extensive remains of Palaeolithic fauna which Buckland found; curiously, the bones showed a mixture of species adapted both for warm and cold climates, confirming that the cave could have been occupied during warm and cold periods during the last stages of the Ice Age. They included mammoth, woolly rhinoceros, reindeer, great Irish deer, bison, hyena, horse and cave bear, bones of the last two being the most abundant. It has been suggested that the woolly rhinoceros was fairly commonly exploited by British Upper Palaeolithic hunters, particularly during the earlier part of this period when it may have been more abundant. When killed it would certainly have provided much more meat, fat, bones and skin than either a single horse or a single reindeer. Buckland's excavation revealed many implements and other objects in bone and ivory scattered through the cave earth, and at one spot, buried six inches deep, lay the remains of a human skeleton. It had been buried ceremonially in the extended position and apparently in deliberate association with a mammoth skull. The human skull, vertebrae and most of the right side of the skeleton were missing, probably through erosion by the sea. The part of the skeleton, which remained undisturbed, was covered in red ochre which coloured the surrounding earth for half a yard round.

Buckland has described the find: the skeleton was '. . . *enveloped by a coating of a kind of ruddle . . . the body . . . entirely surrounded or covered at the time of its inter-ment with this substance. Close to that part of the thigh bone where the pocket is usually worn . . . surrounded also by ruddle . . . about two handsfull of small shells . . . At another part of the skeleton . . . in contact with the ribs [were] forty or fifty fragments of small ivory rods nearly cylindrical, and varying in diameter from a quarter to three quarters of an inch, and from one to four inches in length . . . some small fragments of rings made of the same ivory and found with the rods . . . The rings when complete were probably four or five inches in diameter. Both rods and rings, as well as the Nerite shells, were stained superficially with red, and lay in the same red substance that enveloped the bones; they had evidently been buried at the same time with the woman.'*

The slender frame of a young person had deceived William Buckland into identifying the skeleton as that of a woman: *The Red Lady of Paviland* is the name used to describe the find today, even though W.J. Sollas successfully challenged Buckland's identification of the body as female following his re-excavation of the cave in 1912.

Under the auspices of the National Museum of Wales – having secured permission from Miss Emily Charlotte Talbot to re-excavate Paviland Cave – W.J. Sollas assembled a team to go through the deposits in the cave with a view to adding to Buckland's discoveries. Apart from the expert assistance of the Abbé Breuil, Arthur Loveridge, Dr Marett, Henry Balfour and C.J. Bayzand (who was Sollas' assistant), made up part of the team which was completed by Mr Ward *'who proved a mighty man with the spade'*, and two local workmen, Harry Long and Jack Gibbs. Sollas pays a tribute to the last two:

We were extremely fortunate in our workmen, Harry Long and Jack Gibbs, who entered fully into our plans, and watched for specimens with eagle eye; very little that was of value was allowed to escape their hands.

The completeness of the two excavations is revealed in the total find of over 5,000 artefact types; by cutting a section across the floor of the cave, 9 metres from the finds. Over 3,600 flakes and fragments were found, and between 700 and 800 of these were implements. These remain today the most important collection of earlier Upper Palaeolithic artefacts known from Britain. Many of the other finds complemented those made ninety years earlier by William Buckland – numerous fragments of the ivory rods he had described, several well-shaped and finely pointed bone awls, the fragments of an ivory amulet found by Buckland. An ivory punch, marrow scoops or spatulas made of bone and perforated teeth of wolf and reindeer were identified, together with an ivory pendant which was ovoid in shape. This last object was the source of a story which was one of extreme coincidence – one which was, however, demonstrably true. In the course of his explorations Buckland found part of a mammoth tusk in which had been formed an irregular cavity about two inches in diameter, encircled with bony matter. It had been formed probably by the effect of a blow or fracture received while the tusk was in a pulpy state and within the socket. It gave rise to a deformity in the ivory. While Sollas' team were digging *an incursion of the sea washed out of the cave earth a curious egg-shaped body, the nature of which was not obvious to inspection.'* It was later found that the irregular cavity in Buckland's tusk matched the ovoid object:

> *We were therefore able to compare them, and found they tallied to a nicety, the egg-shaped body obviously fitting into the cavity of the injured tusk. Thus, after a lapse of many thousands of years, we were able to bring these objects once again into their natural relations.*

Sollas demonstrated, too, that the Red Lady of Paviland was a Cro-Magnon man. All the evidence suggested that in all the discoverable characters of the skeleton the same racial peculiarities were present. He was a little over twenty-five years of age, probably a little taller than the man of Cro-Magnon itself, confirming that the hunters who found shelter in the cave were men of large stature. They had capacious brains, were more skilled in fashioning tools and jewellery and able to survive sometimes in a tundra-like environment. The picture has been drawn of Paviland Cave as an Upper Palaeolithic base camp – it faced south commanding an excellent view all the way to Exmoor and Lundy over the Bristol Channel plain. The finds described confirm that it was the centre of the most intense Upper Palaeolithic activity known so far in Wales, if not in the whole of Britain. Rhossili appears in the early story of man as a focal point, where Paviland Cave makes a major contribution to our understanding of human development in Britain roughly midway between 30,000 BC when there were perhaps 500 persons in the whole of Britain, and 8,000 BC when there were 5,000 people.

The ability to place discoveries such as those at Paviland Cave within a time scale has been enhanced in the last sixty years by the development of a new scientific technique. Professor W.F. Libby, just after the Second World War, made his discovery of radiocarbon – this was perfected to provide a refined measuring technique called radiocarbon dating. The horizons of archaeologists were expanded by this dating technique which can be used to establish the age of objects found, for example, in caves such as Paviland where the mixture of bones and implements in different strata may create difficulties in establishing a sound time scale. The application of radiocarbon dating techniques to some of the discoveries made many years ago by Buckland and Sollas has brought valuable and fascinating results. In 1967 Kenneth P. Oakley felt that an effort should be made to date the Red Lady of Paviland by the carbon-14 (radiocarbon) dating method, since material from the skeleton would be well within the range of the method's use. He approached the Curator of the Geological Collections in the University Museum, Oxford, where the Paviland skeleton had been preserved. It is now on display in the Pitt-Rivers Museum in Oxford. He secured permission to take samples of bone powder from three bones: left femur and tibiae. After preparing X-ray photographs and casting the bones in silicon-rubber moulds adequate samples were removed by means of a dental drill. Some 62 grams were secured, lower than the quantity of 100 grams which was the ideal minimum weight for material of such antiquity. The 62 grams of bone powder were then submitted to the Radiocarbon Laboratory of the British Museum for measurement, and then the bone powder was replaced in the bones, an invisible repair being possible. This sample was by far the oldest human skeletal material which had been radio-carbon dated on internal carbon up to this time. It put the Red Lady of Paviland firmly in the Palaeolithic period some 18,000–19,000 years ago.

The most recent review of Paviland Cave (1991) comes in a valuable assessment by Stephen Green and Elizabeth Walker – under the auspices of the National Museum of Wales which has its own Palaeolithic Research Project. As part of their research programme into the Palaeolithic Settlement of Wales the roles of Neanderthals and Early Modern Hunters in Wales have been examined in a booklet entitled *Ice Age Hunters* and the age of the Red Lady of Paviland burial has been re-assessed.

The authors of *Ice Age Hunters* point out that the Lower Palaeolithic period in Wales *'is represented only by one living site, Pontnewydd Cave, occupied by early Neanderthals 230,000 years ago & and by half a dozen stray finds of handaxes, from Penylan in Cardiff; Rhossili in Gower; the Severn Estuary; Rhiwbina, Cardiff; Blaenafon, Gwent; and from the valley of the Afon Marlais near Narberth in Dyfed.* Paviland is described as the *largest and most imposing of all Welsh Palaeolithic caves.'*

The original age of 17,460 BP for the Red Lady burial has been re-assessed, as it was made at a time when the radiocarbon technique was less highly developed than at present. A new determination gives an age of 26,350 BP. This date is close to the one of 27,600 BP obtained on an animal bone which now might be possibly, but not certainly, regarded as a food bone. So we now have an even earlier date for human settlement in Rhossili, and the pre-eminence of Paviland Cave is confirmed. But there were other caves along the cliffs of South Gower – including ones at Pitton, Middleton, and Rhossili – where traces of early man have been found.

Medieval Settlement

The medieval village of Rhossili can be identified from a study of two land charters found in the *Liber Landavensis* or Book of Llandaff. The 158 charters which make up the bulk of the Book of Llandaff purport to record grants of land to the Bishopric of Llandaff from the mid-fifth century to the twelfth century. Disputed churches in the Deanery of Gower had, it was claimed, been separated from Llandaff in the sixth century during *the time of mortality, that is of the yellow pestilence.* The earliest charter relating to Rhossili locates *podum/cella Cyngualan* there with three churches dependent on it. It has been dated as around 650 A.D. with the bounds of *Lann Cyngualan* being given at the end: *below the ditches at the sea, following the two ditches to the mountain, along it the boundary of Llangeni.* The second relevant charter refers to the monastery of St Cynwal with a date of around 925 A.D. This is the *podum Cyngualan* of the earlier charter. They both refer to the same institution, a settled community at Rhossili, devoted to religious life, which was ruled over by an abbot or other principal officers. The implication of the two charters is one of continuity from 650 A.D. to 925 A.D., a significantly long period which places an ecclesiastical settlement at Rhossili at a single location but linked with other cells. One has to speculate about the connection between this settlement and the medieval monastic grange later established at Paviland. The medieval church and glebe land which feature from the twelfth century on the land called the Warren, on the terrace of land above Rhossili Bay, were certainly in close proximity to two other religious settlements at Burry Holms and Llangennith. The sixth century monastery at Llangennith founded by St Cenydd was linked with the island hermitage at Burry Holms. Documentary sources refer to *The Church of the Isle* and *the hermitage of St Kenydd-atte-Holme.*

The founding of a monastery at Llangennith from which other saints emerged to convert the people of Gower – Madoc, Rhidian – is well documented, as is the destruction of the church in Viking raids.

The Chronicles of the Princes – *Brut Y Tywysogion* – dramatises the events by the brevity of the entries as in 860 A.D. when *'the black pagans came to Gower, and were driven out with great slaughter.'* In the fateful year of 986 A.D., *'the black Danes came with fleets to the Severn sea and landed in Cornwall, Devonshire, and the Summer country, and landed in Gower, and there burnt the choir of Cenydd and other churches, and spoiled the men of the country.'* One can draw from this a picture of the Viking longships drawn up on Rhossili Bay's long, golden stretch of sands, the smoke rising from the pillaging of the neighbouring village of Llangennith and the inhabitants of Rhossili wondering if they were to meet a similar fate. It may be a little too imaginative a picture but the events did occur. In Glamorgan the following year the Viking raiders *'devastated the choir of Illtud, the choir of Catwg, and the choir of Cyngar and Llan Dav, and others of the best churches, so that a dreadful famine ensued in the country, and many men died in consequence.'* The Norse names of Worm's Head and Burry Holms reflect the use of these features and landmarks, to these could be added the Sweyne's Howes and Sweyne's Eye from which Swansea derived its original identification.

The existence of a medieval settlement in the area known as the Warren was the subject of speculation until a sequence of circumstances led to excavations by the Glamorgan-Gwent Archaeological Trust which removed the sand and earth of centuries before and, in similar fashion to the discoveries at Paviland Cave, highlighted Rhossili again as an intriguing settlement site. Erosion along a footpath leading to Rhossili Bay was compounded by a stream being diverted because its channel was blocked by debris. The flow of water cut through the floor of a building, medieval walling and bones being uncovered close to the cliff edge. The identification of a medieval building and church in this area of the Warren was accompanied by a series of finds which are described in the technical reports.

After the principal excavations in 1980, the sites were re-covered, but some further erosion has taken place since. The site lies just below the cliffs at Rhossili, on land which belonged at that time to Mr David Wilfred Beynon; he also farmed at one time the greater part of the Glebe land in the Warren, together with the upper fields of Well Acre and Church Park. This land is not as good as that found on the main plateau, and the name *Warren* may be indicative of the more profitable use to which the land was put, that is, as a rabbit warren. The principal building excavated was the one badly damaged by the flow of rainwater which had removed about two-thirds of its floor. The building identified as the church was partially examined. It had fine exterior and interior plaster rendering, wall paintings on the cross wall between the chancel and the nave, and lombardic lettering on the east wall of the chancel. The two structures were built in the early twelfth century – documentary evidence supporting the excavation finds. There was also the unexplored possibility of there having been an earlier settlement on the site comparable to the timber predecessor of the church at Burry Holms. The feature mentioned as having been possibly transferred to the new church on the plateau was a doorway – the architectural character of the doorway seen in the present day church being earlier than much of the rest of the building. It could have been part of an earlier church at Llangennith or the one in the Warren. The chevron moulding is normally of twelfth century date, the dog tooth moulding above the chevron pattern being in an Early English style.

The majority of the pottery from the site came from the damaged round-cornered building, also a bone comb and a casket key of iron. The remains of a young child's skeleton were found in a steep-sided pit, confirming, perhaps, the view that this spot in the Warren was holy ground, used for burials as well as being the site of a church. Further discoveries included the remains of a sixteen to eighteen-year-old person, and the bones of three adult males, who might have been shipwreck victims buried near where they were found on Rhossili Bay. The animal bones found included one of a red deer which, with its suggestion of a hunting economy, was both rare and interesting.

The examination and interpretation of the finds confirmed the possibility of this site being established between 1135 and the end of that century. The round-cornered building is consistent with this date range; the iron casket-key was 12-13th century, as was a small horse shoe; the composite bone comb consisted of more than twelve separate toothed units held between two side-plates fastened together by iron rivets – it was thought to be 10-13th century. A whetstone perforated by a hole near the top was also found. The existence of a church and what could be construed as a large domestic house strongly suggested that the site was part of a village. Other explanations, such as that it might be a manorial site under monastic control, are regarded as less likely.

The reasons for the abandonment of the site can be briefly considered: in Glamorgan there are instances such as Kenfig, where villages have been submerged by sand, and a new location sought at higher levels. In Gower, it has been suggested that because of coastal erosion new settlements were established at Penmaen, Pennard and possibly Nicholaston as well as Rhossili. On the site of the Penmaen Burrows might have stood a village called Stedworlango. There were, too, economic reasons why villages were abandoned and Luke Toft has suggested this could have happened at Rhossili. The richer land on the plateau was brought into use, and the impoverished, less valuable land on the Warren vacated. In the exchequer accounts detailing the monies received by the Duchess of Norfolk 1399/1400 the section dealing with rents from Rhossili records *newly arrented lands* leading to the conclusion in Luke Toft's view that it was around this time that cultivation of the lower land on the terrace above Rhossili Bay was phased out. The two centuries of concurrent use of both churches is implied in his view by the retention of the glebe land designation for the fields around the Old Rectory. Coupled with this we have, in my view, the extra evidence of Church Park which was glebe land around the new church, and the name of the adjacent farm which was Glebe Farm. The total acreage of around 52 acres of glebe land at the time of the Tithe Survey and Award 1845-47 reflects the way in which the single church – by the early eighteenth century – had a value as a living above £50 per annum as did Porteynon, compared with Reynoldston which was £35 and Llangennith which was £15.

A new church was built next to a triangular piece of ground called the Green. One of the features of the old medieval church was incorporated into the new structure: the ornamentation surmounting the Norman chevron design above the main door. The small cluster of houses may not have conformed to a distinct pattern, but the patchwork seen today includes the sites of some of the oldest dated buildings in Rhossili. On the Green is a structure identified and illustrated in J.D. Davies' book on West Gower as the base of a village cross; it looks more massive and imposing in the drawing of a century ago. Nearby is Glebe Farm and next to the church is the New Rectory, completed by 1924 at a cost of £2,000. It was built in part of Church Park, which was land attached to the church and forming part of the glebe land held by the incumbent of the living; the remainder of the glebe land is next to the old medieval church site, running along the terrace of land beyond the Old Rectory. The development of an exclusive field system with the strips in the large open-field called the Vile can be analysed to show, as Margaret Davies did, that their use is confined to farmers from one part of the community – that is, Rhossili, the part of the village which developed first. The strips in the fields near the settlement, in the area called the Little Vile, were later enclosed by dry stone walls, hedges of hawthorn, and banks. They made up the infield: the outfield was left and is partly visible today – a series of open strips separated by landshares. The scene is completed by looking at Pound Croft where, as an old survey reminds us, straying animals were impounded and payment had to be made for their release. *There is for pounding – for ox, cow, or bullock, one half penny, and for every horse one penny.*

A more precise portrayal of Rhossili in its medieval, manorial Gower framework can be attempted. The nucleus of English settlement in Gower lay in a group of manors which dated in law from before the death of Henry I in 1135. These were described as *old knights fees* in a charter of 1306: Penres (Penrice); Porteynon; Oxewyche (Oxwich); Hentles (Henllys); Webbelegha (Weobley); Scorlaggeskastel (Scurlage Castle); Renewardestoune (Reynoldston); Knoylestoune (Knelston); Penmayn (Penmaen); Nicholastoune (Nicholaston); Forshulle (Furzehill); Vernhulle and Pyltoune (Fernhill and Pilton); Steentebrugge (Stembridge). The lordship of Gower was divided into two sub-lordships, known as the Englishry (Gower Anglicana) and the Welshry (Gower Wallicana) Within the lordship of Gower, Landimore and Rhossili was included by Clarence A. Seyler under the heading of 'Exceptional Manors' in his study of *The Early Charters of Swansea and Gower* – a label which might be regarded as indicative of the importance of these manors or, more likely, the exceptional difficulty they pose! Later surveys enable us to sharpen the focus for Rhossili: the manor of Rhossili is defined as stretching from Diles Lake – the river which formed the boundary with Llangennith – to *Talgarth's Well* and along a boundary next to the Manor of Fernhill and Pitton *alias* Pilton. There is no hamlet of Middleton, which appears to develop in the seventeenth century. Paviland was included in the manor of Penmaen some seven miles away; Pilton (or part of it) was included in the manor of Porteynon. At one time there were two manors of Pilton – one held by the Mansel family and one by the St John family.

The picture of the distant 'planet' of Rhossili orbiting around the large 'sun' of Landimore is a puzzling feature of the medieval history of the village. It is referred to by Rice Merrick, writing in the sixteenth century in the reign of Queen Elizabeth I: a member of the Turberville family in the early thirteenth century (1217-1220) married the daughter of Morgan Gam and part of the dowry which went to the Turberville family was the Manor of Landimore and Rhossili. The translation of Latin given by Rice

Merrick reads: *'To whome the said Morgan Gam, with the consent of Matilda, his Wife, gave in ffranke marriage, with Maud their eldest Daughter, Landymor, Rossilye the great and the lesse, as the same deed, registred in the book of Neth, testifyeth.'* The intriguing reference to *'the great and the lesse'* which follows the name 'Rossily' has led to speculation that at this time there were twin medieval settlements at Rhossili. One would have been abandoned as a settlement but the church could have remained in use in the Warren, the new settlement was in the process of being created on the plateau overlooking Rhossili Bay where the present church and green are found today. This may be a misreading of the translation since the original Latin is not recoverable, as the *'book of Neth'* has disappeared since Rice Merrick's time.

The Manor of Pilton and Vernel was held by the service of one knight's fee and Vernel (part of it), was held by sub-infeudation by the service of a fourth part of a knight's fee and six swallow-tailed arrows, or in default by payment of 6d. Lands in Pilton appear to have been held by a similar service. The Manor of Landimore and Rhossili was held by one knight's fee and a pair of golden spurs, or 20 shillings annually. Actual extracts from a survey of the time of Queen Elizabeth I confirm these dues – they reliably convey a picture of the dues and services required many years earlier although the tenants' names would have changed:

> *Sir Edward Mansell: 'The same Sr Edward houldeth thereof the Mannor of Porteynon by one knight's ffee of which the Mannor of Pitton alias Pilton is held by one knight's ffee'.*

> *The Mannor of Paviland parcell of the said (late dissolved) Monastery (of Neath) held by one knight's ffee.*

> *The Mannor of Vernhill held by the heires of Morgan Vaughan, Owen Perkins and Richard Bydder by one knight's fee and six swallow-tayled arrows yearely or vjd.*

> *Several parcells of land at Pilton by the service of the fourth part of a knight's fee and six swallow-tayled arrowes yearely or vjd.*

> *The Mannor of Landimore and Rosilly held by the heires of the late Earle of Pembroke by one knight's fee, a pair of golden spurres or xxs. per annum.*

At the time of this Elizabethan survey Robert Heron, John Taylor and William Grove were linked with Pilton – they held lands which had been held by the Knights of St John of Jerusalem before the dissolution of the order at the time of the Reformation in 1540. We can also see the boundaries of the part of the manor of Landimore at Rhossili in a full version:

> *Also there is a parcel of the aforesaid Lordship of Landymore called Rosilly, whose mears and boundes have been time out of mind as followeth:-*

Beginning at a well called Tall-garth-Well and joining to the hedge of Owen Perkins' land called Freeland, and so as that leadeth southward to Elliot's Cross, from thence and crossing the land as the hedge leadeth to a hallar called Stephen's Torrs, and there hence as a stone wall, being a landseare between this Lordship and the lands of Wm. Price Esq., leadeth to a little creek called Newslade, and so westwards by the side of the sea to the farthermost or point of Wormshead, being within the Lordship afsd. and so northward by the side of the sea to the fall of the Dilly-lake being the landseare between the parish of Llangennith and Rosilly, from there hence to a hedge that leadeth to the northside of a house called Hillend being the lands of Sir William Herbert, and so eastward and southward as the meares leadeth to the Commons of Rosilly down by the house and through the garden within seven feet of the east side Wall.

It can be confirmed that Owen Perkins was the tenant of part of the *Mannor of Vernhill* at this time and the boundary line separates the *Mannor of Vernhill* from the part of the Manor of Landimore at Rhossili. The Manor of Pitton *alias* Pilton adjoined Rhossili as well being marked by a *Hoarstone* with boundary continuing to Mewslade. The boundary continues to follow the seashore to Diles Lake and Hillend but the course of the boundary via the common land was vague until it returned to Talgarth Well at the *house of Gronow*. The word *landseare* to denote a boundary line is paralleled by its use in describing the division between strips in the open-field system at Rhossili where the word *landshare* or *lansher,* in the Gower dialect, describes the turf balk which separated one person's strip from the neighbouring one.

It has been suggested that the manor of Landimore, with Rhossili, had a special status, being kept 'in hand' by the lords of Gower during the twelfth and thirteenth centuries. G.T. Clark refers to *the manor of Landimore which, in its descent apart from Gower, has frequently been a mystery to antiquaries.* The Glamorgan County History refers to William Turberville granting the Templars three churches, namely Llanrhidian, Cheriton and Rhossili, situated in three detached portions of the manor of Landimore. This complex geographical is further described:

The dispersed manor of Landimore, as revealed in documentary evidence of the sixteenth century, consisted of remnants of what was once a single extensive holding in north-west Gower. Its westernmost part was Rhossili, its territory including the pastures of Rhossili Down and the cliff plateau. Landimore proper, centred on the castle on the northern coast, was itself separated into two portions by the manor of Weobley. There was a marked contrast between the wide manor of Landimore and the compact manors of the area south of Cefn Bryn.

In any discussion of 'the Land, Landscape and People of Rhossili' it is an essential starting point that the landowners, whose lease of land to the villagers of Rhossili, Middleton and Pitton enabled them to earn their living, are clearly identified. In the 'play' which begins, appropriately, in the Tudor period when Shakespeare made his mark, we need to know the main 'actors': these were the Mansel family represented at this time by Sir Rice Mansel; the Herbert family, whose acquisition of land in the mid-sixteenth century in Gower and Glamorgan made the Earls of Pembroke leading 'players'; the Somerset family, Earls of Worcester and later Dukes of Beaufort. The Beauforts, as overlords of Gower, play the principal role, with the Mansels and Herbert families in key supporting roles. In fact, it is these two families whose part in the play brings them closest to the other members of the cast. When the curtain rises and the stage is occupied by extras – the people of Gower – it is to the Herbert family and the Mansel family that they address their pleas. It is these two families which receive their services and dues. The sequence of documents in the National Archives and the Penrice and Margam Manuscripts in the National Library of Wales enables us to identify villagers and record their part in the 'play'. The 'play' – the history of Rhossili – has much more authentic dialogue as the characters can be placed much more clearly into their proper context. We can raise the curtain and absorb the performance.

Portrait of a Tudor Village

At the outset of the Tudor period the Mansel family had still to recover the lands they held in Gower, which included the manor of Pitton. We see from a successive grant in tail by Philip Mauncell to his three sons John, Leonard and Jenkyn an attempt to avoid the consequences of his arraignment under an Act of Attainder whereby all his lands were confiscated and granted by Edward IV to Sir Roger Vaughan. The attainder was subsequently reversed and the estates restored to his son Jankyn or Jenkin Mansel early in the reign of Henry VII. The Vaughan family were paid off for releasing the manors and lands which were now to be under the control of Sir Rice Mansel (descendant of Jankyn Mansel) who was indebted to Sir Mathew Cradock for providing the necessary money. The growth of evidence from the Tudor period is reflected in terms of leases which confirm tenancies of individuals, in church records and in the payments of lay subsidies which identify individual villagers. Court records provide another source at the outset of Tudor times: one surviving document is described as *a record of twenty sessions of the county court of the Englishry of Gower held during the period 15 October 1498 to 29 June 1500.* The marcher lordship of Gower was in the hands of a descendant of the Herbert family, Elizabeth Herbert, who married Sir Charles Somerset in 1492. He was made Earl of Worcester in 1514 and a later descendant was created the first Duke of Beaufort. The steward of the family estates was Mathew Cradock, his deputy was Gruffydd ap John; their record of attendance of tenants at the manorial courts included two entries – *amercements* – predominantly sums of 3d, 6d or 12d, were imposed in general county sessions on non-attenders who failed to submit *essoins. Essoin* was an excuse for non-attendance by a tenant who had to perform *suit of court.* Different sums accompany the different names such as *Johannes Stephen de Hardewenesdown* [Hardings Down], *Johannes Heiron* [Heron or Hearn] and *Johannes Tucker de Rossilly* who appear to have been assessed at one shilling [xijd] but the word *essoin* appears as well. In addition to these sources, Rhossili shares in the growing evidence of wills and inventories of farmers which provide names as well as the relative prosperity of Rhossili's inhabitants. The sequence of leases which portray the use made of land by the villagers usually refer to arable land, this tends to disguise the fact that in a mixed farming community the livestock would be partly placed on land leased along with arable land, or the villagers would use the common land.

Several documents can be used to illustrate different aspects of the development of the community of Rhossili in the sixteenth and early seventeenth century – they were granted by the Herbert or Mansel family:

> *30th June 1574: Indented Lease by which Edward Harbert of Hendon leased 7½ acres in the parish of Rossillie for their lives successively to*

Thomas Hullen, Elizabeth Wylly and Nicolas Hullen, nephew of Thomas.
Yearly rent: 16s 8d.

28th April 1579: A lease by Edward Mansel, Knt. Of a tenement of 15¾
[acres] land arable and one acre of furze, in the Lordship of Pytton, for three
lives, to Jenkin Doune, of Rossillye, husbandman, Robert his son, and Juhan
his wife.
Yearly rent: 16s 8d.
Witness: IC [John Cradock].

Each of these leases had note of specified conditions and services.

In an earlier lease of 15th October 14 Henry VIII (1522) the kind of conditions mentioned were normally part of most leases: *'Lease for three lives by "Rice Maunxell, Essquyer, lord of Oxmoche", to John Benett, husbandman, Gwenll'yan his wife, and Genett his eldest daughter, of two tenements, not specified, at an annual rent of 25sh. and two heriots, i.e. the best beast and 5sh.'*, and *'for his custum erying, repyng and ledyng, and for gaddryng of hay 18d.'* Here we have services of gathering and reaping, among others, being commuted for a money payment. In a *'Lease by Sir Rice Manxell, Knt., to Owen Perkyn of Rossylly, of tenements and lands in Portynon, for his life, at a yearly rent of 28sh. 2d. and specified services'* we have mention of an Owen Perkyns – he could be the same family whose name is mentioned in another Elizabethan survey. This lease is from an earlier time of 18th March, 7 Edward VI (1553).

In a final example of a lease from a later period we may have evidence of the emergence of a settlement between Rhossili and Pitton at Middleton (i.e. Middle Town):

20th March 1616: Counterpart of a Chattel Lease by the Rt. Hon. William
[Herbert] Earl of Pembroke of a tenement and lands 17½ acres at Middleton
for 99 years determinable on three lives, to Morgan Creeke of Rossille
parish. Yearly rent 35 sh. Entry fine £10.

The difference here of a fee of £10 for entry to the land was intended to achieve a better flow of cash into the coffers of the lord; the payment by instalments of the entry fine was compensated for by the tenant paying a lower yearly rent than might otherwise be asked. The material made available from the Penrice and Margam Manuscripts is invaluable for studies of Gower villages such as Rhossili. The cataloguing by Walter de Gray Birch of many hundreds of documents from the estate archives, and the printing of the catalogues between 1893 and 1904, has meant that the significant detail is more easily available for study. The diligence and expertise of de Gray Birch in summarising the documents is evident when his synopsis is compared with the original deed or lease. The principal figures are noted, the lease details given and any additional points which the particular document uniquely mentions are included. It is possible to use this evidence to compare the parallel development of the different parts of the community of Rhossili, that is, Rhossili, Pitton and the growing hamlet of Middleton. Although the examples given are drawn from the early seventeenth century to illustrate the growth of the village of Rhossili, it will be found that many of the names are those of families which appear in a lay subsidy return of 1543.

John Longe of *Rossille* and his sons John and Ysaacke secured a lease of tenement and lands 17½ acres for their lives for £10 entry fine and 16s 8d yearly rent, from William, Earl of Pembroke and others in 1610. Elizabeth Emlett of *Rossillie*, widow, Robert Grove and Joane Taylor, his wife, also paid an entry fine of £10 and a yearly rent of 24 shillings for a lease of 12 acres, again from the Earl of Pembroke as are all the leases which follow. One to John Parkins (Perkins?) of *Rossilly* for £7 is of a messuage and lands in *Rossilly* for three lives at a rent of 20 shillings a year. Thomas Rogers, with John and William his sons, secured for £11 a lease of a messuage and lands of 15 acres at a yearly rent of 30 shillings. This name crops up in the history of Rhossili village over the next three centuries or more – one Rogers was the holder of Ashtree Farm before it passed to the Richards family. It is noticeable in this sequence, too, that a figure of 2 shillings an acre seems to be the standard rent. Agnes Emlott, widow, John Longe and Anne Cleypitt crop up in a lease of 1626, in the time of Charles I.

Morgan Creeke, who crops up in the early lease of land in Middleton in 1616, features in further leases relating to this hamlet – with Robert Creeke, his son, and Robert's wife Ann, he secures a lease of a tenement of lands, houses, etc. of 15 acres at Middleton for £8 and a yearly rent of 30 shillings. Richard Creeke, for £15, secured a lease, for 99 years determinable on two lives, of 17 acres at Middleton at a yearly rent of 35 shillings. A later lease in *Rossilly* to Robert Grove, Owen Gamon and Alice Creeke adds to the list of parishioners' names, as does a lease in 1619 to Maurice (*Morrice*) Hodge of *Rossillye*, Jennet, his wife, and William, his son. They leased a messuage in Middleton for £10 and a yearly rent of 32 shillings. Two consecutive leases throw up interesting conjecture on relationships: A lease by William, Earl of Pembroke to Marie Baker, wife of John ap Bynon of *Ross-Silly*, of lands and tenements in *Ross-Silly*, is for three lives for £15 and a yearly rent of £3. In a later lease the two lives named are Mary Baker, wife of Thomas Grove of *Rossilly* and John ap Bynon, her son. The 30 acres leased for £15 are described as a messuage and lands – to be held after the death of Ann Batcocke present tenant, for 80 years determinable on the life of the lessee, then to John ap Bynon for his life at a yearly rent of £5. It appears from this rather convoluted transaction that the earlier Marie Baker has re-married and secured the lease of land, after the death of the then tenant, Anne Batcocke, to pass on to her son John ap Bynon who has the same name as her earlier husband, John ap Bynon. One further earlier lease in 1614 was to Hopkin David Edwardes of '*the island of Worms Head in Landimore*' (with reservations of timber, trees, mines of iron and coal and other royalties). The lease was for twenty-one years at a yearly rent of 3s 4d and 20d increase of rent, and secured for Hopkin David Edwardes grazing ground, it is assumed, where sheep could be taken across the causeway at low tide to graze on the Inner Head. The leases of the Herbert family in the late sixteenth and early seventeenth centuries show the general location of the lands and tenement and help confirm the emergence of the hamlet of Middleton. It is noteworthy, also, that we again have an immense variety of the spelling of the village of Rhossili. The yearly rent of 2 shillings per acre for many of the holdings is matched by one of just over three shillings per acre in the larger holding of 30 acres (for a rent of £5) in the name of Marie Baker for her son John ap Bynon.

The reference to a lay subsidy earlier confirms that evidence from the reign of Henry VIII is available of those villagers who paid this graduated direct tax. The lay subsidy assessments of 1524-5 did not apply to Wales as these were before the Act of Union, so it is those of 1543-45 which are a fruitful source of data, as they give names and amounts paid. The First Subsidy Assessment of the Hundreds of Swansea and Llangyfelach, 1543, has been meticulously transcribed and analysed by W.R.B. Robinson, a leading authority on aspects of Gower's history in Tudor days (*Welsh History Review*, No. 2, 1964-5). The information given in this article can be supplemented by a diligent perusal of the names of Gower villagers found in the return in the National Archives at Kew. This has been done for Rhossili, and for adjacent parishes. Coupled with this fascinating source is a second one associated with Richard Davies, Bishop of St. David's, where a return of 1563 shows the number of households in the *Decanatus de Gower – Archidiaconatum Carmerthen*.

The Lay Subsidy Assessment of 1543 is called by that name to distinguish it from ecclesiastical subsidies such as the *Taxatio Ecclesiastica* noted earlier. It arose from the Subsidy Act of 1543, which provided for a subsidy to be paid in three payments in the three following years. The First Subsidy Assessment was intended to establish the basis of who should pay and how much; the assessments for the second and third payment of the subsidy were to be made separately. Persons whose goods were worth less than £1, and those whose lands were worth less than £1 a year were not required to contribute to the subsidy. Persons whose goods or lands were worth less than £20 were assessed in accordance with a graduated scale shown below:

I. Persons with *goods* worth between £1 and £2 to pay 2d
£2 and £3 to pay 4d
£3 and £4 to pay 6d
£4 and £5 to pay 8d
£5 and £6 to pay 1s 8d
£6 and £7 to pay 2s 0d
£7 and £8 to pay 2s 4d
£8 and £9 to pay 2s 8d
£9 and £10 to pay 3s 0d
£10 and £11 to pay 6s 8d

(Persons with goods worth over £11 paid at the rate of 8d for every pound).

II. Persons with *lands* worth between £1 and £2 a year to pay 4d
                                        £2 and £3 a year to pay 8d
                                        £3 and £4 a year to pay 1s 0d
                                        £4 and £5 a year to pay 1s 4d
                                        £5 and £6 a year to pay 3s 4d
                                        £6 and £7 a year to pay 4s 0d
                                        £7 and £8 a year to pay 4s 8d
                                        £8 and £9 a year to pay 5s 4d
                                        £9 and £10 a year to pay 6s 0d
                                        £10 and £11 a year to pay 6s 8d

(Persons with lands worth £11 and under £20 a year to pay 8d for every pound, and persons with lands worth over £20 a year to pay 1s for every pound).

(Source: *The First Subsidy Assessment of the Hundreds of Swansea and Llangyfelach,* W.R.B. Robinson (*Welsh History Review*, No. 2, 1964-5)

The exemption of poorer people does, of course, call into question the validity of the use of the figures produced, to give an estimate of the population based on the assessments. If poorer classes of employed persons such as those in domestic service, and farm labourers, were excluded from the assessment it will certainly give an under-assessment of the population which cannot be quantified. It is evident, too, that for most Gower parishes the villagers we are concerned with will be those on the sliding scale of payments, whose goods or lands were worth less than £20. In fact, with one or two exceptions, it has been possible to produce the majority of the table, which shows relevant payments from most Gower parishes ranging from 2d to 10 shillings. It does enable comparison to be made between Gower villages although, as W.R.B. Robinson confirms and a study of the document makes clear, the membrane (7) which contains the figures and names for Llandewi and Reynoldston is damaged, so that only the Total Persons Assessed and Total Sums Due figures can be given. These are 36 (£2 9s 2d) for Llandewi, and 24 (£1 0s 6d) for Reynoldston. Four of the contributions due from Oystermouth, and seven of those due from Llanrhidian are also missing or indecipherable.

For reasons given earlier, the 1543 assessment has serious limitations as a basis for estimating the *size* of a given village's population, but will reflect more accurately the *distribution* of the total population. Matthew Griffiths recognises this problem but points out:

The lay subsidy assessments, however, provide the means to calculate the relative wealth of the parishes. . . . One can establish both the average contribution made by the taxpayers of each parish, and each parish's tax yield in terms of pence per acre. In the former case, the results suggest the relative prosperity of the taxpayers in different communities, in the latter, the relative productivity of each parish's cultivable land.

The table given is the basis for the analysis of Gower parishes and prominence will be given to Rhossili's position in the hierarchy shown. Rhossili's 30 persons cluster at 4 at 4d, 4 at 1s 8d and 4 at 2s 4d; these twelve compare with the 12 at 8d, whose assessment is based on goods worth between £4 and £5. It will be seen from the earlier tables that persons with goods worth £5 to £6 would jump at this point to 1s 8d. It is probably true to say that assessors kept the figures within the lower band when they got to a dividing line as at £5 to £6 and, more significantly, at £10 to £11. They may have given the 'benefit of the doubt' to the marginal taxpayer at this point. The total of persons assessed for Rhossili (30), paid a total of £1 11s 2d. Villages such as Cheriton with 34 persons paid less – £1 10s 4d, and one figure here was a contribution of 10s 8d. Porteynon with 35 persons paid far less than Rhossili – £1 2s 8d. Each of the two villages has clusters at the lowest figure of 2d: Cheriton had 18 at 2d, Porteynon had 10 at 2d, and 7 at 4d. The implication here is that the two parishes were poorer at the time, but in the case of Porteynon the converse was true at the time of the Hearth Tax returns of 1670/73. Porteynon was relatively prosperous – in Rhossili over 86 per cent of the households were of one hearth, making it with Reynoldston (80 per cent of one hearth) one of the two poorest parishes in Gower.

In this later Stuart period, Rhossili had an estimated population of 170-190 people: this estimate may be too high. Nevertheless we do know that for Chargeable Hearths there were 22 names and 24 hearths: Not Chargeable were 16 names and 22 hearths. So nearly half the village hearths did not warrant charging the payment of 2 shillings because of the poverty which made 16 people ineligible. The total number of contributions due from the hundreds of Swansea and Llangyfelach is 1,292 which can be compared, as will be seen later, with the total of 1,253 householders for these two hundreds shown by the Return to Bishop Richard Davies in 1563. Most of the 1,292 contributions were based, or assessed, on the value of *goods*; they do not include the contributions of the Earl of Worcester, lord of Gower, who was assessed with other peers in a separate assessment, or Sir Rhys Mansel who was probably assessed at Margam.

The calculation of the individual population of each Gower parish, in Tudor times, can be done in two ways. The less valid method would be to take each person shown in the 1543 subsidy assessment as a householder: using a conventional, but acceptable, multiplier, which assumes that each householder can be counted as 4.5 or 5 persons, we can get a population total for each Gower parish which makes no allowance for poor persons exempt from paying the subsidy. A comparison can be made by using the figures given by a certificate dated 12 October 1563 in which the Bishop of St David's, Richard Davies reported the total number of householders in each parish of his diocese. This return is shown by Lewis W. Dilwyn in his *Contributions towards a History of Swansea*. It is twenty years later than the Lay Subsidy Assessment of 1543, but is likely to be more accurate. It is valid, however, to compare these two sets of figures as W.R.B. Robinson notes: the total number of householders in Bishop Richard Davies' return is 1,253. *'The total of 1,253 householders may be compared with the 1,292 persons included in the assessment for the same area in 1543 twenty years earlier'*. We can apply the conventional multiplier of 4.5 or 5 to the figure given of number of households in Bishop Richard Davies' return.

Lay Subsidy Assessment, 1543

Parish	Number of Persons Assessed	Population Estimate
Oystermouth	59	265-295
Rhossili	30	135-150
Llangennith	57	256-285
Llanmadoc	15	67-75
Cheriton	34	153-170
Llandewi	36	162-180
Ilston	37	167-185
Llanrhidian	119	535-595
Pennard	42	189-210
Bishopston	51	229-255
Nicholaston	27	121-135
Penmaen	16	72-80
Reynoldston	24	108-120
Knelston	17	76-85
Porteynon	35	157-175
Oxwich	35	157-175
Penrice	45	202-225

Households in Gower, 1563 – 'Decanatus de Gower'

Parish	Households 'Howsholdes'	Population Estimate
Capella de Oystermowth	60	270-300
Parochia de Rossylle	22	99-110
Parochia Llangynneth	67	301-335
Parochia de Llanvadog	19	85-95

Parish	Households 'Howsholdes'	Population Estimate
Parochia de Chyryton	29	130-145
Parochia de Llandewy	21	94-105
Parochia de Ilston	40	180-200
Parochia Llanrydyan	162	729-810
Parochia de Pennarth	26	117-130
Parochia de Byshopston	40	180-200
Parochia de Nycholaston	16	72-80
Parochia Penmayne	13	58-65
Parochia de Reynoldston	18	81-90
Parochia de Knowlston	14	63-70
Parochia de Porteynon	17	76-85
Parochia de Oxwich	17	76-85
Parochia de Penrys	27	121-135

The comparison between the two tables gives points of agreement and also inconsistency: Oystermouth, with 59 persons in 1543 paying the lay subsidy and 60 households in 1563, is an example of a good match. Llanmadoc (15 persons and 19 households) is also consistent; Knelston (17 persons and 14 households), Ilston (37 persons and 40 households) and Cheriton (34 persons and 29 households) come quite close. The difficulty of explaining why Oxwich and Porteynon with 35 persons assessed for the lay subsidy in 1543, only appear to have 17 households each in 1563 is matched by the need to find why Llandewi, with 36 persons only had 21 households twenty years later. It seems that the danger of using the figures for persons as if they each represented householders is confirmed – it is probably safer to use the figures of households in 1563 as the base line for population calculations. It does, however, need to be emphasised how close the *total* figures are:

First Subsidy Assessment, 1543	1,292 persons
Second Subsidy Assessment, 1544	1,300 persons
Bishop Richard Davies' Return, 1563	1,253 households

This makes the figures relatively reliable in projecting the distribution of persons and houses at the respective dates, but caution has to be used in assuming we can quantify with certainty the population of each parish. For Rhossili the parameters of population appear to be:

1543	1563	1670s	1801
30 persons	22 households	38 names	36 houses
135-150 people	99-110 people	171-190 people	158 people

It is very helpful to find that 36 houses and 158 people in 1801 gives a figure of around 4.5 per house; we should perhaps link this certain figure with the lower one of around 100 people in 1563, to allow for growth in the seventeenth and eighteenth centuries. In this respect the calculation of population for the parish of Rhossili in later Stuart times from the 38 names (46 hearths), given in a Hearth Tax Return would appear to be too high.

The numbers of those who contributed to the Lay Subsidy of 1543 or, more accurately, who were assessed to pay various sums has been noted. Thirty persons in Rhossili were assessed to pay £1 11s 2d. Petty collectors were authorised to collect the money due from each person. In the 1543 Lay Subsidy Assessment Roll for the Hundreds of Swansea and Llangyfelach (E179/221/236) the parish of Rhossili had a Particular Collector, *Robert Perkin,* who was himself assessed for xxd (1s 8d). Reference to this family in the later sixteenth century is part of our story. The upper limit for Rhossili of 2s 4d was paid by 4 persons who appear to be *John Grove, Robert Grove, Nicholas Taylor* and *John Taylor.* Lesser amounts were assessed for *David Gamon* and Howell ap innon (1s 8d). *John Curteys, William Harry, John Myrike, David Emlot, William Myrik, John David, David Clement, William Hogge, Izabell Thomas* were also members of the Rhossili village community in 1543 as were two people with the same name – the intriguing one of *Yoman. Philip Yoman* and *John Yoman* each were assessed for viiid (8d). Their due sums, it is suggested, reflect the value of the *goods* they were assessed as having rather than land. As well as extracting the names of Rhossili villagers from the Lay Subsidy Assessment of 1543 an opportunity was found to decipher names from other village lists: among the 35 persons for *Parochia de Portynon* were *Nicholas Button, John Emlot, Robert Benet, John Benet, John Enderby, John Gamon* and *John Gamon the Younger.* These last two were assessed for iiijd (4d) each, compared with their namesake David Gamon who was assessed for xxd (1s 8d) in Rhossili. *Symon Barret, Nicholas Barret, John Hopkin* and *Thomas Longe* appear for Porteynon, along with *Robert Lanpbey* or *Lamphey. Catryn Enderby* and *John Enderby* each were assessed for viiid (8d).

A similar effort was made with the *Subsidium* of 37 Henry VIII (1545). This subsidy differed from the previous ones in that the assessment, according to W.R.B. Robinson, contained less than a quarter of the total number of names included in the earlier assessment. *'The fall in numbers is probably largely explained by the fact that persons with goods worth under £5 were not liable to contribute to the subsidy granted in 1545, whereas only persons with goods worth under £1 were free of liability to contribute to the 1543 subsidy'* (Robinson). By referring to the earlier tables, it will be appreciated that this would eliminate all those who paid 8d or less in the earlier subsidy arrangements – unless they had acquired additional wealth in the meantime. This took out possibly 20 of the 30 persons who were liable – leaving some 10 who might be assessed on goods valued at £5 to £6 or more. In the event there are nine names: *Robert Grove, Hoell ap Inon, David Gamon, Thomas Gamon, Nicholas Taylor, Robert*

Perkyn are familiar names, but *Isabell Dawkyns, Annie Maunxell* and *John Thomas* are new ones. John Thomas could have taken over payment of the earlier member of his family Izabell Thomas, whose assessment in 1543 might have been 2 shillings.

The references to the Gamon family in the parish of Porteynon as well as in Rhossili give an opportunity to add a little further detail. J. D. Davies mentions John Gamon of Monkeyland in *Historical Notices of West Gower Part IV:* 6 June 1483 – John Gamon held, or had held, a tenement at *'Scurla Castell'* to which, for 10 shillings fee, on this date, another tenant was admitted. W.C. Rogers in *Swansea & Glamorgan Calendar II* notes John Gamon of Monkyn Land, in 1575, was holding former land of Neath Abbey in the parish of Porteynon. The David Gamon mentioned in the Lay Subsidy Assessments for 1543 and 1545 probably appears again in 1548: *'Grant by David Gamon of Rissilley to Henry Thomas, of lands and tenements at Leystanston in the fee of Wible, and a tenement and lands (called Mountebrough) in the fee of Penrees, co. Glamorgan, to the use of John Gamon his son and Beytton Thomas his wife, in tail. Dated at Swansea, 5th June 2 Edward VI (A.D. 1548).'* We also have from the seventeenth century: *'A true copy of an aunciente deed of the Tenement of Mountebroughe at Penreece co. Glamorgan, whereby David Gamon of Rossilli grants to Henry Thomas a tenement of lands (called Mountebrough) in the fee of Penrees, to the use of John Gamon son of the said David and Beytton Thomas his wife, in tail, with remainders to the heirs of the said David.'* Date as above.

It is immensely valuable to know the names of many of the villagers of Rhossili in 1543 and 1545 – the later return narrows the focus so that we can identify the relatively prosperous members of the community. If we accept the rough guide of the Lay Subsidy Return then the population of 135-150 can be compared with the initial census return of 1801. At this time the figures of 36 houses and 158 people accords well with the values used in earlier calculations, as the average household would be 4.4 people. Three of the farming families at the end of Elizabethan times and in early Stuart times were those of Nicholas William of Rhossili, John Curtys shown as Llandewi but later they are found at Paviland and John Taylor *Husbandman* at Rhossili. They are described in articles by F.V. Emery, *West Glamorgan Farming circa 1580-1620 Parts I and II* (National Library of Wales Journal 1955-6 and 1957-8). The inventories of John Curtys and and John Taylor were both over £60, Nicholas William was a more modest farmer. John Taylor, 'Husbandman' of Rhossili is shown as having a personal estate worth £62 2s 4d in 1609, including 24 head of cattle worth over £18, 160 sheep worth over £20 and crops worth over £13. The eight horses, mares or colts valued at £7 which John Taylor had would undoubtedly have been needed for ploughing, as his crops of over £13 were produced without the use of oxen for this purpose. He had none, whereas John Button at Porteynon had six oxen valued at £6. John Beynon of Llandewi had nine oxen and 200 sheep and lambs when he died in 1576, as well as 26 head of cattle. The more modest holding of Nicholas William at Rhossili included four dairy cows, four heifers and calves and two oxen; he also had 36 sheep, and crops valued at £6 1s 8d, which again reflects the pattern of mixed farming, although on a more modest scale. John Curteys of Llandewi had 25 head of cattle, including one bull, together with three oxen worth £5. His 65 sheep and crop value of £14 10s contributed to his overall inventory total of £60 13s, as did his total of £13 18s 4d in Implements and Household Goods, the highest in the total of six examples given by F. V. Emery.

The Taylor and Curtis families appear throughout the seventeenth century – it is a great help to be able to establish the links between members of the families through the will of John Taylor, the husbandman described earlier whose will is dated 27 July 1609. The list of beneficiaries includes the Poor of Rhossili Parish, his daughters Margaret Taylor and Elin Taylor, together with three of his younger sons – Rowland Taylor, John Taylor and Jenkin Taylor. Ann Beynon, servant, and Arnold Reese, servant, are mentioned, as are Margerie Beynon and Elizabeth Steaphan. Anne Grove, daughter of John Grove, and William Grove, son of John Grove follow, then Ann Curtes, his wife, and Phillip Taylor, his eldest son. There is an intriguing mention of Phillip Courtes, tutor and overseer, and Jenkin Taylor, tutor and overseer. Executors are Ann Curtes, his wife and Phillip Taylor, his son; the witnesses are Thomas Rosser of Rhossili, Richard Bydder, William Jenkin, together with John ap Jenkin and John ab Jevan. The last two names are reminders that even at this time patronymics persisted in this part of anglicised Gower.

Documents and Dynasties

It is a little surprising, perhaps, to find Rhossili mentioned in a variety of documents in the state archives. The manor of Landimore and Rhossili was, however, one of the principal manors of the marcher lordship of Gower and Kilvey. It was kept in hand as one of the demesne manors of the lord of Gower – that is, it was managed directly by the lord and as such assumed a special status. The attachment of Rhossili to be part of the manor of Landimore meant that although it was not an important possession of the lord of Gower in its own right it was invariably linked with Landimore in state documents. These range from Inquisitions Post Mortem to Patent Rolls and Close Rolls. Ministers' Accounts, Charter Rolls and Pipe Rolls contain references to Gower and to the extensive and valuable manor of Landimore and Rhossili. Ministers' Accounts of 1399-1400 show that Duchess Elizabeth of Norfolk had assigned to her as dower one third of the revenues of the manor of Landimore and Rhossili following the death of her husband, the first Duke of Norfolk in 1399. The various state documents relating to Rhossili, as well as Pitton and Pilton, are often in Latin with an established formulary which allowed the scribe to abbreviate the Latin words in several cases. This can pose problems but some of the documents have been transcribed, translated and calendared. They serve to highlight some episodes in the descent of the lordship of Gower as well as the manors of Landimore, Rhossili and Pitton.

Pipe Roll 30 Henry II: [1184] *'Brunus Judeus Londoniensis.......Et in quietantia comitis de Warewic' pro terra de Guhier .xliiij l. per idem breve.'*

Bruno the Jew, of London, owed a fine of £1,000 to the King, Henry II, and was ordered to pay it off in part by absolving various members of the nobility from sums which they owed to Jews. This item acquits the Earl of Warwick of debts which he had acquired and secured by pledging the land of Gower. Successive kings held Gower until it was granted to the de Breos family by King John. The Earls of Warwick were to hold the lordship briefly again in the fourteenth century.

The Great Charter of Liberties granted by William de Breos in 1306 was an attempt by the Lord of Gower to avoid action by the King in the affairs of his tenants: extracts from the document show its purpose:

> TO ALL THE FAITHFUL OF CHRIST who shall see or hear the present writing WILLIAM DE BREOS lord of the honours of BREMBRE and GOHER greeting in the Lord. KNOW ALL YE that we have granted and by this charter have confirmed, for us, our heirs and assigns, to all abbots, priors, hospitallers, templars, knights, free tenants and their men as well English

as Welsh or holding land within the precinct of our English county of Goher, all and singular the liberties underwritten, to hold and to have for them, their successors and heirs and assigns for eve.

There is early mention of the manors of Ostermouth [Oystermouth], Landymor or Rossily and a later recital of the ancient knights' fees including held by the lord of Forshulle, Vernhulle and Pyltoune. The translation of the Charter from the Latin shows how decisions were to be arrived at:

All decisions and records in the said county howsoever arising shall be returned and published at the discretion and judgement of the suitors holding ancient knights' Fee namely, the lord of PENRES [Penrice], the lord of PORTEYNON, the lord of OXEWYCHE [Oxwich], the lord of HENTLES [Henllys], the lord of WEBBELEGH [Weobley], the lord of SCORLAGGES-KASTEL [Scurlage Castle], the lord of RENEWARDESTOUNE [Reynolds-ton], the lord of KNOYLESTOUNE [Knelston], the lord of PENMAYN [Pen-maen], the lord of NICHOLASTOUNE [Nicholaston], the lord of FORSHULLE, VERNHULLE and PYLTOUNE [Furzehill, Fernhill and Pilton] and the lord of STEENTEBRUGGE [Stembridge], not with-standing the opposition of any other tenant of the same country, and according to their decisions executions shall be made.

On the death of William de Breos one of the daughters and co-heiresses inherited his lands. Alina de Breos had married John de Mowbray and it was this family which held the lordship of Gower until the Beauchamp (Bello Compos) family, Earls of Warwick, resumed their claim at a time when Edward III was likely to favour them. The Earl of Warwick had been created Earl Marshal of England by Edward III in 1337. In the roll of pleadings John de Mowbray put forward that the Earl of Warwick had demanded against him the castle of Sweynesey and the land of Gower but had not included in his demand a vill or vills within the land of Gower as was required by law and ancient custom. By not fully giving the names of the properties he could have demanded, the Earl had jeopardised his claim, it was suggested. Within the land of Gower vills, which the Earl might have demanded were:

27 Edward III, roll 14,132 [1353]

. . . the vills of Sweynesey, in which were the castle and 10l. of rent; of Milwodwesketty, with 10 carucates of land; of Ostermuth with the castle and 10 marks of rent; of Thistlebon, with 8 carucates; of Morton, with one carucate; of Kythull, with 3 carucates and a moiety of one knight's fee; of Kilbrogh, with one knight's fee; of Iltwitteston, with one knight's fee and a half; of Pennarth, with the castle, 3 carucates of land, and 2 acres of wood;

of Penmayn, with 1½ knight's fees; of Nicolaston, with one knight's fee; of Penrys with a castle and 1½ knight's fees; of Oxenwich, with a castle, and 1½ knight's fees; of Reyneswardeston, with one knight's fee; of Knoyleston, with one knight's fee; of Porteynon, with a castle and 1½ knight's fees; of Pylton, with a moiety of a knight's fee; of Pavylond, with one knight's fee; of Pitton, with one knight's fee; of Russely, with one knight's fee; of Hentles, with one knight's fee; of Langeneth, with 1½ knight's fees; of Lanmadock, with one knight's fee; of Landymore, with a castle and one knight's fee; of Leyshanston, with a castle and one knight's fee; of Lanndrydian, with one knight's fee; of Louchwarne, with a castle and one knight's fee; of Talband, with a castle and one knight's fee; and of Walterstone, with one knight's fee.

In the order in which they appear in the pleadings we can recognise the manor of Millwood, the manor which combined the properties of the Knights Hospitallers or Order of St John of Jerusalem together with manors such as Oystermouth, Norton, Kittle and Kilvrough. Ilston and Pennard follow with the west Gower components of the lordship such as Rhossili, Pilton and Pitton. In terms of measurement a carucate was a ploughland, usually of 120 acres in the 'large hundred' but sometimes 100 acres or 80 acres in the 'small hundred'.

Within a short time the Earl of Warwick was involved in a further dispute with Edward, Prince of Wales as to whether parts of the lordship of Gower were held directly of the Crown or came under Carmarthen, which was held by the Prince of Wales. Again the proceedings are voluminous, as found in a Roll filed in the National Archives as Roll 9 in the Parliamentary and Council proceedings, Chancery, dated 28 and 29 Edward III [1355-56]. In the proceedings: The Earl [of Warwick] produces evidences of his holding Gower in demesne and in the service of the King in Chief as of the Crown, and that it has never been held of Carmarthen; and that the manors of Kilvey, Landimore and Rhossili are within and are held of Gower. The findings in favour of Edward, Prince of Wales were mitigated by his magnanimity in quit-claiming his rights – this gesture is recorded in a state document of 1360.

Calendar of Charter Rolls 34-35 Edward III [14 July 1360] Westminster

Whereas Thomas de Bello Campo, earl of Warwick, lately in the king's court before the justices of the Bench by a writ of right recovered the castle of Sweyneseye and the land of Gower in Wales against John de Moubray of Axholm, knight; and whereas after this recovery the said Thomas was impeached by Edward, prince of Wales claiming that certain parcels to wit Kylvey, Landymor, Rossully and Kitehull within the lordship of Gower were held from the said prince as of his lordship of Kermerdyn in the principality of Wales . . . whereupon matter of dissension arose, and the said prince considering the right of the said earl with the king's assent by letters patent for him and his heirs quitclaimed all the right he had. . . . The king ratified the quit-claim and also grants to the said earl that he and his heirs shall hold the said castle and the land of Gower with the parcels of Kilvey, Landymor Rossully and Kitehull with the royal liberties and jurisdictions thereto pertaining from the king as of the crown of England by the services due therefrom.

The success of Thomas de Beauchamp, or Bello Campo, earl of Warwick in recovering Gower can be attributed to his valiant service to Edward III and his son the Black Prince. At the Battle of Crecy (1346) he fought alongside John de Mowbray in the company of the Black Prince. He was at Poitiers in the battle which the Black Prince won with an army of 4,000 against 20,000. His family were to enjoy the fruits of the Gower lands from 1360 to 1396 but Earl Thomas died in 1369. In addition to giving details of Sweyneseye, Oystremouth and Kylveye other parcels of the land of Gower are given in the Inquisition taken at Hereford.

Calendar of Inquisitions Post Mortem 15 December, 43 Edward III [1369]

Lanymore. A carucate of land, two-thirds of a watermill, and a court held every month. Pennarth [Pennard]. A carucate of land, 20 marks rent, and a court held every month. Lougherne [Loughor]. 8 marks rent. A hundred court held twice a year, two forests, to wit, Clune and Kylveye, and the park of Bruse. Knythall and Rosselly. 100s rent. Pennarth. A mill. Blakepulle. A mill.

In the same way that the friendship of Thomas de Beauchamp, earl of Warwick, with Edward III enabled the family to recover their lands in Gower it was the enmity between Edward's grandson, Richard II, and a later earl of Warwick which led to the reversal of the judgement made in 1360. This came in 1396 when, as Leland records:

*1397   Thomas Comes Nottingham per billam erroris quam tulit contra
Thomas Comitem Warwic: recuperavit terras de Gower.*

This recovery of lands in Gower is set against the turbulent background of Richard II's attempts to deal with powerful nobles such as the Duke of Gloucester, the Earl of Arundel and the Earl of Derby. Thomas Mowbray, Earl of Nottingham, who was to be created Duke of Norfolk by Richard II, was implicated in the murder of the king's uncle, Thomas, Duke of Gloucester in 1397. By this time he had already regained the lands of Gower which the earlier Earl of Warwick had recovered for his family in 1360. The fate of the Earl of Warwick was to be condemned to the scaffold but as he had given useful incriminating evidence against the Duke of Gloucester to help justify his imprisonment he was condemned to perpetual banishment on the Isle of Man, but later brought back to England and imprisoned in the Tower of London. He had, according to one source, upbraided Richard II with the murder of Thomas, Duke of Gloucester, *'his unckle, for which he was ever hatefull to him.'*

Close Rolls 20 Richard II refer to the discontinuance of proceedings in the King's Bench in 1396, upon a writ of right brought by Thomas de Beauchamp, Earl of Warwick, against de Mowbray and record that the former released to Thomas de Mowbray, Earl of Nottingham and Marshal of England, the whole of his right to the castle of Swansea and lordship of Gower, as well as to the manor of *Kylveye, Landymour, Russelby [Rhossili] and Kythil.*

Despite the favour in which he was held the first Duke of Norfolk almost immediately fell into disgrace. His quarrel with Henry Bolingbroke, Duke of Hereford led to the two powerful nobles riding out to engage in personal combat at Coventry in September 1398. The King's intervention at the last minute stopped the contest taking place and the two contestants were banished from the realm – eventually for life. Thomas de Mowbray, first Duke of Norfolk, died at Venice in 1399. An Inquisition Post Mortem confirms that Gower and Kilvey at this time was worth 700 marks.

By this time Richard II had been deposed by Henry Bolingbroke, Duke of Lancaster who became king as Henry IV. The Duchess Elizabeth, widow of Thomas, first Duke of Norfolk was assigned dower out of the proceeds of the lordship of Gower in these words:

> *Of which said land and demesnes the third part is assigned to the Lady Elizabeth, Duchess of Norfolk, in the name of dower, by the writ of the Lord the King, from the twenty-ninth day of May, in the first year of the above-said King Henry [IV].*

The custody of the lordship and land of Gower had been committed to Hugh Waterton, Knight, *'by reason of the minority of Thomas, son and heir of the late Duke.'* Accounts of divers Ministers and Bailiffs were prepared and we have the Assignment of Dower of the Lordship of Gower made to Elizabeth, Duchess of Norfolk, by John Maunce, Escheator of the Lord the King for County of Hereford and in the March of Wales annexed, on the ninth day of July, in the first year of the reign of King Henry the Fourth.

Duchess Elizabeth had been granted as dower the third part of the manor of Landimore as well as of other manors and possessions of the late Duke her husband. The copy of the writ for the assignment of dower in Gower is to John Maunce:

> *We have taken reasonable dower for herself out of all the lands and tenements which were of the aforesaid Duke . . . in your Bailiwick on the day on which he died . . .*

The relevant portions of this important medieval document are available in translation thanks to the indefatiguable Vicar of Cheriton, Rev. J.D. Davies, who produced them in his four-volume *History of West Gower.* Landimore, with Rhossili, was a demesne manor, so the Ministers' Accounts of 1399/1400 give considerable detail which can be used to illustrate three themes: the damage and 'decay of rents' caused by natural disasters such as encroachment of sea or sand and the losses caused by the death of tenants, the taking in of new lands in some parts of the manor of the manor of Landimore and Rhossili and the assignment to the same in dower of five knights' fees.

Ministers' Accounts 1399/1400

A lengthy list of allowances and default of rents commences:

> *Of which the accounts in default of rent and sergeanty of diverse tenements of Richard de Turberville of Landymore in the hand of the Lord which were wont to render sergeanty . . .*

The details which follow confirm the deaths of tenants or the giving up of tenancies – many of the tenancies previously rented out had to be kept in hand by the lord of the manor:

> *And in decay of rent of 2 acres of land late of Thomas Kiste.*
>
> *And in decay of rent of 2 acres of lands late of William Bemond in the hand of the Lord, by the years 2s 9d.*
>
> *And in decay of rent of 4 acres of land and 1 acre of hill-meadow which Cristina Sutton lately held on the day on which she died . . .*
>
> *And in decay of rent of 5 acres of land and 1 acre of meadow, late of Henry Willym . . .*
>
> *And in default of rent of one tenement and 1½ acres of land, late of David Wether . . .*
>
> *And in decay of rent of 1 messuage and six acres of land there, late of John ap Riez....*
>
> *And in decay of rent of lands and tenements late of John Testarde which are called the Mardre(?) within the fee of Landimore in the hand of the Lord, whence issues nothing as appears by the Court-Roll for the same time, 6s.*
>
> *And in decay of rent and tenements late of Maurice Seward, within the fee of Landymore, being in the hand of the Lord for default of tenants by Court-Roll, 3s.*

And in decay of rent of one weir lately in the tenure of John de la Bere wholly lade waste by the sea, and nothing can be levied thereof, 6d.

The defects in rents and customs caused by the deaths of tenants in earlier times – at the time of the Black Death in south-east Wales during the winter of 1348-49, in 1361-62 and in the Second Pestilence of 1369 – had not been overcome by the beginning of the fifteenth century. The proceeds from heriots (payment made to the lord on the death of a tenant) and fines (payment by a new tenant to a lord for entry to his tenancy) were only temporary gains. The example of Landimore shows that a number of escheated lands in Gower were still vacant at the opening of the fifteenth cenury and the situation was made worse by the revolt of Owain Glyn Dŵr. Gower under the Beauchamp family was worth £300 in 1316 and £386 in 1400 but following the rebellion it was recorded that:

The two main parts of the lordship are worth £100 and no more because the lordship in great part is destroyed by Welsh rebels.

Separately mentioned, with rents, is new land at Roselly:

And of 105s 9d for Easter term, part of 10l 11s 6d by the year at the terms of Easter and Michaelmas, of rents of tenants of Roselly, coming into the hand of the Lord from the dower of Lady Cecily de Saint Mour [Seymour] who was wife of Sir Gilbert [de] Turberville for the manors of Landymore, Knythull and Roselly . . . and not more here, because the lands and tenements of Roselly, whence the said 10l 11s 6d were wont to be paid in the year are wholly assigned from the 9th day of July by the aforesaid Escheator unto the Lady the Duchess, in the name of Dower for the Manor of Landymore and its appurtenances, and other lands contained within the account of the said manor, together with 42s 2d of yearly rent and farm of divers parcels of demesne lands there in the hands of divers tenants below specified and allowed – Title, allowance – for the said Dower also assigned, because the said 42s 2d are charged above in the titles; new land arented, and land and pasture demised to the Gavel, as more fully appears by the extent made thereof, and are not drawn back from the sums of the titles aforesaid because of the said Dower.
Sum – 105s 9d.

The specific assignment of rents of demesne lands at Rhossili to the dower of the Duchess Elizabeth confirms that as part of the manor of Landimore it was normally part of the land kept by the lord for his own use. By this time it was *'in the hands of divers tenants'*, a practice which was prevalent in other manors at this time. There is indication, too, that new lands had been taken in and it has been suggested that it was at this time that additional land was taken into cultivation on the headland at Rhossili. The first church – the medieval church in the Warren – was abandoned and a new one built, it is argued. The carrying of windblown sand led to the original settlement being buried and a new foundation established at the present site of Rhossili Church which incorporated the Norman doorway from the abandoned church. Two fields called *Clerksland* and *Priests Hay* are indicative of new, more productive land being taken into use with some being allocated for the support of the parish priest.

Further entries in the Ministers' Accounts refer to increases of rents:

> *And of 10d, increase of rent of 2 acres of hill-meadow which were of Owain ap Griffith, and formerly by the Lord demised to Thomas ap Mric and John David, this year 4th.*

> *And of 19d, increase of rent of four acres of hill-meadow called Scurloke-mead, so demised to John Muric this year.*

> *And of 8s increase of rent of 2 acres of meadow, which were of Owen ap Griffith, so demised to John de la Mare, Vicar of Llanrhidian, this year.*

> *And of 2s 1d increase of rent of Wormshed, so demised this year.*

> *Sum – 12s 6d (approved).*

The last entry is an intriguing one – although it was common practice to lease the pasture ground on Worm's Head for grazing of sheep the figure of rent appears to be high. Farmers who were prepared to drive their sheep over the causeway to Worm's Head at low tide found their efforts were rewarded – the taste of the mutton being superior in some people's opinion. The salty grass on the Inner Head gave a better *tang* or flavour to the meat than that of sheep grazed mainly on the mainland. The Penrice and Margam Manuscripts include a copy of a warrant by Sir Edward Mansel dated 1st December 1689 to make a lease of Worm's Head. It was to *George Thomas – a steward there* and allowed him to make a lease to John Beynon senr. of *Rossilly.* The lease, which dealt with *pasture ground and island called Wormeshead in the Parish of Rossilly* was for 99 years for a yearly rent of 5 shillings. Mathew Bynon of *Rosilly* was able to secure the use of *'Waste and rocky ground called Worms-head in Parish of Rossylly Manor of Landymore'* by a chattel lease for three lives. He paid £12 initially but the yearly rent was only 6d.

Parts of the accounts for Landimore and Rhossili have curious phrases such as *'pasture demised to the Gavel',* which are unusual in ancient deeds but, according to J.D. Davies, *'are frequently met with in those relating to the County of Pembroke.'* It refers to tenancies which have been commuted to a money payment instead of service. A *gafol* was rent in commutation of service and a *gafol-man* was a customary tenant whose services had been commuted into a money payment.

Ministers' Accounts: Knights' Fees. In the account these follow the words *Sum of the whole Dower – 128l 8s 11½d*. Also assigned to the same in dower the Knights' fees underwritten, namely:

> *The manor of Porteynon which John Penrees holds for one knight's fee; also the manor of Nichollaston and Mauncellisfield which Richard Mauncell holds for half a knight's fee; the Manor of Webbeley which John de la Biere holds for a third part of a knight's fee; also the Manor of Langenythe which John de la Mare holds of the said John de Penrees, who holds of the Lord for one knight's fee; also the Manor of Vorsehull and Vernehull which John Bounte holds for the fourth part of a knight's fee.*

The *Manor of Vorsehull and Vernehull* is a notable change from the Charter of William de Breos in 1306 where the lord of *Forshulle, Vernhulle and Pyltoune* appears. The first two names are now combined in one manor, without Pilton, suggesting that they were geographically linked as well as administratively in the Rhossili area of Gower.

The material which can be extracted from the Ministers' Accounts of 1399/1400 reveals the story of the manor of Landimore and Rhossili at a time in history when sources are sparse. The son and heir of the first Duke of Norfolk, who had recovered the lordship of Gower, should have succeeded his father but was involved in a rebellion against Henry IV, was convicted of treason and executed at York before he became of age. His brother John became the next lord of Gower and owner of the manor of Landimore duly becoming the second Duke of Norfolk. During the time this lord of Gower was away serving King Henry V and King Henry VI in France and Normandy his estates were administered by wardens or receivers under the supervision of the king who occasionally made appointments in Gower on his behalf.

Patent Roll 424, 7 Henry VI, part 1, m.16 (29 November 1429) shows a *presentation* (appointment) by the King to the hermitage on Burry Holms at the far end of Rhossili Bay:

> *For William Bernard. The king to all whom, etc., salutation. Know that of our special grace we have granted to our faithful William Bernard the hermitage of Sancti Kenyth atte Holmes in Gowerlond, to have with all the rights and appurtenances thereto belonging, etc. Witness the king at Westminster, xxvij. Day of November [1429] By the Council.*

On 31 May 1439, the king at Windsor granted to Thomas Norys *'the hermitage of Holmes in Gowersland, Wales vacant by the death of Philip, the late hermit.'* Even appointments to a distant, lonely hermitage on the coast of west Gower occupied a place in the affairs of state.

In the **Inquisition Post Mortem** taken on 12 May 1462, it is shown that the Duke of Norfolk at the time of his death held *'the castle and manor of Swaynsey and the land and lordship of Gower and Kylvey, with their appurtenances except the lordship manor and fee of Landimore and thirty-four acres of arable land and six of meadow in Oystermouth, these having been given to Sir Hugh Johnys.'* This was the third Duke of Norfolk, John, who is named in the well-known brass in St Mary's Church, Swansea dedicated to Sir Hugh Johnys. The latter was *'knight marchall of Ingland under the good John duke of Norfolke, which John gave unto him the mano' of landymo' to hym & to his heyr' for ev'more.'* It was the most valuable of the marcher lord's manors in Gower and produced nearly £53 in cash in 1448-49.

Despite the gift to him, however, during the Wars of the Roses the lordship of Gower, with the manor of Landimore and Rhossili was to pass into other hands; a century later it was the Herbert family, Earls of Pembroke, who controlled the destiny of the tenants of this large and important manor. The Mansel family lost and regained the manors they held in Gower before emerging as the principal family in terms of landholding from the time of Charles II. Through later medieval documents these dynasties which played a role in Gower can be brought to the front of the stage.

We see from a successive grant in tail by Philip Mauncell to his sons John, Leonard and Jankyn the extent of the lands he held in Gower: it is a **Margam Charter dated 10 October 38 Henry VI (1459)** and shows what happened when, in the fluctuating fortunes of families who supported the Lancastrian or Yorkist cause, a local family finished on the losing side. It is an attempt to avoid the consequences of Philip Mauncell's arraignment under an Act of Attainder whereby he would lose his lands and, perhaps, his life. The document refers to *'Oxenwhich, Penryse, Nicholaston, Skorlocastell'*, Porteynon, Horton and lands, tenements and mills at or near *Burry* and Pitton as well as other property in Swansea and Loughor. The attempt to transfer his lands safely to his sons did not succeed so although Philip Mauncell appears to have kept his life his lands were confiscated and granted by Edward IV to Sir Roger Vaughan. William of Worcester in 1479 noted the annual value of Philip Mansel's land as being 5 marks but his valuation has been described as "excessively low". The attainder was reversed and the estates restored to his son, Jankyn or Jenkin Mansel. He appears to have been indebted to his brother-in law Sir Mathew Cradock for financial help in restoring the family fortunes. The extent of the Mansel family's debt to him is seen from a **Margam Charter dated 10 January 11 Henry VIII (1520)**. It is an acquittance by *Sir Mathyas Cradock, Knt,* to Sir Rice Mansel [descendant of Jankyn Mansel] of all claims on certain manors in Gower; the reimbursement included the sum of *'oon hundred markes whiche I the said Sir Mathie have paied to Watkyn' Vaghan' of Tretowr' for a dede wherby the same Watkyn released all the right that he had to the said Rice in the maner of Penrice and Porteynon and othre manerz landes and tenements in Gower.'* Paying off the Vaughan family removed any possible claim this might have had to the lands which reverted to the Mansels early in the reign of Henry VIII. The family, through

Rice Mansel, built up their position; he was a loyal soldier-servant of the crown and the brilliance he showed in royal service earned its reward. As Sir Rice Mansel, he acquired the lion's share of the estates of Margam Abbey at the time of the dissolution of the monasteries, putting up no less than £2,600 altogether between 1540 and 1546 to acquire lands which secured a place for his family in the forefront of the country gentry.

In what were to be the closing years of the turbulent struggle called the Wars of the Roses an influential role was played by Sir Rhys ap Thomas in support of Henry Tudor, earl of Richmond, the future King Henry VII. It was his 1,000 horsemen and three thousand footmen whose efforts in support of Henry VII were rewarded by a knighthood and estates in Gower which included Landimore and Rhossili. The estates later held by his grandson Rhys ap Griffith in 1531 included Weobley Castle and half the manor of Weobley, the valuable manor or lordship of Landimore which included outlying properties in Llanrhidian and Rhossili and the manor of Caegurwen on the northern boundary of the lordship of Gower. The total value of all the estates was £48 12s 5½d at the time of of the execution of Sir Rhys ap Thomas' grandson, Rhys ap Griffith, for treason in 1531. The Act of Attainder was passed in the following year, 1532; it made provision for *'Dame Jane (Jenet) late Wyff to Sir Ryce ap Thomas Knyght Graundfather of the sayde Rice ap Gruffith'* and also for *'Lady Kateryn, Wydowe, late the Wyff of the sayde Ryce ap Gruffith.'* Lands, including the manor of Landimore and Rhossili, were allocated for *'the use of the sayde Dame Kateryn, for term of her lyff'* and did not revert to the Crown under the Act of Attainder until her death. She later married *Sir Peers Eggeccombe Knyght.* This explains the entry in the Calendar of Patent Rolls for Elizabeth I (1558-1560) of a Grant to William [Herbert], Earl of Pembroke, of the Manor of Rhossili, Landimore and Llanrhidian in the County of Glamorgan (January 1560). It is included in the Patent Roll as a *'Grant in fee simple, for 3,199l 16s 6¼d paid at the Exchequer to Roger Alford, a teller there, to William, earl of Pembroke'* which deals with all the lands granted – these were in the county of Monmouth as well as in Glamorgan. The lands acquired in Glamorgan were already being leased by *William Herberte, knight* and were listed as being *late of the late Catherine Edgecombe and formerly of Rice Griffith, attainted:*

The manor of Rosillie, Llandmore and Llanrydian	*Yearly value: 35l 13s 7¾d*
The manor of Webley	*Yearly value: 11l 12s 5¼d*
The manor of Cregurwen	*Yearly value: 50s*

The manor of *Rosillie, Llandmore and Llanrydyan* was to be held by the service of the twentieth part of a knight's fee as was the manor of Webley. The sum of £35 13s 7¾d which was the Yearly Value of the manor of Landimore, Rhossili and Llanrhidian included:

all that our rent of assize of four pounds, ten shillings, six pence, one half penny and one farthing, and the service belonging and appertaining to us of our free tenants there. And all that our yearly rent of thirty-one pounds, three shillings and one penny, and the service belonging and appertaining to us of all our tenants at will there.

It was by this transaction that the earls of Pembroke, of the second creation, became a major influence in Gower and Glamorgan. It is the Somerset family, earls of Worcester and later dukes of Beaufort who play the principal role as overlords of Gower with the Herbert family, earls of Pembroke and the Mansel family in key supporting roles. In fact, it is these last two families who are closest to the other members of the 'cast' when the curtain rises on the 'extras' – the people of Gower – as the 'play' begins. It is to these two families that they address their pleas and pay their services and dues – through sequences of documents in the Penrice and Margam Manuscripts we can follow the villagers of Rhossili as they play their part in the story.

Descriptions and Dialect

Edward Lhuyd, in order to begin his revision of the Welsh sections of Camden's *Britannia*, was obliged to build up a network of correspondents throughout Wales, as well as traversing the country on journeys in Wales between 1697 and 1699. Two of his major correspondents in south Wales were the Venerable John Williams of Swansea and Isaac Hamon of Bishopston. Isaac Hamon has been described as *'below the squirearchy of the Seyses, Bowens, Lucases or Bennetts',* but he did hold offices in the manor of Bishopston during the time he completed his detailed survey of Gower for Edward Lhuyd. He appears as the valuer and drawer-up of a kinsman's inventory around 9 May 1676 when probate was granted and the document shows William Hamon's mixed husbandry – cattle, sheep, horses and corn – had given him a comfortable sum of £82 to leave. In a Hearth Tax Return of 1670 for Bishopston the 38 names – the same number as a Hearth Tax Return for Rhossili around the same time – show *Isaac Hamon one & forge.* He later appears in the court rolls as deputy steward for the manor of Bishopston, February 1677, later as under-steward and recorder, and from 1684 as Steward of the manor. He held this office until at least 1702. His complete account of Gower survives in seventeen closely-written pages in the Carte manuscripts at the Bodleian Library, Oxford and covers twenty-three Gower parishes.

It is to the late Frank Emery, who was the doyen of historical geographers in his research into Gower's history, that we are indebted for a transcription and discussion of Isaac Hamon's survey in *Edward Lhuyd and some of his Glamorgan Correspondents: A View of Gower in the 1690s.* This was published in the *Transactions of the Honourable Society of Cymmrodorion.* 1965. It can be used to illuminate Gower's past, in terms of landscape, land use and the speech and vocabulary of its inhabitants – in this way it also serves to show what villages such as Rhossili were like three hundred years ago.

Isaac Hamon was meticulous in what Emery has called *'the formal geography of the Gower parishes, their size, shape and relation to each other. . . . In fact his word picture of the lay-out of the parish geography is so near the mark that one might suppose he had drawn his own map, based perhaps on Speed's representation in the map of Glamorgan.'* He uses sources such as the manorial surveys arising from the Domesday-like survey of the seigniory or principal lordship of Gower, dating from 1650, when it was commissioned *by the Right Honble. Oliver Cromwell Lord Gnrall of the Parliamts forces.* The eventual result of his labours was the compilation of a literary account, composed at a time when basic changes were taking place in the economic and social life of the region. Hamon confirms that:

> *The South pt. of Gowersland (being Swanzey hundd.), being in length from Swanzey to Worms head about 12 miles is for the most part corn ground*

with store of limestones, & limestone cleeves [cliffs], wherein are many great holes or Caves, here are also divers places from Mumble rode west-ward divers harbours & Creekes where they doe transport much limestones and other goods.

Isaac Hamon's record of the preponderance of arable land in limestone Gower is both a reflection and confirmation of manorial surveys: the broadest tracts of arable land in *'the south part of Gowersland'* grew the range of crops which are familiar to us from the inventories of Gower farmers in the seventeenth century – wheat, barley, rye, white and grey oats, peas and vetches. Isaac Hamon had, at Bishopston, a closer view of the changes:

The Corn & grain that growes in all pts. of Gowersland & therabts. are wheat, barley, Ry, oates white and gray, peas and fitches, and in divers pts. of Swanzey hundd there are much Clover grasses & seedes especially at & near Bpstown.

The significant changes in patterns of land use would, one hopes, spread.

In addition to the detail of farming practices, Isaac Hamon conveys a very sound knowledge of parochial organisation, provided that we remember that although *'his distances for the length and breadth of parishes give the correct proportions . . . his units sometimes seem to be long miles'* (Emery).

Thus Pilton is about *'a mile or more'* from the rest of the parish of Penrice – it would be several miles! The three entries which mention parts of the community of Rhossili today refer to Paviland (parish of Penmaen at this time), Pilton (Penrice), and Rhossili. Hamon describes how:

These pishes followeing doe ly in West Gower, and also in Swanzey Hundd: Penmain lyeth between Penard & Ilston on the E: Llanridian on ye north, Nicholaston on the west, & the sea on the S, it is but a small pish, not much more than 3 qurs of a mile each way . . . this pish is for ye most pt Corn ground, pt Limestones & pt Mill-ston. Another pcell of lands or hamlet called Pavyland belongeth to this pish & is pt of the same, but it lyeth about 4 or 5 miles of, from ye Rest of the sd pish, & is adjoining to Rossilly pish . . . Penrees lyeth between ye sd pish of Nicolaston on the E: Reynoldston & Landewy & Knoyleston on the N: Porthynon on the west & Oxwich on the S: . . . The Church is dedicated to St Andrew, and they say that this ought to be pt of ye vicarage of Llanridian, But both lookes like Imppriacons [Impropriations] here hath been time out of minde a great fayr kept upon St Andrews, but ever since ye year 1665 there hath been 3 fayres more kept & a market upon Friday, by a charter purchased by Sr, Edw Mansell Ld of ye manor . . . As for the Soyl it is corn ground & limestone land except the midle pt thereof, To this pish belongs a remote hamlet called Pilton, & it lyeth near Rossilly, about a mile or more from ye Rest of the pish.

The tithe map for the detached part of Penmaen parish suggests that Paviland is seven miles away, but Isaac Hamon is well-informed and clear in his descriptions of parochial organisation – Pilton and Paviland were not part of the community of Rhossili until 1879. At this time, three hundred years ago, the farming families in these two hamlets registered their baptisms and marriages in the parishes of Penmaen and Penrice, although using the churchyard of Rhossili Church to bury their dead in many cases, as the Parish Registers show.

Isaac Hamon also wrote about:

The people of Gowersland in general: as for stature &c. they are as in many other places some tall, & some of a midle stature but many of them long livers, as well male as female, for of late divers psons (& in most pishes) attained to abt 80 yeares of age & some to 100, or very near, and divers psons this day there (in most pishes as aforesd) yet liveing, that are near the said age of 80, & some upward.

The longevity of Gower villagers was commented on by Reverend J.D. Davies in his *History of West Gower* and from 2006 we have a recording giving memories of Rhossili a century and more ago. Mrs Annie Jenkins was born in 1890, appearing in the census of 1891, so is able to recall scenes of her childhood growing up Rhossili at a time when Queen Victoria was still alive.

Isaac Hamon writes of:

the Holmes Island (near Llangenyth) where an old religious house standeth, & some memorialles there are of St. Kenyth. 'Rossilly or Rose-hilly lyeth between Pilton (pt of Penrees) & Llandewy on ye East, Llangenyth on the North: the sea on the W & S, it is in length about a mile & ½ & about a mile in breadth. The Church is dedicated to the Virgin Mary, and on Candle-masse day they keepe their Mapsaint or Patron day, This is a psonage & in the kings gift, as for the soyle it is all Corn-ground, as all the other pishes are in West Gower.

Both Isaac Hamon and the Venerable John Williams provided Edward Lhuyd with a description of the blow-hole on Worm's Head:

Here is a small Island called Worms-head, in which there is a certain chinke or small cleft in the Rocke that doe Continually blowe like a pair bellowes, & it hath such force & strength, that it will blow & cast of, small stones that lye neare it, as it is reported.

The description *'as for the soyle it is all Corn-ground, as all the other pishes are in West Gower',* is often quoted as an indication of the priority given by farmers in this area to the growing of barley, oats and wheat. Although the economy had an export trade in coal and, as Hamon notes, *'they do transport much limestones . . . along this coast',* it was the rearing of beef cattle, dairy cattle and sheep which complemented the acres of corn. The farmers of Rhossili, Middleton and Pitton used the rough pastures as well as the common land to supplement their meadow pastures in the rearing of livestock. The arable land was too precious to be laid down to grass so it might have been waving fields of corn which greeted the eye when the strips of land in the Great Vile at Rhossili were viewed early in the eighteenth century. We know that by agreement at this time the villagers used the strips for corn at the appropriate season, before allowing stock back on the stubble, with the clover undersown under the corn providing further pasture after all the corn had been harvested.

The glebe land at Rhossili and the adjacent fields such as *Well Acre* were the probable location of a warren at Rhossili – the very name *Warren Close* is indicative of this feature. Two areas have the name Warren Close as well as further names such as *Burrows* and *Harepits* which denote favourable conditions for the rabbits and hares which were trapped by nets, ferrets or, in the case of hares, by dogs. The farm track which leads down to the Warren through *Well Acre* comes to the solifluction terrace which has enough width for decent-sized fields; here are the remains of the *hall-house* excavated with the remains of the medieval church and then reburied under a mound of sand and earth which might be mistaken for a pillow-mound. The ideal conditions for rabbits here were confirmed at harvest time, when the cutting of corn by reaper and binder in adjacent fields brought a good crop of rabbits, caught by human speed and greyhounds as they left the dwindling area of corn. No use was found for the skin in the modern era, but the meat of the rabbit made a very tasty dish to supplement wartime rations of food in remote villages such as Rhossili.

The value of Isaac Hamon's meticulous description of Gower is seen, too, in the evidence he presents of the speech and vocabulary of its villagers – not surprisingly a number of the linguistic features he comments on can be identified in characteristic vocabulary and dialect of villagers in the twentieth century. As Frank Emery points out, one of the most specific of Edward Lhuyd's queries, *'Wherein doth the English of the Vulgar in Pembrokeshire and Gowersland differ from that of the Western Counties of England?'* inspired Hamon to make his invaluable survey. The fascinating details of old dialect words and their pronunciation are seen in the work of authors such as Frank Emery and Horatio Tucker, which enables us to examine how the villagers of Rhossili might have spoken three hundred years ago. Their speech, like that of other Gower folk, brought echoes of the West Country: it was distinctive enough to be noted by A.G. Bradley in *In the March and Borderland of Wales,* 1905.

But the Gower man outside the Welsherie is no more Welsh than a Devonian, though he is not like a Devonian. His voice and virtues are entirely his own, and his language, like that of South Pembrokeshire, is an English vernacular evolved in isolation.

The forty-six words of *The Old English of West Gower, Which is Now Out of Use* were produced by Isaac Hamon as examples of the Gower vocabulary which had disappeared by corruption or lack of use.

The people that were born in Qu: Elizabeth's time and dyed about 30 or 40 yeares ago, used these words & some other words besides.

The examples of words which Isaac Hamon suggested had disappeared include *Churchgoin* for a Christening, *Hay* meaning yard, as Church hay and *weest,* meaning dismall; it could be suggested that they still had usage in the present century, however, as when a person was not looking particularly well he could be described as appearing *weest* or unwell. Few of the other words bring echoes of dialect words in Gower fifty years ago, so Hamon was largely right it seems.

And further as touching ye old dialect in Gower, the Southern pt, about Oxwich, Penrees Porthynon & all the pishes in that pts did pnounce their words something like the West of England, as v: in steede of f or z for s & the like.

He also confirms that 'o' was pronounced as if it were 'a', with a long field called *Longlands* in the glebe land above Rhossili Bay being called *Langlands.* In a contrary way *hond* for hand, *lond* for land were sometimes used, together with terms and phrases which Hamon could not have heard of, as he suggests that *'many such sort of words & terms they had, but all this is strange to ye people now that are under 50 yeares of age.'* A similar fate has overtaken words used by older Gower folk, which would not be understood by people under fifty in villages in Gower today. *'Yet in former times,'* as Hamon concludes, *'all people both highe & lowe did talke the old English.'* The similarities of Gower speech with local village dialects found in rural Wiltshire has been obvious to someone brought up in Rhossili who spent nineteen years in Wiltshire.

The Reverend John Collins produced *A List of Words from the Gower Dialect of Glamorganshire* which was printed in *Philological Transactions, IV, No. 92,* 1850, where a far more recognisable sequence of Gower words appear. 'Caffled' refers to entangled as with a ball of string, or a length of binder twine which had become tangled up; 'Cammet' meaning crooked was used by Gower people to describe someone who was awkward or cack-handed. 'Clit' to stick together and 'Charnel' which was a place raised to the roof for hanging bacon were also used. 'Nesseltrip' might be the smallest pig in the litter, or the youngest member of the family! A 'seed lipe' used for sowing corn was, according to Collins, *'a matted basket of peculiar shape'*, it had to fit around the waist of the sower or on his hip. As you listened to a speech by a raconteur of the calibre of George Tucker of Horton – who could pack more dialect Gower words into an after-dinner oration than most in Gower – you could be transported back to former times: the field became *vile* or *viel* as in the *Great Vile* and *Little Vile* the area where the strips of land of Rhossili villagers lay in open fields. Sheep were penned in fields near the cliff which have the name *Vold,* which is Fold, they could be released to graze on the cliff common land through holes left in the drystone walls. The word *shoord* would be a gap – a sheep-hole in some cases – but also a field entrance filled by a gate or hurdle when not in use. *Colley cows* as Horatio Tucker confirms in his writings, were milking cows, *faayer* was fair; *flathin* was an egg-and-milk pudding, sweetened and spiced and baked in a pastry-lined dish. 'Gloy' was the unbruised wheaten straw selected for thatching, and a 'mawn' was a large wicker basket used for carrying sliced-up root crops to cattle in their stalls, or in a smaller version it was used for potato picking where the expert picker could get exactly half a hundredweight in one.

Corruption of a number of place-names and field-names is always likely where vowels and consonants are altered in the characteristic Gower dialect – so *Mon Acre* becomes Monica. *Furzey-land* might become Vurze-land. Within the open fields, the balks or strips of land separating the individual strips from each other are landshares in Gower, but are described as 'lanchers'. Sometimes in other areas the word, or a similarly corrupted version of it, is used the describe the individual strip itself. *Quar* would be quarry as in the floating quarries or *vlotquar* which were the locations where limestone was dislodged from the cliff face by picks or explosives and then loaded on to ships tied up at the cliff anchorages near Kitchen Corner. The word *tallat* was given to a loft, usually a storage place above the stalls where cattle were kept. It would be heated by the warmth from the cattle below, so it was not unknown for farm labourers on the poorer farms in the nineteenth century to sleep there. One Middleton farmer, ready to go *quat* (sleep), used to say that he was going up to the tallat; he was going up the stairs to his bedroom, but in the case of some early Gower farmhouses the bedspace would be open and reached by climbing a ladder, exactly as you would go up to the tallat above the stock by a ladder from the barn. *Zull* was a wooden plough, *zi'thee* meant see you and *zi'thee knaw* meant do you know. In his article on *The Dialect Speech of Gower* in *Gower III* (1950), Horatio Tucker confirmed the reasons for the distinct nature of Gower speech and vocabulary, as Hamon had done many years earlier. He suggested that:

> *The vocabularies of Gower speech which have been compiled, while not very comprehensive, nevertheless show a richness and variety of words not usually met with in other districts in Britain Separation and isolation from the parent speech for many centuries has resulted in characteristics peculiar to*

Gower and wide variations in the form of words of West Country origin, but on the other hand it has contributed to the retention of some words which have dropped out of dialect speech elsewhere in Britain.

Rining meaning mooching or scrounging is a lovely Gower word, as is *culfe* or *culfer* for a slice (of cake). *Pilm*, meaning dust, has been retained from Cornish; *cluppit* is broody; and *jibbons* or *chibbons* are spring onions.

John Evans was able to point out in 1804 in *Letters Written During a Tour Through South Wales,* the inescapable similarities noted between the linguistic features of the West of England and Gower:

The language of the Gower people is English, the dialect broad and coarse, so that a traveller might fancy himself in the West of England.

When linguistic returns were first collected in the census of 1931 they showed Gower as one of the most completely anglicised parts of South Wales: in ten of its eighteen parishes more than 90 per cent of the population was unable to speak Welsh. As Isaac Hamon noted in his account written over three centuries earlier: in Oxwich, Penrice and Porteynon they *'did pronounce their words something like the West of England'* whereas in North Gower *'about Llanrhidian, Cheriton . . . they inclined more to the Welsh, and mixed some Welsh words among their old English.'*

In Isaac Hamon's day we find, too, descriptions of disputes between landlord and tenant over infringements of the manorial rights of the lord. In turn the lord of the manor might be alleged to have infringed the rights of the lord of the Seignory of Gower. William Richard was the lord's bailiff in Rhossili in the later seventeenth century. The steward was also expected to keep his ear to the ground to ensure that, if any wreck took place on the shore of Gower, representations were made and investigations begun so that items from the wreck reached the right custodian for a year and a day when, if they had not been claimed, they became the property of the appropriate lord. Even if they were claimed, there was financial benefit to the lord from whose manor the items were recovered. Writing to a lord to secure the handing over of articles of wreck recovered by his tenants and acquired by him although they rightfully belonged to the lord of the Seigniory, was a matter for diplomatic courtesies, but if the argument presented by the steward did not prevail there might be a resort to litigation.

The ninth article of a roll entitled *Manerium de Landimore* which was a survey made for the Rt. Hon. Phillip Earl of 'Pembrock' and Montgomery in September 1657 before William Seys and George Lucas, confirmed that *'Wreck of the Sea doth belong to the Lord of this Mannor.'* This ignores the superior claim of the overall rights of the Lord of the Seigniory, so when several manors of Gower including Landimore, Weobley and Reynoldston passed to the Mansel family by purchase in 1666, it gave them control of additional areas of the coast where a claim to *wrack de mer* might be made. The correspondence of the Mansel family in Volume II of *A Schedule of Penrice and Margam Muniments not hitherto catalogued* (National Library of Wales, 1942) gives details of a letter from Richard Jeffreys for the Marquis of Worcester, 9th March 1677/78 to Sir Edward Mansel, Bart., Vice Admiral of South Wales:

> *David Evans informs him that French wines and brandy washed ashore in Gower-land in February were seized by Sir Edward's agents under the pretence that they were brought ashore within the manor of Oxwych and Porteynon. His Lordship is 'much injured' because wrecks on that coast belong to him by virtue of his Seigniory of Gower. The writer is commanded to desire Sir Edward to cause restitution of those wines and brandy to be made to David Evans for the lord's use.*

So, although the items washed ashore were part of the *presentments* at the next manorial court it did not always follow that the lord of the manor recognised the superior claim of the overlord of the lordship of the Seigniory of Gower, that is, until 1684. The extra prestige and influence attaching to the Marquis of Worcester when he became Henry first Duke of Beaufort in 1684 may have changed the picture. Shortly after the Duke of Beaufort's triumphal progress through Wales, which brought him to Swansea in August 1684, we find Sir Edward Mansel signing this affirmation:

> *Whereas of late there has happened several Vessels of Wine and other Wrecked Goods to be taken up Floating in the Lordships of Roscilly, Landimore and Webley within the Seniory [Seigniory] of Gower and Libertys thereof in the County of Glamorgan which came thither by occasion of a Wreck Ship which was cast away at Sea and least that any should think that I pretend to any right thereunto I do acknowledge that what came unto my hands which was taken Floating was the right of his Grace the Duke of Beaufort as he is Lord of the said Seigniory and I have it by his favour and not otherwise. Witness my hand this Twentieth day of September 1684.*
>
> *Edward Mansell*
>
> *Witness hereunto Godfrey Harcourt John Watkins David Thomas*

So the lord of the newly acquired manors of Landimore, which included Rhossili and Weobley, acknowledged that he enjoyed the fruits of *wrack de mer* by favour of the lord of the Seigniory. There are presentments in later years: when the manors of *Landymore*, *Wibbley* and *Reignoldston* held a Court Baron at Llanrhidian on 16 September 1690 it was noted *'We present part of a mast taken up on Rociley sand.'* The presiding Stewards were Thomas Mansel and George Thomas. In a later record of 20 May 1717 for the same manors, when they held a *View of Frankpledge with Court Baron* under Thomas Cory, Steward, at Reynoldston, the presentment reads: *'We present two vessels of oyl and a vessel of wine taken up upon Roseily sand and delivered unto Mr Edward Hanchorn [Hancorne] and also a little cag of lime juice as wrack.'*

The regular procedures by which tenants presented at the manorial court wreck found on the foreshore of Rhossili Bay is a reminder of the traditional rights exercised by the lord, provided of course that the discoverers were prepared to declare it. Interpreted:

by stewards such as Gabriel Powell, who was the Duke of Beaufort's Steward for the whole of the Seigniory of Gower, and his son, Gabriel Powell, junior, who succeeded him, the ancient rights and prerogatives of the Lord invariably meant payment by tenants for the simplest permissions:

Oystermouth: There are others who fish for and take Lobsters and Crabs on the Rocks, or on the Sea Shore for which they pay the Lord sixpence a piece yearly.

Bishopston: A few of the Inhabitants of this Manor pay Sixpence yearly for fishing in the Sea, to wit John Webbern and William Phillip for fixing Nets on the sands, and David Hugh for catching Crabs and Lobsters in the Rocks.

Furze Cutters; pay yearly for Cutting Furze on the Hill 6d.

Source: *A Survey of the Seigniories of Gower and Kilvey 1764 by Gabriel Powell.*

In view of these charges – which include one for cutting Furze which was normally a manorial right in some manors exercised freely – it is easy to see why the regime of Gabriel Powell, senior, and his even more unpopular son, did little to ease the burden of the Duke of Beaufort's tenants. The Mansel family exercised similar control over fishing and crabbing rights in the manors of Oxwich, Porteynon and Pitton *alias* Pilton, the difference may have been that the tenants could freely catch lobsters and crabs but could not sell them without permission. The Court Baron held at *Oxwhich* on the 27th day of May 1702 records tenants who were present, and a Jury which included Thomas Lucas, gent., Will. Richard, John Beavan, James Taylor, John Gamon and Samuell Grove, as well as Morgan Beynon and George Long. Courts such as these could hear cases involving property or disputed sums up to the value of £2, which is why one of the early cases involving Jenkin Jenkin, plaintiff, *versus* John Lewies, defendant, for '*goods sould*' shows only the sum of £1 19s 11d *Recovered 10 shillings*. An inserted sheet in these Court proceedings reads:

May ye 27th 1702

The presentment the Grand Jury of ye severall Lordships Porteynon Pitton alias Pilton at a Cort barron held under ye Honorable Edward Mansell of

Margam Baronett Lord of ye said Manors before Thomas Mansell Esq. Steward There

A case is heard and the judgement signed by Thomas Mansel, Esquire, and John Hopkin, Edward Hoskin, John Gamon, George Bach, Henry Lucas, John Jones, and Nicholas Hoskin. In the next case the phrase *sould by* is crossed through where it appears by each defendant's name; instead of *sould by* is written the phrase *selling without leave*

Penrice and Margam Manuscripts 7444

The document continues: *by the oath of Robert Thomas we present*

Joan Clement for selling without Leave fined 2s 6d.	*3 lobsters & 4 Dozen of crabs*
we present John Grove for selling without Leave fined 2s 6d.	*3 lobsters & 3 Dozen of crabs*
we present Samuell Grove for selling without Leave (No fine put in)	*2 lobsters & 2 Dozen of crabs*
we present Ann Gamon for selling without Leave fined 2s 6d.	*2 Dozen of boiled crabs*

We have to assume that Samuell Grove paid the same fine as the others. The entry of 2 dozen boiled crabs indicates they were ready to eat, this in the later era of Gower crabbers usually meant a higher price was charged. It also appears from the insertion of the phrase *selling without leave* that the two men and two women crabbers might have secured.permission to sell their catch if they had gone about it in the right way. Altogether the total catch of 8 Lobsters and 11 dozen crabs, caught in May, represented a formidable achievement, judged by recent standards, when anything remotely near these plentiful hauls of shellfish would be unlikely. The later entry, again mentioning John Grove, suggests that he did not have a very happy day: John Grove and Griffith Prison [Prisson], being overseers of the highways, were presented for '*suffering the way that leadeth from Rosily to Swansey within the Manor of Oxwhich is to* [be] *Repaired by the inhabitants of the parish of Oxwhich by the 2nd day of June next.*' The entry dealing with highways ends: [if not], '*then £1 19s 11d performed.*'

These entries in the manorial court rolls are quite informative – John Grove and Griffith Prisson had their responsibilities as overseers of the highways to see each parish maintained its road system. The onus was on them to organise repairs with materials and labour provided by the villagers who were duty-bound to play a part. The villagers of Pitton *alias* Pilton were also involved in an incident concerning the wreck of the *Shepton Mallett* in 1731, which prompted investigations which uncovered what had happened to part of an earlier ship which was wrecked under Pilton Cliffs in 1677.

The summary of the incident given by de Gray Birch in his Catalogue of the Penrice and Margam Manuscripts refers to an affadavit or deposition of Moses Thomas, of the Parish of Oxwich, county Glamorgan,

> *respecting a figure-head of a Lion, of a ship, found under the cliffs at Pilton, in Gower, in the Parish of Rossilly about A.D. 1677, taken by Francis Bevan of Reynoldston, and afterwards taken by Sir Edward Mansell's bailiff as wreck belonging to the said Sir Edward as Lord of the Manor of Pilton; and respecting the wreck of the Shepton Mallett of Bristol.*

Sworn at Penrice, 8th November 7 George II (1733).

The wreck of the *Shepton Mallett* on the rocks or cliff of *Pilton Clift* about February 1731 eventually led to investigations as to what had happened to her cargo and the *'Mast, Cables, Sayles and other things belonging to the Said Shipp.'* John Creek of the parish of Rossilly in the County of Glamorgan, Yeoman; Edward Tucker of the parish of Llandewy in the said County, Mason, and Thomas Griffith of the Parish of Penrice in the said County. Yeoman, eventually made depositions respecting the circumstances, and the disposal of items from the ship which washed ashore. The three men *'Joyntly and Severally make Oath'* and describe how in February 1731 *'The Shipp called the Shepton Mallett was Wreckt on the Rocks or Clift called Pilton Cliff.'* This was within the land of the Right Honourable Thomas, Lord Mansel, who could claim custody of items from the wreck – they did not come under the jurisdiction of the freeholder tenant, Maysod Dawkins, who had sub-let the property to John Harry. John Creek and Edward Tucker describe how *'severall things on board the said shipp and great parte of the said shipp as alsoe of her Taibles, Furniture and apparell came on Shoar.* The *Mast, Cables, Sayles and other things belonging to the Said Shipp'* were in the custody of John Harry at this time, having been taken *'from the waterside by the said John Harry, Robert Bydder of the parish of Rossilly . . . Richard Owen of the same parish and George Taylor of the parish of Langenith and severall others by Ower Direction.'* Thomas Griffith confirmed that he was present at Pilton at the time and *'did see Richard Owen with a Rope fixed by the Mast of the said shipp haleing* [hauling] *the same on Shore before the Tide.'* The three principal villagers – John Creek, Edward Tucker and Thomas Griffith – placed their marks by their names at the end of their depositions. They were sworn at Penrice on 23 September 6 George II, A.D. 1732. These details of what had happened to the *Shepton Mallett* clarified the question of custody of the wreck, which would belong to Thomas, Lord Mansel, in whose custody it would remain for a year and a day, unless claimed in this time. It could then be disposed of by the lord of the manor of Pitton *alias* Pilton, provided of course he had come to an agreement by this time with the lord of the Seigniory of Gower, the Duke of Beaufort, that he could retain wreck which came ashore on the coasts of the manors in Gower which he held. The willingness to exploit opportunities presented by wrecked ships is one which recurs in the eighteenth century along the coast of South Wales – along with the tales of smugglers come the stories of the 'wreckers'.

The contribution of Moses Thomas came during investigations as to what had happened some fifty-five years earlier to wreck from a ship wrecked under Pilton Cliffs in 1677. Moses Thomas, gentleman, who was then sixty-eight years of age, was able to give full details of the removal by Francis Bevan of Reynoldston of the Head or Lyon of this ship to his house at Pilton, from where it was taken away by the Bailiff of Sir Edward Mansel, William Richard. Mr George Lucas, whose tenant Francis Bevan was at Pilton, is shown as holding a freehold (socage) house and 14 acres in East Pilton, and the same in West Pilton, around 1640.

The glimpses of the past afforded by literary accounts such as Isaac Hamon's are very valuable in that they show the rural landscape of Gower in Stuart times. To this picture we can add the evidence of Parish Registers for Rhossili which date from 1642, and the picture of Rhossili's villagers as shown in Hearth Tax Returns.

Restoration Rhossili

The start of the Civil War in the seventeenth century is dated usually to 22 August 1642, when King Charles I set up his standard at Nottingham and called on his loyal subjects to come to his aid in his struggle with Parliament. In the years which followed, the individual tragedies of divisions within families, divisions within villages and within counties are inextricably merged in many cases with the constitutional, military and religious struggles within the nation. Although the unremitting support of nobles and gentry to their respective causes can be clearly chronicled it is less certain, for example, how the ordinary villagers viewed the campaigns which led to battles in various parts of England and Wales. One suspects that they were detached from deep consideration of the arguments which brought about the Civil War, and were caught up in it only through loyalty, as a tenant or follower of a lord who had answered the call to arms. Everyday life no doubt continued, in the remoter rural areas, in its normal course, with occasional awareness of the national events which were to lead to the execution of Charles I on 30 January 1649.

Charles II landed at Dover on 25 May 1660, and entered London in triumph four days later, on May 29 1660, his thirtieth birthday. One of the first measures to combat a deficiency in the royal finances was a *Free and Voluntary Present* to King Charles II which was made up of *ye free guifts* of the wealthier members of the nation. These included, in Gower, five of the wealthier members of Rhossili whose contributions in the schedule totalled £2 1s 8d. An acknowledged deficiency of £300,000 in the revenues of £1,200,000 per annum projected by the Convention Parliament as being necessary for the King to run the country properly was also to be remedied by the proposal to introduce a Hearth Tax. This was imposed from 1662 and continued until its abolition in 1689. The returns for this tax, which can be viewed at the National Archives at Kew in London, are notably lists of assessments of how many hearths each householder had in their dwelling; this created liability for each householder of 2 shillings for each hearth. We can identify the relative prosperity of some 38 Rhossili villagers: many were noted as *Chargeable*, that is, liable to pay the tax, while those assessed for their number of hearths but unable to pay for a variety of reasons were deemed to be *Non-Chargeable*. Either way, we can identify a large number of the householders who lived in Rhossili three hundred and twenty years ago. Their names are given, some evaluation of the size and standard of the houses in Rhossili can be attempted, reasons offered for exemption from the Hearth Tax can be studied, and these shown as being in arrears can be sympathetically considered!

This variety of sources from which a number of themes can be illustrated has a valuable addition from the time of the Civil War – the Parish Registers of Rhossili. By law Parish Registers should date from Tudor times:

The keeping of registers of baptisms, marriages and burials was made compulsory in 1538 and some date from then. Many more, however, record registrations from 1558, for in 1598 the keeping of such records was again ordered and the copying into books of entries as far back as the year of Elizabeth's accession was encouraged. (W.B. Stephens, *Sources for English Local History*).

The only Parish Registers in the Swansea Hundred which go back to the seventeenth century appear to be those of Ilston (1655), Llandeilo Talybont (1662), St Mary's, Swansea (1630) and Rhossili (1641). Reynoldston has Bishop's Transcripts where the earliest entry is 1682, but the Parish Registers date from 1713. The fact that Rhossili's Parish Registers date from the time of the Civil War makes them an invaluable reference for family history for over three hundred and fifty years, always assuming the researcher can distinguish between all the Bidders, Beynons, Thomases, Bevanses and Stotes!

The illegibility of a number of the earliest entries means that it is not until the Restoration in 1660 that the record of Baptisms, Marriages and Burials affords us the opportunity of gleaning sequences of names to match up with Hearth Tax returns and leases. Even then there is an occasional hiatus, as shown by an entry in Latin in the Parish Register around 1668-69. In 1668 and 1669 the Rector declined to write up details in the church registers because the fee for this service of three shillings and four pence was unpaid. The Register of Baptisms dates from 1641, Burials from 1642 and Marriages from 1665. It is rather speculative to interpret the earliest entries but they do appear to reveal names which we can confirm from later sources:

> 1642 *Margaret Taylor the daughter of Phillip Taylor was buried ye xth of*
> *February*
> *David Ball was buried March the xth Anno of 1645*
> *Roger Austin was buried June 9th*
> *Sybill ye wife of Phillippe Grove was buried June 30 (?)*
> *Nicholas ye sonne of John Longe was buried August 10th*
> 1645 *November ye 10th Alfred Hughs was buried*

We are on safer ground by 1662 when the baptisms of Richard Bidder (4th August), and John Beynon (10th September) were recorded. The burials of John, the son of Morgan Mayo, and Elizabeth Gamon, *uxor* David Gamon, appear in 1665 together with the marriages of John Stote and Jane Rees, Morgan Beynon and Elizabeth David, Samuel Taylor and Anne Bydder of around the same period. The entries would be in Latin in the original record. Rowland Taylor and John Stote appear as Churchwardens. So, from these early entries we can list the family names of Bidder, Ball, Beynon, Austin, Grove, Stote, David, Long and Gamon together with Mayo, Rees and Hugh. We can establish that Roger Austin, who was buried in 1645, was the Rector of Rhossili from 1580 until his death. David Ball is mistakenly identified as David Batt in an Abstract of Wills proved in Carmarthen – he is referred to correctly as David Ball of *Rosehilly* in a note of wills for each year which includes 1645. The date of the will which is described as incomplete is 20 January 1643, so that it was made during the Civil War. Among the names mentioned in the will we have:

Robert Done	*Poor Man*	*Rhossili*	*Glams.*
Nicholas Stephen	*Poor Man*	*Rhossili*	*Glams*
Alice Austin	*Poor Woman*	*Rhossili*	*Glams.*
Mary Willy	*Poor Woman*	*Rhossili*	*Glams.*
Anne Creek	*Poor Woman*	*Rhossili*	*Glams.*

David son of his brother Nicholas Ball

Dorothy Ball sister

Dorothy Thomas daughter of sister Anne Ball

Margaret Dawkins   servant

Nicholas Long, the son of John Long or Longe, who was mentioned as having been buried in 1642, was mentioned earlier, in his father's will which was dated 16 April 1626. The date of probate was 27 June 1626. Here we find that John Long, the eldest son, was named as executor; Isaacke and Nicholas, sons, were also named, together with Anne Longe, his wife, and Anne Longe, his daughter. Nicholas Giles, *Stock custodian*, Llangennith, also appears together with Roger Austin, debtor. Among the witnesses is Morgan Creeke the elder, a member of a family we have noted taking up a lease of land in Middleton in the early Stuart period. It is from such sources that the story of the villagers of Rhossili can be built up – Parish Registers, wills and leases all help to illustrate and illuminate the lives of the village community. The major change in the Stuart period, however, was the change in the ownership of a large part of Rhossili. Shortly after the Restoration in 1660, the earls of Pembroke disposed of substantial parts of Gower parishes to the Mansels and other landowning families. These sales extended the land ownership in Gower of the Mansel family. Sir Edward Mansel acquired one third of the total while 45% passed to Evan Seys, Martin Button, John Wyndham and Bussy Mansel. The investment of nearly £4,000 by the Mansel family in acquiring lands in Gower can be seen from a sequence of five documents in the *Descriptive Catalogues of the Penrice and Margam Manuscripts* prepared by Walter de Gray Birch: 'The messuages, lands, privileges etc in the manors or parishes of Rosilly, Lanridian, Landimore, Bishopston, Cheriton, Loughor, Wibly and Reynoldston' are the basis of the transaction. The seal of Great Sessions dated at Cardiff on 4 May 1667 on the final document gave the security of title which the complex sequence of documents was intended to convey. The Mansel family already held the manor of Pitton *alias* Pilton at Rhossili.

In Gower we can still find the leasing of land, the performance of duties relating to the holding of land and the growth of the size of some holdings in the hands of the more prosperous villagers of Rhossili. The names of some villagers have already been noted: Mary or Marie **Baker** who in the counterpart of a chattel Lease is described as being a widow. The Lease, dated 1st December 1648, during the Civil War, secured for £15 a grant of a messuage and lands in *Rossillie* for 99 years, determinable on three lives. It is by the Rt. Hon. Phillip (Herbert), Earl of Pembroke, P.C., K.G.; the yearly rent is £3 with royalties reserved and specified services. Thomas **Hodge** of *Rosillie* had a similar lease for £15 of a messuage or tenement and 15 acres of lands in Landimore, at a yearly rent of 32 shillings; this was dated 12th March 1649/50. A Freehold Lease by John **Long** the elder, of *Rossillie* for £20, secured him 24 acres in the *Parish of Rossillie* at a yearly rent of 50s 8d in June 1656. It is around this last date that we can confirm the names of many of the tenants of the manors of Landimore and *Wibley* from a document entitled:

> *A perfect Extract of all the Tennants, Messuages and tenements with theyr severall termes and estates . . . the severall Rents, Dueties services and Herriotts expressed in theyr severall Leases or grants . . . and due to ye right Honourable Philip Earl of Pembroke and Montgomery in his Manners of Landimore and Wibley.*

William **Seys**, gentleman, is referred to as his Lordship's Steward: he was Steward of the lordships of Landimore, *Wibley* and Reynoldston according to W.C. Rogers, who also notes his receiving a new lease for three lives of Weobley Castle. In a Lease to Seys dated 5th June 1655 *Wormeshead Island* and *one perch of wild furzy and and woody land called Henbach* are mentioned *being 6 acres in my Manner of Wibley*. John **Rogers**, by a lease from the seventh year of the reign of Charles I (1632) had one messuage and 15 acres for a yearly rent of £1 10s. A Herriot of *ye best ox* or 20 shillings, at *ye Lord's choice* was also part of the agreement – this was due when one of the named persons or lives in the Lease died.

Margaret **Gamon** in a lease of the same year is described as *ye wife of Roger Thomas deceased*. It is crossed through as she held only during her own life the one messuage, 10 acres of lands at a yearly rent of 20 shillings. Presumably she had died.

Randolph **Thomas** and Anne Emlett his wife have a Lease of one messuage and tenement of 15 acres at a yearly rent of 30 shillings.

John **Lawrence** *holds by right of his wife, during his life*, 12 acres at a yearly rent of 24 shillings.

Robert **Creak** and Richard **Creek**, as has been noted, also have leases which date from before the Civil War.

John **Taylor** and Elizabeth **Taylor**, one messuage and tenement of 10 acres, yearly rent 20 shillings, is a lease on the same terms as the earlier ones. They also had to find two hens or 1 shilling. This is a feature of all leases, which include the provision of *two capons* or *two hens*, or alternately one shilling, *at the Lord's choice*.

Isaak and John **Long**, for 7½ acres, had to find a yearly rent of 16s 8d. There is also the mention of *suit of Court and Mill*, which are again standard duties requiring the tenants to attend the appropriate manorial court and have their corn ground at a manorial mill which would be under the lord's jurisdiction.

A recital of the details of Leases is not intrinsically interesting but it does enable an assessment of patterns to be made – the yearly rent of land is consistently around two shillings an acre in the early Stuart period. The later leases from the time of Charles II also start around this figure: in 1656 in Rhossili David **Griffith** of *Rossilly*, for £11, secured a chattel Lease from the Rt. Hon. Phillip (Herbert) Earl of Pembroke, of a messuage and lands of 10 acres for a yearly rent of 20 shillings, but this figure for the Interregnum is followed by similar ones in Restoration Rhossili. William **Morgan** of *Rossilly*, for £8, had a messuage and lands of 10 acres – at *Mideltone*, as has been noted earlier – for a yearly rent of 20 shillings. The name Anne **Emlett** in an earlier Lease to Randolph Thomas may well be the Joane [Joanne] Emlett. wife of Randolph Thomas, shown in a Lease of 1664 which also mentions Philip Thomas, his son, and Elizabeth Dame or **Dawe**, wife of Philip Thomas. The 15 acres shown in the earlier Lease is now for their three lives for £6 and the same yearly rent of 30 shillings, as for thirty years earlier. In a final example of a Lease from the Rt. Hon. Phillip (Herbert), Earl of Pembroke, before the sale of the lands in 1666, we find the names of John Stote and Jane Rees whose marriage was noted earlier: here we have Anne Austin, Jane Rees, her daughter, and John Stote, for £12 and a yearly rent of 35 shillings securing a messuage and lands of 7½ acres for their three lives in 1664. A Survey of the Manor of Landimore in 1666 is probably linked with its eventual sale to Sir Edward Mansel, Henry Rumsey is mentioned as one of the *associate commissioners of the said Survey*, and was later involved in the sale proceedings. Ready cash was also raised by means of a Tripartite indenture where the parties were:

(1) *Philip, Earl of Pembroke and Montgomery and the Hon. William Herbert, his son, and heir.*

(2) *William Yorke of the Devizes, John Norden of Badbury, and Francis Wroughton of Wilcott, co. Wilts., and John Borrowdale of London.*

(3) *John Bynon of Rosilly, yeoman.*

John **Bynon** acquired a messuage and 45 acres of land in the parish of Rosilly, county Glamorgan, in the manor of Landimore, for £62, and an annual rent of £2 10s. This high advance payment, and low rent, may denote the need to raise cash to meet commitments and previews the eventual sale of lands for nearly £4,000 which came later.

We are now in position to assess the content of rent rolls of Stuart times which give a summary of the names of tenants of various manors at a defined time – the *Manerium de Horton*, The Manor of Porteynon and the Manor of Pitton *alias* Pilton were part of the holdings of the Mansel family in the south-west of Gower. As such they are dealt with in a sequence of rent rolls for *one yeare ending att Michaelmas 1666*; the very nicely-bound booklet of roughly A4 dimensions with the large figures 1666 on the outside contains not only rent rolls for the Manors of Horton, Porteynon and *Landymore* but also the Mansel manors of Oxwich, Penrice, Nicholaston, and *Scurladge* among others. The *Manerium de Horton* the *rent roll thereof for one year ended at Michaelmas 1666* has names which were well established in Gower at this time: David Bennett, Randolph Knayth, Margarett Baker, John Russell, Robert Griffith, Johan Harry, and Jenkin Phillipp. William Bennett, gent, is shown, with free tenants such as William Bennett (the same man), and George Lucas.

A similar list for the *Manner of Porteynon* would tend to include names familiar from earlier notes on Rhossili: John Thomas, John Grove, Margarett *Emlod* (Emlett), who is shown as a widow, and John Beynon. Morgan Baldwin and Francis Baldwin are followed later by Elinor Baldwin, widow; Thomas Button the Elder is matched by Thomas Button the younger and John Button the elder. William Richard and John Richard come before the intriguing name of John ap John Knayth, with Francis Clement the elder, and younger. Henry Gibbs Esquier, is distinctive, as is the clergyman, Mannasse Matthews, Clerk, and William Gamon of Monkenland; John Beavan and Richard Beavan also appear. It is also worth mentioning the name of John Harry – appearing here in 1666, he may well have been the unfortunate victim recorded in the later Hearth Tax return where we have the exemption of *John Harry burnt down the 7th day of August*

Penrice and Margam Manuscripts 1125: The Mannor of Pitton alias Pilton

Rent roll thereof for the yeare ending att Michaellmas 1666
Rees ap Hugh in right of his wife
Edward Salisbury
Hugh Long in right of his wife
John Stephen in right of his wife
William Taylor
Phillip Long
Owen Gamon
William Gronow
Anne ? Donne widow
John Richard in right of his wife
Phillipp Taylor
John Taylor

John Gammon
John Beavan he more for a Forge
David Gamon
Griffith John
David John
Jenkin Taylor
William Richard

Free Tenants

Bussey Mansell Esquier for a Tenement of lands at Pitton
George Lucas gent, for a tenement in Pilton hee more for another tenement there.

The phrase *in right of his wife* implies that the land being leased has come to the husband through his marriage to the daughter of a previous tenant – the example of Rees ap Hugh who is shown as being married to Elizabeth Hill is one which appears early in the rent roll for Pitton *alias* Pilton. Further light is thrown on this family by a lease of two or three years before the date of the rent roll, that is, 1663-1664. For the Manor of Pitton *alias* Pilton we have a Copy of a Memorandum of a Lease by Sir Edward Mansel, Bart, to Elizabeth Hill, wife of Rees ap Hugh; in an illuminating and intriguing example of the way surnames became standardised and patronymics were gradually replaced, we find that this Lease was to *'Elizabeth Hill, wife of Rees ap Hugh, Nathaniel Pugh and Lydia Pugh their children.'* The holding of a messuage, garden and lands – half an acre, together with 3 acres in *new park* – in the name of the wife, was why Rees ap Hugh appeared in the rent roll in 1666 as a tenant *in right of his wife*. The yearly rent of 6s 6d was mainly for the new land which was being *taken in* at the time of the Restoration. At this time, too, family names were becoming fixed and we can follow the principal families such as the Rogers and Taylor families through following the land they held in, say, 1685. Jeonett and Morgan Gamon, the children of David and Jeonett Gamon leased a messuage and lands of 12 acres for their two lives successively at a yearly rent of £1 16s 4d in 1664. David Griffith the younger of Porteynon, Anne Thomas his wife and Jane Griffith, their daughter, leased 9 acres in the Parish of Rhossili for £14 and a yearly rent of 16s 8d in 1671-72. Thomas Jones of Rossilly leased a messuage and lands, *now held by Elinor Williams,* for two lives; the ¾ acre holding was held for a yearly rent of one shilling only, which implies that this part of the land did not warrant an entry fine. The small size of the portion may have been compounded by limited fertility perhaps. In fact, Thomas Jones did pay a fine of £2 16s, and would have secured the reversion of the Lease from Elinor Williams. Henry Alien of Marwood Parish, county Devon, Anne Creeke, his wife, and Robert Creeke her son by Robert Creeke her former husband, secured a Lease for their lives of 17 acres at Middleton in 1673 for £15 and a yearly rent of 30 shillings.

Two further families can be studied: William Taylor, with two others, paid a Fine of £2 6s, and a yearly rent of four shillings for two houses, *heys* and garden which came to 21¼ acres in the Pitton *alias* Pilton part of the community in 1673. Sage Taylor and Mary Gronow, spinsters, had a house and garden in the same manor in 1684 at a yearly rent of 2 shillings, with a Fine of £1 4s. A Bond by John Taylor, and Philip Taylor, son of the *said John of Rossilly* was to William Richard and describes them as *yeomen* – we see this family extending their holding in 1698 in an adjacent part of Gower by a substantial investment which suggests they were relatively affluent. If this is the same family then we see from a Lease for three lives by Edward Mansel of *Henllis* in the Parish of Llandewy that they were taking up land on the boundaries of Pitton *alias* Pilton manor. John Taylor of Rossilly and his brothers Samuel and Joseph Taylor surrendered a Lease for two lives and for £43 6s secured four parcels of land called *Higher Nockfields* and High-Walls in the Parish of Llandewy at a yearly rent of 50 shillings. The John Bevan who paid more for a forge in the Manor of Pitton *alias* Pilton is probably the same person who gained a grant of 12 acres, with two others, for their lives in 1681, paying a fine of £23 and yearly rent of 21 shillings. The willingness and ability to pay relatively large sums shows that, like the Taylor family, the Bevan family may have been reasonably affluent villagers.

The collation of all the names which have been mentioned – in leases, in rent rolls and in the Parish Registers – needs to be attempted if we are to gain a clearer picture of the relative standing of members of the Rhossili community in Stuart times. The amount of land they held, the number of hearths they had in their houses and their ability to make voluntary contributions to the king, Charles II, can be gleaned from a study of documents found in the National Archives, Kew and in the National Library of Wales, Aberystwyth. The initial glimpse we can get of the wealthier members of the community in Restoration Rhossili comes from the Free and Voluntary Present 1661, mentioned earlier. Glamorgan, Gower and Rhossili people volunteered to contribute, as seen in the document which is partially reproduced below:

GLAMORGAN   A perticuler of ye free guifts, of ye Inhabitants of ye hundred of Swanzey, taken ye One and Twentieth day of November, One Thousand Six hundred Sixtie & one, Before William Herbert, William Thomas and Walter Thomas, Esquires, Commissioners for his Majesty in that behalf

Schedule of contributions (Free and Voluntary Present)

Parish	Names	£	s	d
Porteynon	Thomas Button		2	6
	John Richard		5	0
	Owen Richard		6	8

Rossilly	Phillip Taylor	10	0
	John Thomas	10	0
	Morgan Gammon	5	0
	Richard Bidder	10	0
	William Richard	6	8

(The National Archives, E179/264/47)

The most significant offer came from a Mr Rowland Dawkins of Pennard (Kilvrough), whose £10 contribution might have been partial mitigation for his positive support of the Parliamentary cause, when, with Colonel Philip Jones and Bussy Mansel, he was a key figure in the clique who ruled Swansea during Cromwell's Protectorate. He is also referred to as Major-General Dawkins in some contexts. The three Commissioners involved with the Swansea Hundred were William Herbert, William Thomas and Walter Thomas. The last two names appear to be those of loyal Royalists of Swansea restored to prominence after the Restoration. Two totals given for the Swansea Hundred were £84 14s, to which later sums appear to have been added, to give a final total of £101 1s 6d.

It is worthy of special mention that in Gower the number of contributors at Ilston came to 8 – this total exceeds that for Porteynon (3) Reynoldston (6), Penrice (2), Oxwich (1), Nicholaston (1), Llangennith (2), Llandewi (3) and Rhossili (5), although much bigger numbers of contributors are found at Oystermouth (10), Llanrhidian (15) and Bishopston (6). Ilston, usually regarded as a small village today but the main centre of nonconformity in Gower around 1650 when John Miles founded the first Baptist Church in Wales, appears to have, nevertheless, contributed substantially to the Free and Voluntary Present to Charles II. The 8 contributors – George Harry, Leyson Davies, John Austine, Thomas Richard, Jenkin Hoskin, John Davies, Hopkin Bowen and Morgan Harry – promising a total of £2 18s 6d, which was higher than all the other small Gower villages except for Reynoldston's £4 10s. We have the signs of a potential hierarchy in Rhossili, not just in the manor of Pitton *alias* Pilton but in the community as a whole. The picture is widened further by a document dated the following year, 1662. It is one of the most valuable and informative sources of information on Restoration Rhossili, as the thirty-three names of villagers in Rhossili are followed by the acreage of land they held nearly three hundred and fifty years ago in 1662.

Penrice and Margam Manuscripts 7141

> *1662 A true valuation of all Lands Tenements Tithe and Gliebe within the Parish of Rosehilly*

The list of names, the number of acres each person held, and the assessed valuation for tithe purposes of the land held – all these details were the work of six of the villagers who were called Surveyors. It is no surprise to find Phillip Taylor, John Thomas, Morgan

Gammon or Gamon, Richard Bidder, William Richard – the five contributors of the *Free and Voluntary Present* to Charles II – were five of the six Surveyors whose names appear at the foot of the document. The sixth name is that of Thomas Hodge. At the top of the list comes the village clergyman, Mr Edward Gamage – His *tithe & gliebe* totalled £50. He had recently been restored to the living of Rhossili with the return of Charles II in 1660, having been expelled from the living a decade earlier. The next name is that of Mr Richard Saise (whose name is normally spelled as Seys); he was the Lord's Steward whose role covered manors such as those of Landimore. The thirty-three other names appear below in the order they are shown on the document, together with the number of acres they held. The assessed valuation for tithe purposes has been left out for the purpose of simplification: *The summe is £161 12sh. 8d* is the total given at the bottom, *& the tithe & gliebe £50*. The total given at the top is an approximation of these two figures added up – £210.

Rhossili Villagers 1662:

Phillip Taylor	76 acres
Elizabeth Beavan widow	30 acres
John Thomas	60 acres & a Clift
Morgan Gamon	34 acres
David Gamon	15 acres
Elizabeth Gamon	20 acres
Richard Creeke	17 acres
Thomas Hodge	15 acres
John Stote	15 acres
David Griffith	10 acres
Richard Bidder	60 acres
John Taylor	10 acres
Ann Austine widow	17 acres
William Morgan	10 acres
Isaack Longe	7 acres
John Beynon	30 acres
John Longe	24 acres
Randolph Thomas	30 acres
Avis? Creeke	12 acres
George Harry	15 acres
Rowland Taylor	30 acres
David Hopkins	30 acres
Margrett Austine widow	2 acres
Richard Austine	2 acres
Mr David Bennet	7 acres
George Philip	2 acres

Edward Salsburie	*3 acres*
David Ball	*1 acre*
Morgan Vaghan [Vaughan]	*10 acres*
Griffith John	*3 acres*
Ann Stephen	*1 acre*
David John	*3 acres*
Reese Pugh?	*14 acres*

These villagers would appear to be the principal householders who held land in Rhossili, Middleton and Pitton *alias* Pilton under either the Earl of Pembroke or the Mansel family. When we come to the Hearth Tax Returns of a decade later we can compare the acreage of each tenant with the number of hearths shown in their houses – it is likely that Philip Taylor would have 4 or 5 hearths; it is more than probable that Margaret Austin would have lived in a 1 hearth house. The thirty-eight names given in one Hearth Tax Return complement the thirty-three names found in 1662 – many of the families will be identical so that we gain a very convincing of the villagers who lived in Restoration Rhossili.

The Hearth Tax records date from 1662 to 1689, when the payments were abolished. The sum of two shillings had to be paid yearly at the Feast of St Michael the Archangel (29 September) and the Feast of the Annunciation of the Blessed Virgin St Mary (25 March). The best returns for Glamorgan, Gower and Rhossili appear to be the later ones of 1670-1673 when the names of those chargeable for hearths are coupled with the names of those deemed non-chargeable. The total of names has been regarded as indicating the number of households or, more accurately, household units in a village such as Rhossili where the total of thirty-eight names should represent a similar number of *householders* or *household units*. It is tempting to take each name as representing one household unit or family and use a conventional multiplier to calculate population totals but this is by no means a straightforward task. We can, however, normally assume that the richer the person the more hearths and stoves he might possess – giving a rough idea of the relative wealth and status of members of the community. Conversely, houses with one hearth have been regarded as an indication of the humbler inhabitants, and this humble role might also be assigned to those with two hearths in less prosperous communities. Those with seven or more hearths lived in some affluence it is assumed, in a house of some size befitting the status of the pillar of society. We would not expect too many of those in villages such as Rhossili.

The focus on the population of Gower can be achieved by an examination of the Hearth Tax Returns at the National Archives: Class E179/221/294 for 23 Charles II (Michaelmas 1670). At Pennard, the assessment for Rowland Dawkins (Kilvrough) was for 8 hearths, Mr Charles Bowen was shown with 9; Robert Bydder with 4 and David Hopkin with 4 also appear. For Reynoldston we would anticipate Mr George Lucas 7, John Lucas Senior 4, and John Lucas Junior 4; Thomas Jones had 2. The twenty-one names for Porteynon had a total of 39 hearths. It is unusual to find, at the end of the Porteynon return, examples of the names of those who were exempt, which does not occur in any other of the villages around Porteynon. The entry reads:

The persons underwritten are under the value & poore:
John Richard William Hoskin

This was certified at the end as having been examined by Rowland Williams who was the Collector, and John Richard, Constable. The entry for Rossilly among the 45 membranes which make up the County Assessment for Glamorgan in 1670 gives 27 names who have a total of 35 hearths it seems, although the number of hearths for persons at the top of the list is indistinct. John Taylor at the top is followed by Richard Bevan, John Thomas and Jenetta Gamon, who is possibly the *relict* of David Gamon as shown in the Parish Register. Whether they had 2 hearths or more is not clear. William Richard, William Castle and John Rogers certainly had 2 hearths as had John Beynon Senior. Richard Portrey, Rector of Rhossili at this time, had 1 hearth, Thomas Griffith, vacant 1, and Sir Edward Mansel, *Knight & Barronett*, vacant 1 were also accountable for empty properties. The indistinct figures for hearths is not a problem – we cannot plausibly claim, however, that the 27 names given do represent the house-holders of Rhossili in 1670 when we have no knowledge or clue as to the numbers and names of Rhossili villagers who secured exemption by dint of poverty or for other reasons. We are better placed to assess the relative status of Rhossili's inhabitants, and its possible population from another return in E179; it is 221/297 (Charles II) which is made up of 96 membranes giving details of Assessments for the county of Glamorgan. For the Swansea Hundred the *Swanzey Town and libertie* starts at membrane 89 and the first name is that of Lewis Jones *portriffe* (Portreeve).

The 38 names shown can be successfully compared both with the names of those shown in *A true valuation of all Lands Tenements Tithe and Gliebe within the parish of Rosehilly* made in 1662, and the Hearth Tax Returns of 1670. Changes in actual Christian names will be seen but if surnames are compared the picture is quite clear: for example, William Castle (2 hearths in 1670) is shown as 1 hearth in the comple-mentary return, but does not feature in the list of tenants in 1662. John Taylor, Richard Bevan, John Thomas, Jenetta Gamon, John Rogers, William Richard and Richard Bydder were mostly in the 2 hearths or more category in the Hearth Tax Assessment of 1670; in the detailed return produced we have Phillip Taylor 3, John Rogers 2, John Thomas 4, Richard Bidder 2, John Stephen 2. We can find Phillip Taylor 76 acres, with Rowland Taylor 30 acres, in the 1662 list, with Morgan Gamon 34 acres, David Gamon 15 acres, and Elizabeth Gamon 20 acres, also appearing. If David Gamon is the more modest landholder with 15 acres then it would explain his one hearth category a decade later. John Thomas, it is evident from other sources, was a successful and influential member of the village community during the Interregnum – it is significant that in a village of 33 one hearth homes he appears as assessed for 4 hearths, the highest figure for Rhossili. Only five properties were of more than one hearth – Richard Bidder had one, to go with the 60 acres he is shown as holding earlier, with John Thomas holding 60 acres *and a Clift* to give him a similar size. We have not noticed among the earlier names the ordinary mortals such as Morgan Mayo and George Phillip – one member of the family of Mayo is involved in a Lease of 1689, a member of the Phillip family is involved in a Lease of Talgarth's Well. We do not have William Richard as a landholder in 1662, yet he is shown in 1670 as having a 2 hearth property in 1670 and appears in a Penrice and Margam Estate document of 1672. We get a significant clue from a deposition made by Moses Thomas in the year 1732 about a wreck which occured under Pilton Cliffs around 1677, where a William Richard of Pilton is shown as *Bayliffe* to Sir Edward Mansel of Margam. His family were later involved in limestone extraction under a Lease from the Penrice and Margam Estate.

It is worth pointing out the names of some of the Rhossili villagers who lived in one-hearth homes: Rowland Taylor (30 acres), Richard Creeke (17 acres), Thomas Hodge (15 acres), Randolph Thomas (15 acres) and Ann Austine, widow (17 acres), were among them. The picture is of modest dwellings, but surely not poverty; the taking up of leases readily in the later Stuart period which involved commitment to pay entry fines as well as rent suggests a modest degree of affluence. Morgan Mayo, who died in 1677, did not pay the Hearth Tax, but we find someone with the same family name – David Mayo – taking·up a successive lease in 1689: David Mayo, Rhossill', Margaret Taylor his wife and Thomas Griffith her son, secured a messuage and lands of 10 acres in Middleton for their lives for £14 and a yearly rent of 20 shillings. David Mayo is shown as a Churchwarden later. George Phillip did not pay Hearth Tax but it may be a member of his family, Thomas Phillip who received a grant for his life of a house and 2 acres in the Manor of Landymore in return for a modest investment. The property was one on the fringes of tile Manor of Rhossili which always featured in Surveys of the Manor of Rhossili: *Talygarth's Well*, where a spring continued to give a supply of very cool, pure water to the settlement for centuries. The grant, dated *November ye 2nd* 1686, reads:

> *Granted then unto Thomas Phillip All that Cottage and two acres of ground now or late in ye tenure of Jeremiah Bond or his Assignes Scituate & being near a place called Talgas well in ye said Mannor* [Landimore] *. . . for and dureing the terme of his naturall life and no longer. At the yearly rent of two shillings of lawful English money . . . Suite of Court and Suite of mill unto such of my mills as my heires shall appoint.*

This abbreviation of the document covers the main elements – Thomas at the end agrees to pay all rates and taxes as shall be imposed and *keep ye same in tenantable reparation.*

> *Fine for changeing of ye life £1. 1sh. 6d.*

It has to be admitted that Thomas Phillip may not have had a bargain with his two acres for a yearly rent of two shillings: some of the ground here is rough grazing, with gorse, bramble bushes and soggy ground preventing its use for anything more than the stocking and feeding of beef cattle. Not far away is Sorry Bargain!

The three families which have not yet featured fully in the snapshots of Restoration Rhossili are the Richards, Bidder and Thomas families – we have *Gulielmus Richard* buried in the last decade of the seventeenth century leaving a will, and an inventory valuing his possessions at over £75. Various Richard Bidders and Robert Bidders are among the seventeenth century villagers of Rhossili, but we also have mention of an ancestor at *Vernhill* in Tudor times where *'The heires of Morgan Vaughan, Owen Perkins and Richard Bydder . . . held the manor by the service of a fourth part of a knight's fee and six swallow tayled arrowes yearely or vjd.'* We find William Richard in the Hearth Tax Return for 1670 where he is assessed on 2 hearths; two years later he features in a document which highlights the presence of a limestone trade at Rhossili. A further nineteen years later a William Richard of *Rhossilly* secures a Chattel Lease to dig lime at Stephen's Torrs. Earlier, in 1661, we find a William Richard who agrees to pay 6s 8d in the *Free and Voluntary Present* to Charles II. It is almost certainly the William Richard mentioned here who appears in 1663 as having his name submitted to the Archdeacon's court. At this time he was charged with not paying the church rate towards the upkeep of the fabric of Rhossili Church. He was one of five parishioners of Rhossili recorded as being fined for non-payment of church rates. It is possible to take a closer look at the name William Richard as it crops up over a period of 30 years – we can conjecture that in his various roles a William Richard was a prominent man in the Rhossili community.

As one of five parishioners who were fined for non-payment of church rates in Rhossili in the 1660s he appears with David Griffith (1662) and John Thomas (May 1663), the entry being William Richard (1663). A document noted earlier gives the clue that he was the bailiff of Sir Edward Mansel. In 1677, according to a deposition made by one Moses Thomas over fifty years later, William Richard at that time was involved in a search for a *Head or Lyon* from a ship which had run aground under Pilton Cliffs. He was described as William Richard of Pilton *Bayliffe to Sir Edward Mansell of Margam*. It is in this capacity that he appears in the *Catalogue of Penrice and Margam Manuscripts* by Walter de Gray Birch: Document 1700. The summary in the Catalogue suggests it is a *'Paper, apparently relating to a wreck at the Worm's Head about those who loaded limestone'*; it records payment of 4d per day to the thirteen named person who carried out the work – some of the names appear more than once. William Richard is one of the witnesses of the will of Richard Bidder who died in 1681 and probably appears for the last time in a lease of 1690. Two geese and two capons have to be provided or three shillings, 2s 6d for *Custome* the *Herriot or best beast* being 40 shillings. Although the Lease is for three lives the Lives in Being are noted as *Himself and Mary his sister*. A transcript of the Lease shows that William Richard and his sister

Mary acquired *'A Messuage & Tenement containing 22 acres in Rossilly Parish with Liberty of Ingress Egress and Regress to break Dig & take up Limestones on a piece of Stony ground called Stephen Torres for to burn Lime for manureing of said Tenement.'* Lime could also be used to make mortar to repair the house, there was provision for *'paying the Tenant of Stephen Torres 1 shilling per weigh for ye Cole'* which had to be brought across his land*, 'for burning the said Lime.'* The William Richard of *Rhoshilly* who died in 1691 – *Gulielmus Richard* is the entry in the Burial Register for Rhossili – had his will probate established at Carmarthen on 10 September 1691. W.C. Rogers notes his Inventory as giving a total value of £75 18s 2d.

In 1661 a Richard Bidder was baptised on the fourth day of August; we find a later reference to Richard Bidder, Senior, as a Churchwarden, so this is likely to be one of his sons. Twenty-four years later, in 1686, a Richard Bydder married Ann Griffith, with earlier marriages of Anne Bydder to Philip Jones and Maria Bydder to Howell Bennett also appearing in the Rhossili Parish Register. The even earlier marriage of Anna Bydder to Samuel Taylor may be a reference to the Anne Bydder who later married Philip Jones. *Richardus Bydder* is buried in 1681 and we can see from his will brief details of the family relationships: his death on 6 March 1681/2 was followed by probate being granted on 23 March. The details help clarify the family group.

Anne Bidder, eldest daughter, has a share of a barque, Joseph Bidder, the second son has a Leasehold house and Tenement called the *Exchange of Porteynon.* There is a reference to Richard Bidder, eldest son, Nathaniell Bidder, third son, and Daniell Bidder, fourth son. John Creekie is a tenant; Rachell Bidder and Mary Bidder are his second and third daughters. Gwenlian *now wife* is shown as one of the Executors with Richard Bidder the eldest son. The witnesses are William Richard, Richard Gamon, John Beynon and Joseph Richard. The reference to a s*hare of a barque* is a reminder that investment in a small trading ship for cross-Channel trade was not unlikely for a Rhossili villager although the principal quays would have been at Porteynon and Oxwich.

It is John Thomas, living in a four hearth house in the 1670s, who appears to have been a man of influence in the local community – he may be the John Thomas who appears on the list of those presented at the Archdeacon's court for refusing to attend the parish church and who was among those fined for non-payment of church rates. He was in the company of William Bynon, Rees ap Hugh and John Taylor in 1668 for refusing to attend church and in the company of David Griffiths (1662), William Richard (1663), Richard Bevan (1666) and David Gamon (1666) for non-payment of church rate. It may be an earlier John Thomas who was an associate of Colonel Philip Jones, the principal figure in the government of Swansea during Cromwell's rule. As such he was the agent for tithes. Edward Mansel described their activities:

> *Jones the chief, Dawkins and Bowen under him, and the rest understrappers*, these *managed the whole deanery of Gower. These livings worth three score and ten pounds a year.*

John Thomas was the tenant of *60 acres & a clift* and was one of two tenants who held most land in Rhossili; Richard Bidder was the other. For Rhossili, the number of nonconformists was 45 in the Compton Census of 1676, the largest group of dissenters in Gower. The number of conformists, 99, gives a figure of 144 for the population of Rhossili so it appears the numbers included all members of families. The licensing of meeting-houses under the Religious Toleration Act 1689, as shown in the records of the Quarter Sessions, show use of the house of Caleb Thomas at Rhossili in January 1721/2 and the house of David Beynon at Middleton around a century later (1812).

The Landscape of Rhossili

The visible evidence of Rhossili's past is an illuminating feature of its landscape today and the eighteenth century is the time from which we can describe aspects of the village and compare the scenes of yesterday with the scenes of today. The earliest dated houses in the village come from this time: Rhossili Farmhouse, Ship Farm, Riverside Farm and High Priest. The farming patterns of Gower villages are shown in the superb maps of 1780 by John Williams for the Penrice and Margam Estate and can be compared with the tithe maps in the middle of the nineteenth century for the same villages. We are within touching distance of Rhossili's past and can view with greater certainty features which in earlier centuries might have been shrouded in mist. A change in approach is required, not discarding documentary evidence but using it with field evidence; not merely studying maps but closely viewing the present-day landscape and intepreting its features.

It was W.G. Hoskins, whose invaluable pioneer work was *The Making of the English Landscape*, who demonstrated the techniques required in following this approach; his evocative pictures of the landscape of past centuries are not an exercise in imagination but are based on sound evidence. When he introduced, as editor, *The Making of the South Wales Landscape* by Moelwyn Williams, he made his philosophy abundantly clear:

> *The landscape itself, to those who know how to read it, is the richest historical record we possess. There are discoveries to be made in it for which no written records exist, or have ever existed.*

He gives the flawless advice: *'To write the history of the landscape requires a combination of documentary research and of fieldwork, of laborious scrambling on foot wherever the trail may lead.'* Along the Heritage Coast trail from Rhossili to Paviland are visible reminders of the past, whether they be lime-kilns or dry-stone walls, Iron Age promontory forts or open fields. They are all there to be seen. The growing band of adherents to the study of landscape history has been matched by the growing use of words such as *palimpsest*. Originally used to describe writing material used for a second time after the original writing has been erased, it is now used to evoke the idea that past features in the landscape have been buried or eroded – erased – but can still be detected by a judicious mixture of fieldwork and research.

One of the principal difficulties which bedevilled the work of surveyors and tithe map compilers at Rhossili was the boundary between Llangennith and the parish of Rhossili at the western end of Rhossili Bay. It came up through Hillend and across some fields of Sluxton Farm, so that for tithe purposes it was not always possible to establish which fields were titheable for Llangennith and which for Rhossili. The boundaries of Rhossili, with detail of the adjacent manors of Pitton *alias* Pilton. Paviland and Pilton, together with *Vernhill* are given in a Survey dating to the mid-eighteenth century (1764). It was made by Gabriel Powell, Junior from the *observation and Experience of Gabriel Powell (his late Father deceased) and Himself for above Sixty-three years*. The description of the boundaries of the Manor of *Roscilly* follows on from the description of the Manor of Landimore of which it was still part: Landimore formerly held by *Sir Rees ap Thomas, Knight of the Garter, came to the Crown by his attainder*. It was granted by Queen Elizabeth I to William Earl of Pembroke and sold by one of his descendants to Sir Edward Mansel, Baronet. The boundaries of Rhossili follow on from the Survey made in Elizabethan times. An earlier one dated 1 May 1713 involved several people completing a Survey about the *Bounds of Langenith*: the signature of Edward Mansel of Henllys, Steward of Gower for the Mansel family at this time, heads the gentlemen's list. It was followed by the signatures of David Thomas and Edward Hancorne. The list of parishioners is headed by Richard Portrey, Rector of Rhossilly, followed by Richard France, Francis Jones, John Taylor, Matthew Jones, John Higgin, John Tucker, John Rogers, Thomas Rogers and George Taylor.

The Document reads:

Certificate About the Bounds of Langenith

We the Minister and Several of the Parishioners of the parishes of Rossilly and Langennith Do humbly Certifie whom it may Concern That where the Dyles Lake falls Into ye Sea Northward upon the sands is the Boundary of the Parish of Rossilly and theare Joynes the parish of Langenith and from theare up by the said Lake to the Pill Lake, and so along the North side of the Lands, called the Legg, up to the Cross at Hillend, taking In all the Lands of the Right Honourable the Lord Brooke In ye Possession of John Taylor to the Southwerd of ye sayd Legg, Pill Lake, and Dyles, are within the said parish of Rossilly; all which we humbly Certifie this first Day of May In the twelfth year of Her Majesty's Reign over Great Brittain &c and In the year of our Lord 1713

So, with the western boundaries of Rhossili fairly securely established at Diles Lake, where the stream runs out on to Rhossili Bay, we can proceed eastwards towards one of the landmarks in the landscape of Rhossili today – the Old Rectory with its associated out-buildings and glebe land.

The rectories or vicarages of Gower are often described in glebe terriers, whose value extends beyond a simple decription of the main buildings; tithes, other dues and details of glebe land also appear. One for Llangennith is described as *A terrier of all and singular, the houses, buildings, tythes, dues, and profits whatsoever of and belonging to the Vicarage of Llangennith, in the County of Glamorgan and Diocese of*

St. David's made the 20th day of December in the year of our Lord 1720. Earlier in the same year, one had been compiled for Rhossili which refers to the Rectory of Rhossili: Rhossili had a Rector at this time while Llangennith had a Vicar. The Reverend Richard Portrey had been instituted as Rector of Rhossili from 26 June 1665, but he was also to be the Vicar of Llangennith and Rector of Ystradgynlais. He died in 1714 and had widened, it seems, his landholding beyond the glebe land to take up a lease by which he paid £2 a year for Worm's Head. At the time of the terrier in 1720, which can be read in the Rhossili Parish Registers, Thomas Pardo was Rector of Rhossili and John Evans the Curate.

The glebe terrier is valuable as a source of description of the tithe practices of Rhossili, and of the main buildings, which can be compared with the Old Rectory as it is today:

> *A Terrier of all and singular the Houses, Buildings, Glebe Lands Tithes Dues and profits whatsoever of and belonging to the Rectory of Roschilly in the County of Glamorgan and Diocese of St. David's; made the fourth day of October 1720.*

> *A Parsonage House, containing Two Rooms upon a Floor and lofted throughout; a Barn about a Perch and a Half in Length; and three small outhouses under one and ye same roof, about Three Perches in Length. Also a Garden, containing about Five Square Perches; a Hay yard, containing about ye Fourth Part of an acre; and a small croft ye North side of ye House, containing about Four and Thirty Square Perches. Also Twenty Acres of Tillable Land in eight several Fields, and a Warren, containing about six acres. The whole is bounded on ye North, by My Lord Brook's Land, on ye South by My Lord Mansell's Land, on ye East, by Rosehilly Down, and on ye lest by ye sea.*

Although it was necessary to engage in extensive renovation of the Old Rectory in the nineteenth century, the essential structures remain, together with the land of course. The large barn is still intact; the three smaller outbuildings appear under one roof for their entire length, with a step in the roof where it joins another building. The walled gardens give shelter from westerly winds and are able to enjoy the sun from the east and south, making them warm spots on any sunny day. The small Hay yard and the lengthy croft on the North side of the house lead out on to the glebe land. The Iley stream runs between two of the fields labelled Isly and Emless Lays in the Tithe Apportionment Schedule for Rhossili which dates to 1847. At this time the total acreage of glebe land (over 51 acres) was almost exactly the same as the 50 acres shown for Edward Gamage in 1662. This might make the figure of *Twenty Acres* given as part of the glebe land a little suspect, but the words are *Twenty Acres of Tillable Land* in eight fields, in the terrier of 1720. *Horse Land, Sheepen Park, Long land,* with *Field under the House, Isly and Emless Lays* made up most of the cultivable land adjacent to *Parsonage House* in 1847. *Burrows* and *Cliff* covered another twenty acres of rough pasture for livestock, with *Well Acre* and *Church Pa*rk making up a further seven acres.

At the time of the Tithe Award procedures, under the Tithe Commutation Act, the Reverend John Lloyd was the Rector of Rhossili. He had been Rector of Rhossili since 1838, and Vicar of Llangennith from 1852. John Lloyd found the parsonage house in a dilapidated state, so he lodged in the village, leasing the parsonage to a farmer, Mr Lewis. When he took on the two livings in 1852 it is thought that he had the parsonage rebuilt for his own convenience as it was part of the way towards Llangennith. The location of the Old Rectory was not due originally to it being midway between Rhossili and Llangennith, as Robert Lucas points out in *A Gower Family*:

> *The reason why the Rectory and the church glebe land lay at the foot of the Down, between the hillside and the sea, was that it was the site of of the early medieval village.*

Its isolated, somewhat romantic, position could not disguise the fact that the only way to reach it was along a footpath around Rolling Tor or along the old cart tack, which ran outside the high stone wall at the top of the glebe fields which was nigh impassible! John Ponsonby Lucas, grandfather of Robert Lucas, was instituted as Rector of Rhossili and Vicar of Llangennith when John Lloyd's failing eyesight led him to resign the two livings and take the vacant living at Oxwich. He rented the majority of the glebe fields in the Warren to George Beynon, my grandfather. My father, David Wilfred Beynon, whose family moved down from Sheep Green to the Ship Inn around 1906, when it closed as a public house, described in *Yesterday's Gower* how his family came to farm this land:

> *My father had a small farm, with most of the fields on the beach – thirty feet above it really. With the big bay below. They were originally glebe land and he rented them from the parson.*

The Beynon family came to own the glebe lands, together with the Old Rectory, but the buildings eventually passed into other hands. More recently, the National Trust acquired the land above the bay and the Old Rectory. A new rectory was built, in 1924, adjacent to the church, at a cost of £2,000. Memories of farming the fields, picking new potatoes and carrying corn from the glebe land fields land fields to Ship Farm are part of the personal history of the Beynon family; my father, Wilfred Beynon, made up the ricks of corns in the rickyard, to be thatched and kept until required – then the threshing machine would arrive, together with helpers from other farms to share in the work. This communal help was part of the pattern of threshing the corn in the days before combine harvesters. The solitary building – the Old Rectory – with its outbuildings and walled gardens is still evocative of the past. The atmosphere has been captured recently in a sequence of paintings by Christopher Last. There has been work to restore parts of the buildings – one of the first to be tackled was the old outside privy! The abiding memory, though, will be the atmosphere, which is shared by anyone who has sat on the front door steps of the Old Rectory, looking out upon Rhossili Bay, Worm's Head and Burry Holms in the fading light of a balmy summer evening. The view, the ancient features in the landscape, all enhance the feeling of timelessness as the waves roll quietly in on Rhossili Bay a short distance of one field away. It is one of the rare visions which the landscape provides of how little has changed in parts of Rhossili over several centuries.

The landscape here does not tell the full story but enough of the hidden evidence has been uncovered to confirm that the earlier settlement of Rhossili was here, and the features below the surface are part of the early history of Rhossili, complemented by the new buildings above the bay. These took over the functions of the besanded buildings – on the plateau a small group of thatched cottages huddled around the church, with the Green and Pound adjacent to the farms whose buildings reflect today their earlier history. Next to the church was a farmyard which shared a wall with the churchyard. Rhossili Farm House, on the other side of the narrow road, to which the farmyard belonged is a dated building with an inscription showing 1729. Long before this time, however, Rhossili Church with its unique doorway had been built. The arch over the Church door, with its outer dog-tooth moulding and inner moulding of deeply cut chevrons reflects a style of the later Norman period, and was probably put there in the late twelfth century; it is the only one of its kind in Gower. The late nineteenth century view of Rhossili Parish Church is taken from the *History of West Gower* by the Rev. J.D. Davies; to appreciate the context in which the church might have appeared at that time it is necessary to remove the features beyond the church which now are present in the landscape. Ashtree Farm and Ashtree House would be on the left as you looked out from the elevated churchyard; the new rectory with a bungalow – recently built in Church Park – the Worm's Head Cottage which preceded the Worm's Head Hotel on the same site-all these would have to be mentally removed from the present landscape. The handful of farms, farmhouses and cottages at Rhossili would not have significantly impaired the view of Worm's Head seen by visitors such as Sir Stephen Glynne Bart, whose *Notes on the Older Churches in the Welsh Dioceses* in *Archaeologia Cambrensis*. Volume XIV, Fifth Series (1897), includes his description of Rhossili Church:

RHOSILLY: September 24, 1848.

A long church consisting of a chancel and nave, with small western tower and a south porch. The east window is modern Pointed, of two lights, the north and south windows of the chancel each a wide lancet, now closed. There is a trefoil-headed niche on the south side under a window, but there is no remaining trace of a piscina. There is also a lychnoscope on the south, now closed. The chancel arch is a very plain Pointed one. The roofs are open; the floor is bare clay. The south door within the porch is Norman, but pointed with chevron mouldings and shafts. Within the porch, stone benches; also a stone bench along the east.end of the chancel. The windows are very few in the nave, and those very narrow and small. The steeple has the north and south sides gabled, and only a few slits for openings. It has an outer west door, and another opening into the nave. The font has a square bowl, scalloped on two sides, upon a short stem scarcely to be seen, and set on a square plinth. There is a glorious view from the churchyard over the sea, to the Worm's Head.

The only point in the description of Rhossili Church which touches on its condition states that *the floor is bare* clay, but we know from other sources that the fabric of the church was in a sorry state which led to urgent work being carried out on the roof of the building and the interior. In 1890/91, with the substantial support of Miss Emily Talbot who contributed £500 towards the repairs, improvements were made at a cost of £800. The church was re-roofed, a new porch was built, a pulpit, lectern and choir stalls, and pitch pine seats for the congregation were installed. The altar rail was erected, the floors tiled and a vestry created below the tower.

In considering the foci which are the obvious landmarks in the story of Rhossili's past, we cannot ignore other elements in the landscape which have been marginally altered in some cases, and fundamentally altered in others. The examples to be seen on the way towards Worm's Head, following the track which leads from Rhossili car park along the cliff top are the dry-stone walls; further along the coast the visible relics include lime-kilns. Both relate to the farming patterns of earlier years, the dry-stone walls providing a means of separating cultivated arable or pasture land from cliff common land and the lime kilns providing a vital supplement to the soil. The dry-stone walls have to be admired as ingenious relics of a bygone era, when the dearth of trees, and the reluctance of hedges to grow in the salt-laden air of Rhossili meant resorting to other means. The persistent south-westerly winds inhibited the growth of hedges as well, so the commonest field boundary would be a sequence of modest earth banks, no more than four feet high, crowned with a low thorn hedge, which could still be blown by the prevailing wind into a growth pattern which sees the hedge overhanging the bank away from the persistent south westerlies. These stone walls, readily built of native limestone quarried on the spot, are a distinctive kind of field boundary in the more exposed coastal landscapes of southern Wales where it is far from easy to secure the growth of live hedges. They extend in some form or other all the way along the coastal footpath from Rhossili to Paviland and beyond.

The dry-stone walls which skirt the edge of the cliff from the National Trust Centre at Rhossili to the old look-out station are carefully repaired or restored versions of the original walls; the original materials have been used where possible or new supplies of limestone obtained where the deterioration has been too marked and the walls have crumbled. These restored walls do not exhibit the full range of characteristics of the original walls which can be seen in un-restored form further along the coastal footpath. At present the walls which enclose the cultivated area of land which goes right to the corner of Fall Bay at Tears Point are good examples of the overhanging walls made by the farmers during the orginal enclosure of the land. They both fulfil their principal purpose: the restored walls and the original walls define and separate the common cliff land from the grass and arable areas inside the dry-stone walls. It is noticeable that many of the fields immediately inside the walls are grassed, with sheep having access to both cliff common land and pasture nowadays through gates but also originally through spaces left in the lower part of the stone walls at intervals. The word 'shoord' or sheep-hole might describe these spaces – the ones visible now have a large lintel stone set in place to prevent the access point becoming unusable as the weight of the stones in the wall above pressed down. Along the dry-stone wall section from Fall Bay to Mewslade Bay the fields inside the walls are named *Fold* or *Vold* in the Gower dialect, confirming that the sheep could be kept there, and released on to the common cliff land as well. It follows that there are, at the inner boundaries of these fields called *Vold*, hedges, banks or further stone walls to prevent the sheep getting into the cultivated areas beyond. The field boundaries in these cases would be low stone walls or earth banks, with a rather stunted but effective hawthorn hedge topping them off. They would be high enough as a barrier to ensure the sheep remained in the fold and did not reach the vegetable fields just beyond.

It is the outer dry-stone walls along the cliff – where they are original -which exhibit the skilful and often artistic work that went into their creation. It is this art which the National Trust is now trying to impart to its trainees who are restoring sections of the walls. The skill of the stone-masons who constructed them from the stones dug from the neighbouring cliffs some centuries ago has to be admired. The stones are mainly rectangular in shape because of the natural jointing and fissuring of the local limestone, and are built up, not only to divide the arable from the open fields, but to protect the whole from the strong prevailing winds. Many of these walls curve outwards at the top to break the wind force and to preserve the stability of the wall structure. The basic strength comes from the large through-stones at the bottom of the wall, with each stone carefully fitted together to give a high wall, built without mortar, but with a life span of many years. The outward curve at the top inhibits the agile, determined sheep which often prefer the vegetable fields or fields of young corn as a change from cropping the short, close-textured grass on the common cliff land where they are normally supposed to be. Robert Lucas, in his concise and immensely informative pamphlet on Rhossili confirms the value of the outward curve: *'Along the edge of the cliff land the old stone walls were cleverly built with an outward overhang or "batter" towards the top of the wall to prevent the sheep from clambering over the wall into the crops.'*

The perception of most visitors to Rhossili is that it is an area of spectacular coastal scenery – the sweep of Rhossili Bay, the unique outline of Worm's Head, the vista of headlands stretching out into the sea all the way from Fall Bay to Porteynon Point. It is only later, after the first impressionistic view, that there is a growing awareness that there are equally attractive and interesting features in the landscape which are distinct from the natural landscape. This is where a distinction has to be drawn between the landscape fashioned over thousands of years by nature, and the man-made landscape which is the product of only a few thousand years. Worm's Head comes into the first category – over countless years it has been part of the natural landscape of Rhossili, it has presided over and made a distinctive contribution to the history of the village. Dylan Thomas apparently enjoyed his visit to Worm's Head: *'There was monstrous, thick grass there that made us spring-heeled, and we laughed and bounced on it, scaring the sheep who ran up and down the battered sides like goats.'* He had also the experience which befalls the incautious visitor to Rhossili, who visits Worm's Head, without checking the tide tables, or in Dylan Thomas' case, falls asleep on the springy grass. *'I was trapped on the Worm once,'* he wrote, *'I stayed on the Worm from dusk to midnight.'* He made his cautious and slightly perilous way back across the causeway in the dark when the tide had ebbed far enough, but he still had an 18 mile walk to get back to Swansea. In his imaginative way, Dylan Thomas described the solitary nature of this famous landmark: *'Nothing lives on it but gulls and rats, the millionth generation of the winged and tailed families that screamed in the air and ran through the grass when the first sea thudded on the Rhossili beach.'* It shows an appreciation of the aeons of time during which this landmark has been part of the landscape of Rhossili.

Two glimpses of Rhossili and Worm's Head come from opposite ends of the nineteenth century: in the first the description is by Benjamin Heath Malkin, who used materials collected during two excursions in the year 1803 to write about *The Scenery, Antiquities and Biography of South Wales*. His topographical descriptions of Gower note that *'Worm's Head forms the extremity of the peninsula,'* and he describes its appearance:

> *Its position on the map in some measure justifies the similitude, however whimsical. It runs more than a mile into the sea, and should be visited at low water, for the purpose of examining its curious rocks, which are inaccessible while the tide is flowing. The low isthmus, which connects it with the land, is then under water, and forms it into a small island. The eligugs [sea birds] visit this promontory, as well as the castles on the grand coast of Pembrokeshire, to which these cliffs bear a strong resemblance, though on a scale somewhat inferior.*

J.D. Davies brings us nearer the present day with his account in *History of West Gower*, written at the end of the nineteenth century: *'I should mention that Worm's Head and the Pavyland Cliffs nearby, used to be a very noted place as the haunt of the Peregrine Falcon; and some 20 or 30 years ago, a gentleman living in Gloucester, who followed the ancient sport of hawking, used to employ old Jeremiah Cox, one of Mr Talbot's Keepers, to procure him annually a pair of these young birds or their egg.'* The *eligugs* of Benjamin Heath Malkin are still on Worm's Head and cliffs such as Devil's Truck and Thurba Head. Breeding peregrine falcons have returned after an absence of some years to bring up their young on the sea cliffs of Rhossili – the eggs and young secure greater protection, through legislation which safeguards them against predatory hawkers, than they did in J.D. Davies' day. The decimation of the seagull colonies and wild pigeons has been an unfortunate, but foreseen consequence, of the return of peregrine falcons to one of their historic haunts. As we enter the twenty-first century other features in the landscape of Rhossili will alter or disappear but the time-less landmark of Worm's Head will remain.

Linked with Worm's Head, and visible at low tide, is another natural feature called Crabart. Its inclusion in a description of features in the landscape of Rhossili is justified by the contribution it has made over the years to the subsistence mode of farming prevalent in remote villages. It contributed crabs and lobsters – to those skilful enough to catch them! The shell-fish caught here, the harvest of winkles and mussels and the seasonal catches of bass and mackerel have all provided a valuable supplement of sea food to villagers in the not too distant past. Other Gower villages had their crabbing grounds too. The area is adjacent to Worm's Head. As the causeway to Worm's Head opens at half-tide,which is some two and a half hours after high water, crabbers can cross from the mainland. The rocks uncovered are known as Crabart; here in the holes in the rocks and pools are the crabs and lobsters, mainly caught in the season from April to September. The unfortunate villagers of the manor of Pitton who were described in an earlier account, had secured good catches of crabs and lobsters but made the mistake of selling their catch without the permission of the lord of the manor, which would have been given perhaps in return for payment to the steward of the manor. The miscreants were fined in the manorial court, each paying a fine of 2s 6d in May 1702. Other villagers in Pennard and Bishopston, manors which came under the Duke of Beaufort, paid six pence yearly *for catching Crabs and Lobsters in the Rocks . . .*

At Rhossili the crabbers would cross the wide causeway which led to the rocky ground of *Crabart*; the seaweed strewn rocks, pools and crevices would have holes sufficiently large for crabs to move into them when they were covered with water. At low tide the opportunity occurred for those villagers with knowledge of the ground to make a good catch; successive generations of crabbers in the Gower villages have learnt the location of the best holes from relatives and those who keep up the art today are often sons of well-known crabbers of the Gower families. The traditional skill of Tom Richard of *Kinmoor* and Sam Ace of Middleton – both famous lobster-men a century ago according to Horatio Tucker in *Gower Gleanings* – was exercised not only on Crabart, but further up the rocky ground towards Worm's Head and ranging down to Tears Point. More recently the expertise of famous crabbers of the past in Rhossili has been more than matched by John Beynon, Vernal, and Margaret Ann Beynon of High

Priest Cottage. They, too, amply demonstrated their skills in turn, both regularly using the fortnightly low tides to make catches of lobsters in good numbers, as well as crabs. They were the best in their lifetimes; few villagers of the present day have equalled their achievements: John Beynon (Uncle Johnny), on one occasion caught a lobster of quite a few pounds which was duly commented on in the local evening paper. The value of a shell-fish diet, to eke out other food supplies, was matched by the value of the exercise involved in catching the crabs and lobsters. The sale of some of the catch, without risk of arraignment in manorial courts and fines, also contributed to family finances in the present century; a lobster sold after it had been cooked might be acquired by a local hotel for its guests, at a price of around £5 per pound in these years. The healthy exercise and diet would have contributed to the longevity of some Gower crabbers: *Uncle Johnny* Beynon (my great-uncle) was still catching crabs and lobsters a few years before his death in 1965, at the age of eighty-eight!

The modern crabbers are more fortunate than those of earlier centuries: they have to observe regulations relating to the size of lobsters and crabs which may be taken (and local courts have fined those caught with under-sized crabs and lobsters) but they no longer have to observe the piscary rights of the lord of the manor. In the same way as rights of *wrack de mer* defined the disposal of items of wreck between high-water marks and low-water marks, the rights of the lord relating to the taking of fish and shell-fish were used to supplement his income

Nestling under the cliffs at Kitchen Corner the flat rock platforms with a wall running through the middle of them denote a further feature in the landscape, but this time it is a man-made one. The rusting remains of iron in holes seen in the rocks reveal the origins of the feature – the flat, rock platforms opposite Coonan's were the location of the *vlotquars*, the floating quarries, as they were called, from which limestone was extracted and exported to the West Country. The ships tied up to anchorage points set in the rocks which can still be seen today; the limestone was loaded on by teams of villagers who had been hired for the occasion. It was back-breaking and dangerous work – falls of rock, and the use of explosives to blast limestone from the cliffs were twin hazards. C.D. Morgan or 'Kit' Morgan described the scene a century ago:

> *We see the dangerous quarries, hear the loud booming of the blasting rocks as the quarrymen ignite the match, and the torn masses tumble from their firm beds. We pause as we view the frightful place, where men, at the peril of their lives, toil for a hard crust. Those quarries are on the side of the precipice, and from shaky ledge to shaky ledge the loosened stones go falling down. How men can ever work in such a place we know not, but necessity drives them to it – necessity, that iron law that yields to no power.*

It is not evident to the visitors who tread the coastal path near the look-out station that near at hand are the remains of one of the major industries of Rhossili in the nineteenth century. The first major census return of 1831, and others later, attributes the growth of population in Gower villages such as Rhossili to the influx of limestone quarrymen who came to earn a living in these perilous surroundings. A typical comment confirms: '*The increase of population in Rhoscilly is attributed to the extension of the limestone trade.*'

The limestone quarries at Kitchen Corner, the unique outline of Worm's Head, and the rocky pools and crab holes of Crabart are left behind as the coastal path follows the dry stone walls to Fall Bay. The landmark of *Tears Point* should perhaps be *Tares Point*, where the dry-stone walls run down towards Fall Bay. Here the cultivated land – used for growing swedes one year or pasture the next – extends very close to the cliffs. Every scrap of cultivated land seems to be taken in, to the extent that we have examples of encroachment on the common land between Fall Bay and Mewslade Bay. In one place, a straight section of wall butts onto the original stonewalls – thus enclosing two small areas, one of which became a potato garden tenanted by Sarah Stote.

The valley of Mewslade, with Mewslade Bay, has natural features which dominate the landscape here such as Thurba Head. The author C.D. or Kit Morgan described the scenery in *Wanderings in Gower: A Perfect Guide to the Tourist, with all the Lays, Legends, and Customs and Glossary of the Dialect* over a century ago in 1886. Here the tour of C.D. Morgan seems to have reached its unrivalled apogee – the purple prose in his distinctive style might well have been banned if it appeared in a modern tourist brochure where claims of perfection and eulogies of beauty have to be substantiated. It is a stunning picture he presents, even if it appears a little contrived; this is how he described Mewslade Bay a century ago:

Mewslade comes next, where there is the finest rock scenery on the island, surpassing anything even in the far-famed Isle of Wight. . . . In the centre of this little valley stands a tower-like ivy-robed rock; turning the winding of this little vale you have a nice peep of the sea. Descending over the rough rocky pathway you are at once on Mewslade sands, one of the fairest scenes in Gower . . . I think this is one of the most beautiful bays on the whole coast. There is a pensive beauty about it – a calm gentleness that throws a strange spell over the soul – to see the blue waves running over the sand; whisperings like angels' whisperings blend with the zephyrs that sigh over the liquid flood; onward the little billows roll, and as they steal quietly over the smiling rocks we think they are rejoicing and seeking for a home; and when they are retreating back to their parent's breast they seem to linger on the yellow sands as if loth to part with this cosey nook. We think they would like to rest here, and bid adieu to the unsettled flood that wanders to every shore. The sun looks with a fond look on this most beauteous spot, warming and shedding its brightest rays here, and the silvery moon floods the sparkling tide with mellow light, and throws many lovely shapes and grotesque forms on rock and crag.

It is to be hoped that the eulogistic quality of this tribute does not prevent visitors from making their own judgement!

Survivors in the landscape might well describe those features of prehistoric times which, in later years, are still recognisable though largely changed. These would be the cairns, the chambered tombs and barrows which invest the higher parts of Gower with an air of timelessness, which is matched along the whole length of Gower's coast by the promontory forts of the Iron Age There is much to see along the coastal footpath from Rhossili to Paviland but the equally frequent features which are not so visible, and not so old, but nevertheless important are the lime-kilns. Built in fields for short-term farm use, built along the coast, where there is evidence to show that some lime was exported, and varying in size and type – the lime-kilns of Gower are a sequence of modern survivors in the landscape. There are some twelve to fourteen sites along the Rhossili-Paviland section of the Gower coast, or inland, plus one on Burry Holms. The extraction of lime from limestone would have been part of the Gower scene for centuries, although many of the derelict lime-kilns seen today would have been built mainly in the nineteenth century.

The most frequent use of the lime-kilns found along the coastal footpath from Rhossili to Paviland would have been to produce lime for local farmers to put on the fields adjacent to where the lime-kilns are located today. There is, however, variation in their size and type, as well as in the frequency of their appearance. The lime-kilns seen today are the successors of those used in earlier centuries: The practice of burning limestone to provide lime goes back in Gower, without doubt, to the twelfth century, and may even have been practised during Roman times. The building of lime-kilns and the use of lime is part of the story of man's attempts to secure the improvement of land by various means throughout the ages: sources confirm the folding of sheep on ground which was to be cultivated later, horses carried marl and manure to the fields, and lime was used to enhance and tone the soil to give greater productivity. Lime also had other uses: one entry in *Ministers' Accounts in South Wales* in the early fourteenth century refers to *'Breaking stones for making lime and mason hired to mend the lime-kiln, 2s 10½d.'* In the construction of stone buildings, sand and limestone were needed for making mortar and in the living apartments interior walls and ceilings might be carefully plastered and whitewashed. The lengthy role of the watcher at the lime-kiln is seen where a large stipend was paid to the man *'doing the burning and watching the lime-kiln night and day, 18 days, 6s 9d.'* The kiln could not be let out during the process and night-time work involved candles or lanterns being used to see to the tending of the kiln with fuel. One of the largest lime-kilns in Rhossili is at the head of the valley leading down to Ramsgrove; it has a niche which has the appearance of having been specially built into the right hand wall as you enter. It could have been put there to accommodate a light of some kind – a candle, or more probably a lantern, judging by its size.

The use of lime, it has been noted, is described by writers in the late sixteenth century such as Rice Merrick – it was used to sweeten the soil in upland areas. *'For the mountaines in those days bore noe such corn as now groweth thereon, because lyming and marling of the ground was not used, and as I think, not known.'* The use of lime was certainly known to writers such as George Owen who was a major advocate and authority; he advocated the use of different types of natural fertiliser, and was an authority on the contribution such additives had to the consistent improvement of the soil. He lived in Pembrokeshire where countrymen believed *'that a man doth sand for himself, lyme for his sonne and marle for his graunde child.'* A combination of marl and lime was able to reduce heavy clay soils to a finer texture, making them easier to cultivate.

An extract from the modern Ordnance Survey map which can be used to identify the locations of the lime-kilns at Rhossili does not show many of them – two more of the prominent ones have to be added, leaving several unidentified: four at Rhossili, four in the the vicinity of Mewslade including the one on Thurba Head, two at Pitton, one at Red Chamber and West Pilton, and three at Paviland including one at Yellow Top. The sequence of lime-kilns in the coastal landscape of Rhossili can be used to identify and pinpoint the more visible ones which are worthy of study. Their location has been verified by fieldwork. The lime-kiln marked on the Ordnance Survey map in Well Acre Field is buried under a mound of earth for the greater part, but the quarrying which is noticeable in the surrounding area and on the cliffs immediately outside the cliff walls lends credibility to its location. The lime-kiln above Fall Bay is open to the skies still and retains its basic form, while the very good one between Fall Bay and Mewslade Bay is easily examined although not very far from the cliff. It is surrounded by rubble and the quarries from which the stone to make the lime was derived. Its location and that of others along the coastline, is sufficiently far from the settlement area to make one wonder how the farmers brought the fuel to this point. It has been suggested that where *'some of these kilns are located a long way from a road,'* as in the Ystradgynlais area of Breconshire, *'fuel clearly had to be carried to them by mule, in the same way that the burnt lime was taken away,'* (Eurwyn Williams). Gower farmers, travelling through lanes and fields, could reach points adjacent to the lime-kilns on the cliffs in a fairly straightforward way. The well-hidden, nearly inaccessible lime-kiln on the eastern side of Thurba Head can only be seen by looking back from a vantage point further along the coast towards Paviland. It is perched on a quite precipitous slope and tucked under the cliff face which makes up part of the defences of the promontory fort on Thurba Head.

It is not necessary to fully rehearse the details of all the promontory forts found intermingled with lime-kilns between Rhossili and Paviland. Old Castle, Lewes Castle, Thurba, Horse Cliff, Yellow Top, The Knave – the features already described are part of the prehistoric landscape of Gower the ramparts and ditches seen today are relics of their Iron Age origins, but are seen alongside features of other eras. The promontory forts are juxtaposed with nineteenth century lime-kilns, remnants of medieval open-fields, limestone quarries and spectacular scenery – all visible from the coastal foot-path which runs alongside dry-stone walls. The most impressive lime-kiln in Rhossili is found in the Red Chamber area at the head of Ramsgrove valley. Its size and location raises interesting questions as it appears to have had a capacity greater than some of the other farm kilns, although this may be an illusion. Tucked up against a bank at the head of Ramsgrove valley it might appear bigger than the lime-kiln between Fall Bay and Mewslade Bay, which is out in the open. Its characteristics cannot be compared with those of the very large lime-kiln at Great Tor, Oxwich, so it was probably not built for commercial use, although the cove below it could have been used by small boats to take away some of its production. It brings an intriguing end to the landscape of Rhossili before we reach Paviland and return in our imagination to the time thousands of years ago when early villagers of Rhossili lived in Paviland Cave for a time.

By the end of the nineteenth century the lime-kilns were becoming disused: the increasing use of cheaper artificial fertilisers including superphosphate of lime, guano brought from South America and a variety of potassic materials hastened their decline, as did the reduction of wheat acreages in the later nineteenth century. Moelwyn Williams in *The Making of the South Wales Landscape*, summed up their fate:

> *As the ruined Norman castle indicated the decline of manorialism and the feudal system, so did the ruined lime-kilns represent, in a less spectacular but in an equally significant way, the changes which agricultural methods were undergoing in South Wales at the close of the nineteenth century. By the end of the First World War, most of the smaller lime-kilns were in "glorious ruins, or becoming so", more especially along the sea coast.*

When Samuel Lewis completed *A Topographical Dictionary of Wales* in 1833 he described Rhosilly or Rosilly in various ways: *'It is situated on a bay to which it gives its name, in the Bristol Channel, and which is enclosed on the south by Worm's Head, a small promontory forming the western extremity of the county of Glamorgan, and stretching two miles into the sea. . . .* [The landmark is familiar but has grown in size.] *The surrounding scenery is agreeably diversified, and the views over the bay and the adjacent country abound with objects of interest and with features of pleasing character. The living is a rectory, in the archdeaconry of Carmarthen and diocese of St David's, rated in the King's books at £9 6s 8d. The church, dedicated to St Mary, is an ancient structure situated near the shore, but is not remarkable for its architectural details.'*

Samuel Lewis does not describe a feature of the landscape of Rhossili which is, in its own way, the equivalent of the Red Lady of Paviland. It would have been, according to estate maps and the later Tithe Map, a clearly visible part of the land and the landscape. Two of the themes of this study now come together in a portrayal of the medieval open-field system known as the 'Viel' or 'Vile'. Its unique character places it alongside Laxton in Nottinghamshire and Braunton in Devon. As one of the principal survivors in the landscape – albeit in attenuated form at the end of the twentieth century – it merits special consideration.

The Open Fields at Rhossili

The most important historic survivor in the landscape of Rhossili is seen throughout a walk along the coastal footpath from Rhossili to Mewslade Bay. Inside the dry-stone walls which separate the common land of the cliff from the cultivated land is evidence of an open-field system. The vestiges of this medieval survivor – still visible today in the twenty-first century – reflects both the continuity of the tenancy of the strips in former years and the uses to which the strips were put in the growing of crops. Although the turf balks which separated the strips have largely survived, the crops grown there are principally corn, no longer reflecting the diverse use to which the strips were put. The agricultural purposes reflect, too, the decline in farming which has overtaken the community of Rhossili in recent years.

It is probable that the strips were a product of the communally-organised colonisation of waste or common land. It was followed by the partition of the cleared land among those who had done the clearing. If this scenario was applied to Rhossili we could speculate that the abandonment of the medieval village site in the Warren led to the taking up of additional land along the headland from the nucleated village around the new church. The rocky limestone soil would have been ploughed and large stones removed; prior to this, substantial areas of gorse would have had to be burnt and uprooted. The acquisition of new land, it could be suggested, took place in the late thirteenth and early fourteenth century: evidence from Ministers' Accounts for Gower at this time refers to the taking in of further land in the Manor of Landimore, including Rhossili. Around the nucleus of the village there would already have been a sequence of fields comparable to those developed further out along the headland. Three aspects of these developments can be emphasised and illustrated: firstly the reference, already noted, when *newly arrented lands* appear in Exchequer accounts allocating payments to the Duchess of Norfolk in 1399/1400. This phrase, which is distinctly related to Rhossili in the accounts, refers to the acquisition of new land to supplement the resources of the village at a time when the abandonment of the medieval settlement had taken place. Secondly, the map of Rhossili produced for the Penrice and Margam Estate by John Williams in 1780 offers a distinct picture: the individual strips in the open-fields are shown in blocks with the names *Great Field, Middle Field* and *Little Field* in use. The terms *Great Viel* or *Great Vile* and *Little Vile* had been in use for some time – the *Great Vile* is referred to in an agreement of the 1730s in the manorial court.

Within the various blocks of open-fields the various tenants who hold strips rarely have two consecutive ones side by side. Where a tenant has two strips next to each other they tend to be near the outer edges of the blocks – here the individual tenant has added on a strip of his own, through encroachment. In a sample of fields – where letters of the alphabet are used to denote different tenants – one block has tenants shown as A, F, D, B, N, G, K and L. Following this block is one with the pattern A, L, I,

M, C, H, and one which runs D, F, G, I, A, B. The appearance of structured, organised patterns of tenantry in open fields, where every tenant has strips in totally different parts of the open-field system, can be taken as evidence of specific, deliberate allocation of land to individuals as it was cleared. As it was brought into use those who had contributed to its clearance received a share of a strip of land in turn. Alternatively, the precise allocation of strips could have resulted from the pooling of the land resources some years later and their re-allocation in an organised way. If this had happened, why was the opportunity not taken to place an individual farmer's strips in adjacent blocks of differing soil quality, instead of scattering them over a much wider area in what now appears to be a more random manner? Thirdly, taking the visible remains of the open-field system as a basis, it is possible to recreate the pattern of possible development: in this model, the early settlement around the green and church, with its accompanying fields, was expanding and cultivation was extended to some parts of the manorial waste along the cliff. The earlier fields were separated by banks of earth and turf, topped with thorn hedges – to protect and enclose the crops in these inner fields. These are now part of the *Little Field* or *Little Vile*. The additional land became known as the *Great Field* or *Vile* with the *Middle Field* as part of it. This, it has been suggested earlier, has every appearance of the infield-outfield system which, in some writers' views, was the fore-runner of the open-fields or common-fields which evolved in many parts of England and Wales from Norman times. The extensive debate on the origins of open-fields has sought to focus on the different interpretations which can be placed on the open-field systems seen in England, Wales and Scotland, but even here there is sufficient focus for Rhossili to be fitted into the same frame as Laxton in Nottingham-shire and Braunton in Devon.

The two seminal studies for Gower, and in particular for Rhossili, came from Margaret Davies and Frank Emery. It is noticeable that the writers who contributed to the debate on open-field systems in the more modern era were prepared to confirm, with certainty, that many parts of England and Wales had an open-field system at the time of the Norman Conquest, or that it became a clear and unambiguous part of the manorial system the Normans effectively introduced into England and the anglicised parts of Wales. D. H. Owen in his own contribution to *Settlement and Society in Wales* was clear that the Anglo-Norman conquest had contributed to the open-fields of Gower:

> *At Rhossili arable strips in a surviving manorial field known as the "The Vile", are still separated by uncultivated balks, termed "landshares", but in some places there are permanent boundaries in the form of dry stone walls or earth banks.*

A particular focus on south Wales, especially Gower, has been provided by the two scholars already mentioned: they provide an overview which offers a wider perspective, together with a parochial view which concentrates on Rhossili.

Frank Emery in *Open Fields in Gower* in *Gower* XXV (1974) focused on the rareness of surviving open-field systems such as the one at Rhossili; in the *Agricultural History Review* (1956). Margaret Davies gave prominence to this feature in *Wales Field Patterns*, and returned to the subject in depth in *Studies of Field Systems in the British Isles* (edited by A.R.H. Baker and R.A. Butlin, 1973). Emery identified that the two most important elements in the manorial economy which emerged in the rural landscape were compact villages such as Reynoldston and the organisation of open fields within which arable land was worked on on a system of inter-mixed strip-holdings separated from each other by turf balks. It will be evident by now that *Vile* is Field (the Gower dialect softens the F to V) as in the example such as *Vold* (Fold) given earlier. Similarly the word for the narrow low balks made up of earth and field stones which separate the individual strips of Rhossili's open-field system has also been corrupted. From the various permutations of the word *landshare* (derived from the Old English meaning boundary), we have *landsherd* at Braunton in Devon, *lawnshed* at Portland, *landscars* or *landskers* in west Wales, and *lanchers* in the Gower dialect. In Gower these are the grassy balks found between the strips in the surviving open fields; elsewhere *land-shares* sometimes refers to the strips themselves. These raised green balks were formerly marked by varieties of wild flowers such as cowslips, as they were never ploughed out; in more recent times, efforts to widen the area of cultivation to make it more accessible to modern machinery such as combine harvesters have led to the ploughing out of some strips. Crop sprays also affected the wild flower population, and the cowslip population dwindled but has now begun to re-appear in one or two places. Frank Emery focused on the medieval evidence for open-fields in Gower but they were also fashioned in many of the medieval manors of the Welsh Marches, with similar features across the Bristol Channel being traced and described by H.P.R. Finberg. Rhossili's *Great Vile* is matched by the *Great Field* of Braunton. At Braunton in north-west Devon an open-field of some 350 acres, divided into arable strips, was made up of 491 strips or lands in 1889. They were divided among fifty-six proprietors at that time, today the proprietors number only twenty, two of them holding each a single land.

In the pages of *Past and Present* in 1964, Joan Thirsk provided a widely accepted definition of what is called the open-field system:

> *It is composed of four essential elements. First the arable and meadow is divided into strips scattered about the open fields. Secondly, both arable and meadow are thrown open for common pasturing after harvest and in fallow seasons. In the arable fields this means necessarily that some rules about cropping are observed so that spring or winter-sown crops may be grown in separate fields or furlongs. Thirdly, there is common pasturage and waste where the cultivators of strips enjoy the right to graze stock and gather timber and peat, and other commodities, when available such as stone and coal. Fourthly, the ordering of these activities is regulated by an*

assembly of cultivators – the manorial court, in most places in the Middle Ages – or, when more than one manor was present in a township, a village meeting.

We can recognise at Rhossili three of the four elements described: first, the division into strips within the open-field system. The names *Little Vile, Great Vile* and Middle Field convey the impression that they are part of the vestiges of a classic three-field system of open-field agriculture: the name *Little Vile* is a description given to enclosed fields which were formerly strips in the open fields, which are nearest to the village of Rhossili. Further out, in the remnant of the open-field system visible today, would have been the *Great Viel*, referred to in a document of 1731. The names of fields in this area shown on the Tithe Survey of 1845 also include a block called Middle Field. We must not press this interpretation too far, but Rhossili certainly displays in its open-field system the characteristics of a model type. Secondly, the arable and meadow were thrown open for common pasturing by the stock of all the commoners. In the early eighteenth century, this was causing problems: tenants with stock could turn them into the arable land after corn sown there had been cut by all tenants but several tenants were '*not regarding the time they turn in, which very often happens when several of the Tenants have their Corne on the Ground, which has often been the occasion of a great deal of disturbance and like to end in Law Suites for divers Trespasses comitted there.*' Thirdly, there was extensive waste and common land – the cliff and Rhossili Down being the principal areas. These two areas of common land had rights of grazing attached to them which related to the numbers of stock which could be grazed (stints) and the locations where different tenants could place their stock. Other rights included the cutting and gathering of bracken at defined times.

In these ways, Rhossili fulfilled the criteria of the model of the open field system in three respects: the missing element was the use of a manorial court such as a court leet or court baron to regulate the use of the open fields through what today might be called community by-laws. These by-laws would be introduced, and invoked, at times when pressures on the limited resources of a village were becoming more tangible. Limits on the number of stock grazed on the fallow arable or meadow might be introduced; the timing of the release on livestock onto the land after corn harvest would have to be agreed. It is the basic problems of harvest and pasture which the by-laws of an open-field village would have to deal with. This fourth element, regulation by a manorial court, was achieved in 1731, when an agreement was enrolled in the manorial court rolls of the manor of Landimore. It is shown in the Penrice and Margam Manuscripts as '*A true Coppy of the Stint or Agreement about the Great Field at Rosilly.*' At Rhossili the *infield* could have been the sequence of fields taken into cultivation near the village church, green and pound. Here the remnants of the strips in the *Little Vile* are enclosed; they have names such as *Cooks* and *Priests Hay*, the latter suggesting that they were set aside to provide for support of a clergyman. These initial strips, it is

Aerial view of Old Castle promontory fort.
(© Crown copyright: Royal Commission on the Ancient and Historical Monuments of Wales).

Lithograph showing method of excavation of Paviland Cave (known locally as Goat Hole)
and location of finds by William Buckland in 1823.
(City and County of Swansea: Swansea Museum).

An early twentieth century postcard of Rhossili Parish Church.
(West Glamorgan Archive Service).

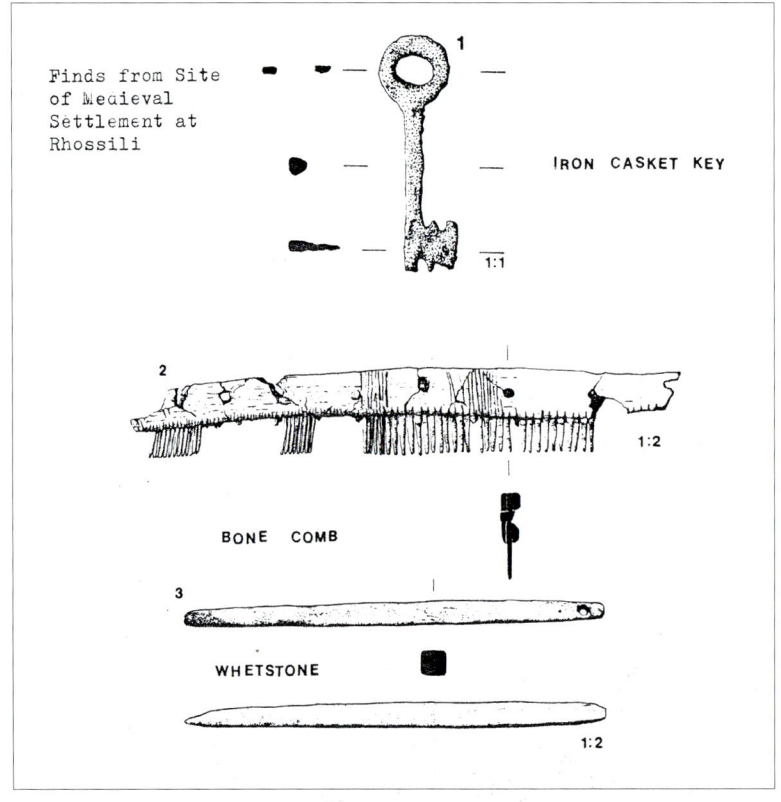

Scaled drawings of finds from the medieval settlement at Rhossili.
(© Glamorgan-Gwent Archaeological Trust and the author).

Two aerial views of Rhossili, the Vile and Worms Head.
(© Crown copyright: Royal Commission on the Ancient and Historical Monuments of Wales).

[Overleaf]: Detail from a Penrice Estate map of Rhossili surveyed by John Williams, 1780.
(West Glamorgan Archive Service).

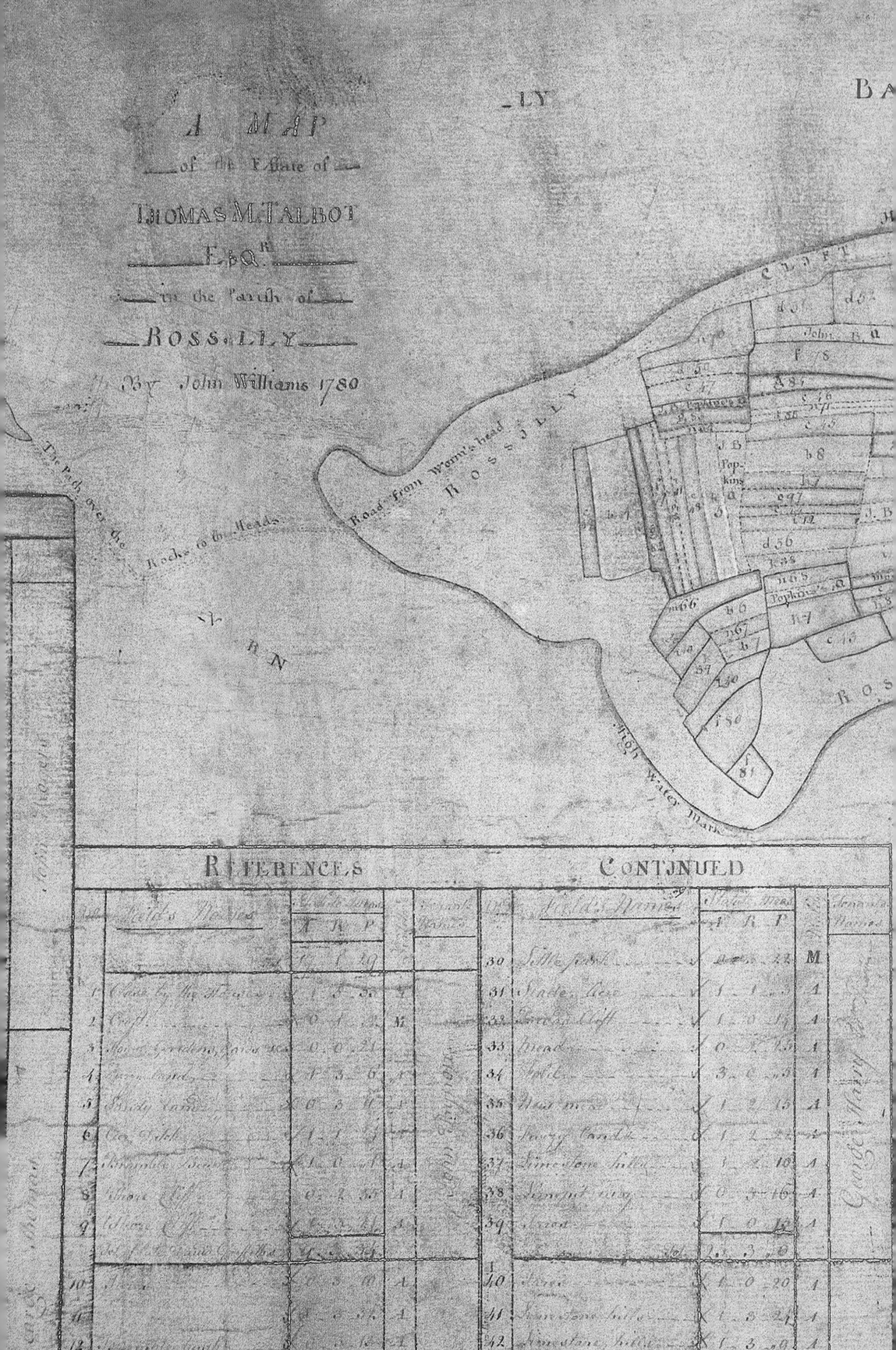

A MAP

of the Estate of

THOMAS M. TALBOT

EsQr

in the Parish of

ROSSILLY

By John Williams 1780

ROSSILLY

Road from Worm's head

High Water Mark

The Path over the Rocks to the Heads

REFERENCES   CONTINUED

	Field's Names	A	R	P				Field's Names	A	R	P	
				19			30	Little field			21	M
1			5	35	M		31	Stable Acre	1	1		1
2	Croft	0			M		32		1	0		1
3		0	0	21			33	Mead	0		15	1
4			3	6			34		3	0		1
5			0	3			35		1	2	15	1
6		1	1				36		1			1
7		1	0				37	Limestone		1	10	1
8		0	1	35			38		0	1	16	1
9			3	31			39		1	0	13	
									1	3	0	
10			3		1		40		1	0	20	1
11					1		41			3	21	1
12					1		42		1	3	19	1

Rossilly Glebe
Rossilly Church

J. B. Popkins

Popkins Ellis

J. B. Popkins

Wm Richard's Ellis

John B. Popkins

J. B. Popkins

CLIFF Containing ...

John B.

George

REFERENCES CONTINUED

Field Names	State ... A	R	P		Owners Names		Field Names	State ... A	R	P		Owners Names
		1	21	A		88	Marsh ...	0	1	7	A	
... land	1	2	30	A		89	Long ...	1	3	6	A	
	0	2	31	A		90	Little ... park	0	3	9	A	
	0	3	20	A		91	...	1	1	6	A	
...	2	1	17	A		92	Marsh ...	0	3	21	A	
... hill	0	3	3	A		93	Smalling	0	1	26	A	
	1	3	16	A		94	... land	1	3	18	A	
	10	0	0			95	Field	2	1	0	A	
	0	1	8	A		96	Sand Cliff	2	0	13	A	
... land	0	3	3	A		97	...	1	0	2	A	
...	1	2	17	A				13	0	12		
... hole	1	3	4	A		98		0	2	22	A	

REFERENC...

An aerial view of Middleton looking west to Worm's Head.
(© Crown copyright: Royal Commission on the Ancient and Historical Monuments of Wales).

*An early twentieth century postcard of Worms Head, posted by a day tripper
on a charabanc outing to Rhossili from Swansea.*
(West Glamorgan Archive Service).

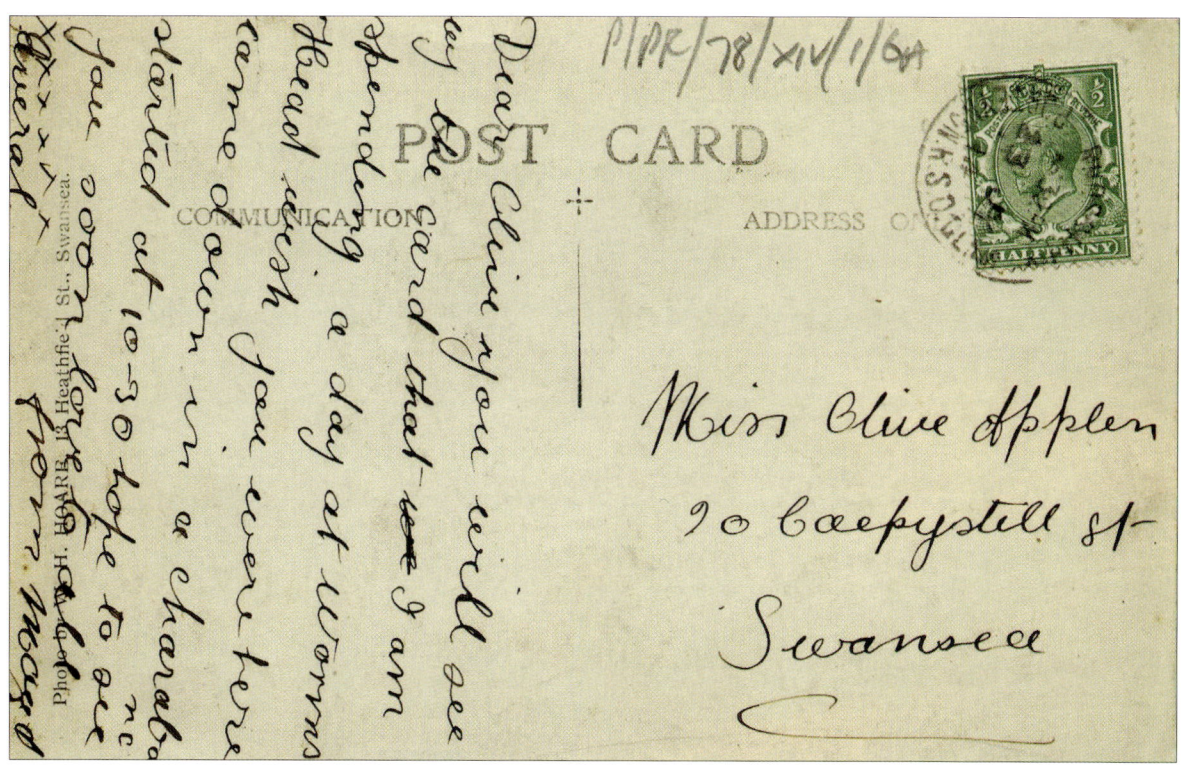

Edgar Evans in the naval uniform of Boy 2nd Class.
(From the collection of the author).

suggested, were gradually enclosed, by putting banks of earth and stone, topped off with thorn hedges. As you move from the village nucleus towards the open fields you find examples of the classic furlong strip. The long, relatively narrow, field in a typical example near the remnants of the open-fields is bounded by the earth banks topped off by thorn hedges as described. Within the narrow but sheltered confines of the former open-field strip, market garden crops such as lettuce have recently been grown. The sparse hedge overhangs the bank as it tries to escape the ravages of the south-westerly wind. With the enclosure of sections of open fields nearest the village, communal rules of cultivation need no longer apply and the better quality of land could be used for more productive cropping patterns. The *Little Vile* being the infield, the outfield would have been land brought into cultivation at a later stage, when pressure on resources required it. The *Great Field* with Middle Field are the two areas which could have developed in Rhossili – here the land has less depth of soil and each ploughing brings its share of limestone rocks to the surface. It would have been originally part of the manorial waste or common land which had to be scrificed to extend the area of cultivated land. With the extension of strips of cultivated land into the outfield a better balance was arrived at between the various resources of Rhossili village – there were still sufficient areas of cliff land and common land on Rhossili Down for livestock. The outfield had to be enclosed in the economic but effective way already described – the dry-stone walls which now demarcate the open-field system at Rhossili from the adjacent cliff land.

The Royal Commission on the Ancient and Historical Monuments of Wales published in 1988 *An Inventory of Ancient Monuments in Glamorgan. Volume III: Medieval Secular Monuments Part II, Non-Defensive*, in which Field Systems were described. In a valuable synopsis the *remains of the open-field layout of the manor of Rhosili*, are described and referred to as an interesting survival of a manorial open field. The principal area today which is unenclosed lies on the headland between the Coastguard Station/ National Trust area and the Coastguard Lookout of former years, overlooking the causeway to Worm's Head. The complete system was much more extensive:

> The area extends from the ravine of the Mew Slade on the East to within 425 metres of the headland on the West, and from the base of Rhosili Down,(the 900 acres of which formed the common pasture of the manor), on the North to the sea cliffs on the South. Most of the open field lies to the South and South-West of the road connecting the villages of Rhosili and Middleton, though some traces extend North of the road as far as the base of Rhosili Down. The main area of arable land is about 390 acres in extent and occupies a plateau falling gently from 90 metres above Ordnance Datum on the north to 45 metres on the South and South-West.
>
> The whole area is sub-divided into strips, arranged in roughly square blocks designated by such names as Sandy Land, Priest Hay, Bramble Bush,

Furzyland. . . . The strips are between 230 metres long and anything from 15 to 70 metres wide; the range of size is thus considerable (two-thirds of an acre to 4 acres), but the commonest size is 230 metres long by 25-30 metres wide (1.5–1.7 acres).

The names of the fields sometimes appear in slightly different form – two of those already mentioned could be described as *Bremhill Bush* and *Vurzeland* in speech. The longest fields are represented on the map by a block of fields called *Furzy-land,* where the appearance of curving field boundaries is related in its more extreme forms in other open-field systems to the reversed S-shape of elongated fields. The influence of the technique of medieval ploughing where teams had to plough over a considerable length is the basis of this feature: it was a long, slightly uphill pull for the horse or oxen teams – hence the curve in the field boundaries. *Vurzeland,* when planted with potatoes in one year, also proved to be a very demanding location for the pickers of the crop – the middle strip leading off Small Way was full of long rows, stretching it seemed into infinity! The young potato pickers in the Second World War appreciated that each row would yield many hundredweights – so only a few rows would be required to make up the several tons required by evening for transport to Swansea. But the longer the rows the less was the respite from the back-breaking chore, which normally came when the potato digger was in action opening fresh rows. Here the row opening, and the rest periods, both came at long intervals – a lesson in appreciating how many back-breaking hours villagers in Rhossili, and later Middleton, spent in hoeing, weeding and picking crops.

The patchwork quilt of the Vile as seen from Rhossili Down still reflects, through the colours of the different crops, the size, shape and pattern of the original open-fields. The individual tenants' strips are shown in 1780 on the map of the manor of Rhossili drawn up by John Williams, surveyor to Thomas Mansel Talbot. John Williams' map meticulously labels each strip with a letter, and also gives other features such as boundaries, including the one between the Manor of Landimore and Rhossili and the Manor of Pitton *alias* Pilton. The key to the map gives the names of the tenants who have been identified by the same letter in each case, so that their total holding can also be ascertained; the estate of John Bennett Popkins is more extensive than that of other landholders – it totalled over 49 acres and was owned by the family at this time. Later, after two sales of property in Gower and elsewhere by the family of Popkins, their major holdings passed to others, including Christopher Rice Mansel Talbot who expanded his Gower (Penrice) Estate. Colouring each tenant's strips confirms the picture already revealed by a study of the letters of the alphabet applied to each strip, although villagers might have strips in more than one of the blocks, within each set of strips the letters are nearly always different from strip to strip. There is convincing support for a scenario which describes how the open-fields developed: each *furrow-long* or furlong (220 yards) was ploughed by a team, after being won from the waste by the clearance of furze, brambles and undergrowth. Each strip was allocated in turn to one of the team who had provided either equipment, or an ox or horse – successive ploughed strips going to a different villager on each occasion until each had received a share of this block of land. Then the team started a fresh block. The pattern is only broken on the outer limits of the open-field strips – holdings such as that of John Rogers (D) have consecutive fields along the edge of the cliff, shown by the same letter or colour. These, it could be suggested, are examples of fields taken in after the main allocation of strips was completed.

Margaret Davies, in her study of 'Wales' Field Patterns' in *Agricultural History Review* (1956), used her version of the John Williams' map of 1780 to show that six farmers of Rhossili village held nearly 142 acres in the Vile and in closes of meadows around their farms: these were Matthew Beynon, John Griffith, John Roger, George Thomas, William Taylor's widow and John Beynon (Letters B-H). Three of the holdings here, together with three more at Middleton, were around 19 or 20 acres, or 22 acres in one case. The sample of seven farmers in Middleton (Letters I-P) held nearly 130 acres in the Vile and, to a greater degree than the farmers of Rhossili, in enclosed fields sloping up to Rhossili Down and gently down towards Mewslade Bay. These seven farmers were William Griffith, George Harry, David Griffith, Sara Stote, Late John Stote, John Thomas and Matthew Morris. Margaret Davies suggested that, *'many of the Middleton farmers held only one or two strips in the Vile, the larger share of open arable land was therefore held, and was probably always held, by the farmers of the older group of farms around the parish church of Rhossili.'* As the settlement of Middleton developed, around the start of the seventeenth century according to one sample of leases of land there, farmers with holdings in the Vile may have moved there. The Stote family were among those who took leases of land in Middleton, as well as holding land in the strips in the Vile. Strips taken in from the land leading down from Middleton to Mewslade Bay might be exclusively in the hands of Middleton farmers in some instances: Matthew Morris had all his holding in Middleton fields. Annual redistribution of strips was unknown at Rhossili, but holdings did have changes of tenant: between 1780 and 1845 the holding of John Griffith (Letter C), which was 32 acres, was added to that of George Thomas (Letter P), who had 19 acres. This made up the fifty-one acres held by the Thomas family in 1845 in the person of Robert Thomas. The holding of John Thomas, which came to 15 acres, passed to Owen Beynon's family through a lease taken by him in 1796; these fields are shown as 'O' on the map of 1780 and have continued to be held by members of the Beynon family through the two hundred years which followed. The present farmer, at Ship Farm, Middleton, is Geoffrey Beynon, whose father David Wilfred Beynon acquired them as part of the land bought when the Penrice and Margam Estate sold land to their tenants shortly after the Second World War. The Beynon family farmed in Middleton but, like other Middleton farmers, had access to the main portion of the open-fields at the Vile by means of a lane from Middleton. This became disused, but has recently been re-opened as a footpath route through the diligence of volunteers under the auspices of the British Trust for Conservation Volunteers.

The holding of John Bennett Popkin or Popkins is not fully shown, although the fields labelled 'A' are part of it. Fifty acres and a farmstead in Rhossili village were once owned by the Popkin family of Forest, Llansamlet in 1780, but this land formed part of a sale in the early nineteenth century, at which time most of the land in Middleton and Rhossili held by the Popkin family passed to the Penrice and Margam Estate. In looking at the tenants shown two centuries ago as holding strips in the Vile, some attempt can be made to show a measure of continuity within the different families such as Rogers, Stote, Thomas and Beynon. The Rogers and Stote families feature as tenants with continuity of leases of the same land from 1780, through a survey of 1814, to the Tithe Survey material of 1845-47. The comparison of family holdings in the Vile at two separate times in 1814 and 1845 formed the first part of Doreen Richards' survey of the open-fields in Rhossili in 1942 in *An Agricultural and Social Study of Rhossili*. A native of Rhossili, now Mrs Doreen Leighton and living again in the village, Doreen Richards demonstrated in her dissertation a degree of continuity of tenancy among the farming families and that, where changes took place, the tenancies often went to someone linked to the vacating family. In the case of Owen Beynon, however, he took over the holding of John Thomas, 15 acres in strips in different parts of the Vile, through a lease in 1796. The family acquired the use of land which was later tenanted by two of Owen Beynon's sons, Edward and William Beynon: they shared the use of the fifteen acres at the time of the Tithe Survey in 1845-47, but later the strips became part of the holding of one farm, and this is now called Ship Farm. The combined holding of George Thomas and John Griffith, mentioned earlier, was farmed by Robert Thomas in 1845, and continued in the Thomas family who had two farms at one stage, both in Rhossili. The Thomas family continue to farm today. In the case of John Rogers (Letter D), the land he is shown as holding near the outer dry-stone walls, is supplemented by strips in the Vile and by land running up to the farm he held (AF). The farm-buildings and farm-house were part of the cluster around Rhossili Parish Church, and the name Ashtree Farm is a reminder that an ash tree grew horizontally in the farm-yard. The house and buildings at Ashtree Farm were occupied – together with all the fields labelled D – by William Rogers in 1814 and 1845. The farm continued in the family until a later Rogers – another John Rogers – retired and lived in the house called Ashtree next to the farm. Harry Richards took over the farm and Harold and Bowen Richards, his sons, then became tenants. The two holdings tenanted by the Stote family also changed hands: the 20 acres in the names of Sarah Stote in 1780 were all part of the holding of Samuel Ace in 1845. Doreen Richards has suggested that the other holding changed hands after the death of Isaac Stote in 1831: further details confirm the lease of the 22 acres, the *lives in being* in 1831 being shown as himself and William his brother, with *Himself* crossed through. Where there is continuity of tenancy, however, as in the case of the Beynon family of Ship Farm, it is possible to trace the individual fields over a period of more than two centuries – from 1796 to the present.

The emphasis on continuity, or otherwise, of landholding has taken us away from the consideration of the missing element in the open-field system at Rhossili – the communal organization of the sowing, harvesting and cropping of the open-fields at Rhossili, which came in the early eighteenth century. The document which reveals how this important omission was rectified is catalogued as 3312 of the Penrice and Margam Manuscripts kept at the National Library of Wales, Aberystwyth. It is summarised by W. de Gray Birch as a *'Record of the Proceedings at a Court Leet and Baron, held for the Manor if Landimore, 24th May 1731. Thomas, Lord Mansell, Baron of Margam, being lord of the Manor. This comprises a true copy of the stint or agreement about the great field at Rosilly.'* It is reproduced in full by Frank Emery in 'Open Fields in Gower', *Gower* XXV (1974): here his transcript, with minor amendments, is reproduced in full, with a commentary on the text. The joint court leet and court baron met at the *dwelling house* of John Williams in the village of Reynoldston on 24 May 1731, then adjourned, and met again at the same place on 14 June 1731. The proceedings were under William Watkins, Deputy to Thomas Cradock, Steward of Thomas, Lord Mansel, Baron of Margam. Several of the tenants within the manor of Landimore, or that part of it called the *Homage of Rosilly* were concerned with current practices in the Great Field at Rhossili, or *Rosilly field,* as it was *'comonly called and known.'* The tenants held *'certaine parcells of Lands uninclosed'* as we have seen, *'being divided by Landshears and **well known of old time'*** (my bold). We have no way, it seems, of finding out how far back the open-field system dates. The tenants could graze cattle and horses *sans number,* that is, without regard to the quantity of land each tenant held in *Rosilly field.* If there was no restriction on the amount of livestock grazed on the Great Field, if the number was *not* proportionate to the amount of land there which each person held, then it is not unexpected that it had caused *'great Detriment, prejudice and losse.'* Also the practice of indiscriminately turning in livestock meant that it *'very often happens when several of the Tenants have their Corne on the Ground,'* which had led to *'a great deal of disturbance'* and a likely resort to law-suits. There was a need to adopt a practice of stinting by which each tenant had rights only to graze a certain number of livestock, coupled with the drawing up of a calendar to control when animals would be allowed to enter, and when they should leave, the open fields. So, the document continues, the *Homage of Roslly* have agreed to Stint each Tenant for the time to come in *Rosilly field* and not to turn the livestock in there, *'untill after Corne harvest yearly and when each and every person or persons holding any Lands there shall have carryed off his, her, or their Corne and Graine from their respective proportion of Lands.'*

The stint agreed: *'For each Acre of Lay or whole Ground: One Horse or two Oxen or Two or three years old Cattle and all other Cattle under that age three for one. For each Acre of Stubble: One Ox, one Beast of three year old, and two Beasts under three year old, but noe Horse to Be allowed to Graze there for stubble.'* The grazing could continue until St Andrew's Day (30th November) but on or by this date all Cattle and Horses had to be removed and *'the land kept free from Grazeing untill Candlemas day yearly* [February 2nd], *and then every Tenant is to Graze his own Land and to Herd for the Sumer Season and untill the first Mow of Corne be raised and carryed of from the said field. The Homage of the said Mannor doe hereby humbly beseech and intreat the Lord of the said Mannor. That the Stint and Agreement aforesaid within Rosilly field may for ever hereafter be a Custome to be observed and kept by the present and all other future Tenants holding any Lands there under the said Lord.'*

The lord by his Deputy Steward agreed and *'Confirmed and Enrolled the same accordingly,'* and a formal presentment was made. The jurors who put their names to it were: Nathaniel Bowen Gent, George Thomas, John Thomas, David Long, John Harry, David Jenkin, John Jones, Randolph Bynon, Thomas Griffith, John David of Leason, Robert Batcocke and William Ace. It was dated 14 June 1731.

In describing Rhossili's open-field system, many previous scholars' work has to be acknowledged because of the significance of the survival of this pattern of medieval agriculture. Its survival into the twenty-first century is a challenge to the villagers and the few remaining farmers to continue to farm it as a living part of the the village heritage. Frank Emery brought together the elements of scenery and landscape in the peninsula and in Rhossili. He emphasised that within the scenery of cliffs and bays, Worm's Head and Burry Holms, the landscape reveals a feature which is central to Rhossili's story – the open fields.

> *Now South Gower is unique not only for the sake of its unparalleled coastal scenery – as in that magnificent run of cliffs from Overton to Worm's Head – but also because it possesses one of the very few relics of open-field cultivation. Perhaps not enough people are aware of this prize, that Gower shares with only another half-dozen sites in the whole of Britain. So complete has been the historical process of hedging that only these few "islands" of the ancient system have not been engulfed: they stand out as remnants of an older order of agrarian management.*

The tangible remains of the open-field system at Rhossili are best viewed from the headland – a vantage point near the Old Lookout gives a view back towards the village. The strips in the aerial photograph clearly show in 1988 the unique pattern of the open-field system – the farming of them on the ground reveals that the variegated crops of earlier days have given way to the growing of corn, with cabbage being the principal alternative. The acquisition of various strips in the Vile has given the National Trust some voice in the management of this unique feature. There is a need to safeguard this tangible relic of Rhossili's past from when farming families exercised their yearly energies to eke a living from the land. It needs to be cherished!

Farming Families and Farmhouses

The origin and development of surnames is an intriguing topic – not least in Wales where there is the added complexity of patronymics and matronymics. It might be expected that in Gower, as in the other anglicised parts of Wales, fixed names would be evident from an early date, but this is not always the case. David Rees in *A Gower Anthology* gives an inscription from Penmaen Church which shows the retention of patronymics in this part of Gower in the early seventeenth century:

> *Here resteth the Body of David, the sonne of David the sonne of Richard the sonne of Nicholas the sonne of Rys the sonne of Leison the sonne of Rys the sonne of Morgan Ychan the sonne of Morgan the sonne of Cradocke the sonne of Iustin ap Gwrgan Sometime Lord of Glamorgan interred in the 21st day of August in the year of our Blessed redemption 1623.*

It is likely, however, that the higher in social class the family was, the sooner would have been the adoption of a family surname which served throughout the later centuries. Even here the practice was not universal; families whose roots lie in a common ancestor might nevertheless have totally different names after their family surnames evolved in different ways.

The social history of Rhossili and its economic development cannot be fully explained without reference to families whose names appear in sources such as the Parish Registers of Rhossili Church. Some names appear over a period from the seventeenth century to the nineteenth century, others, including my family, appear in Rhossili from Oxwich or other villages and these families continued to farm in the village until the later twentieth century. In some cases, the origins of the family in Rhossili lie outside Glamorgan: such a family were the Stotes. The 1992 edition of the International Genealogical Index had around 35 entries for Cornwall of Stote, Stoate or other variations of the family name, but around 450 entries for Devon. Of these, around 100 entries are shown for Braunton, Devon, which lies just across the Bristol Channel from Rhossili, so it could be assumed that if there was migration via the cross-channel trading ships that plied between Gower and the West Country, families such as the Stotes might have found their way into parishes such as Porteynon as well as Rhossili. A search of the same International Genealogical Index for Glamorgan, yielded a sample of over 50 entries for Stote – none outside Gower or Swansea. A few entries for Swansea, four for Penrice and four for Porteynon are found in the sample, leaving over forty entries of Stotes in Rhossili. Although not exclusive to Rhossili, it is this village which is their base in Gower, in which their farming and smuggling exploits took place. The local families, too, play their part in the social fabric of the community of

Rhossili: Ace, Austin, Beynon, Bidder, Bevan, Gammon, Griffiths, Rogers, Taylor and Thomas are among the names which crop up over the centuries.

It will be seen later that, among Rhossili families, the Griffith family became Griffiths, while the Roger family moves into Rogers which is more noticeable in the later parish registers, on gravestones and in the census names which can be checked from 1841-1901. We can also recognise the surnames of families which appear to have developed an occupational name or nickname. Bidder, it has been suggested, was the name for someone who summoned guests to weddings and funerals and its appearance in the Gower peninsula has been recorded in Rhossili from the sixteenth century at least. It appears as Bydder in Pennard and as Bidder in Knelston. Similarly, in the fulling of cloth a person engaged in the trade was usually known in the north of England and Scotland as a walker and in the south-west of England as a tucker. This gave Walker and Tucker, with Fuller, as surnames – with the geographical distribution suggesting the Tuckers could have come to Gower from the West Country. The word *curtois* (courteous) could give rise to Curtis: John Curteys is found in Rhossili in 1543, Thomas Curteis of Penryce, Isabel his daughter and Thomas his son appear in a Lease dated 1 April 1579. John Curteys of Llandewi had a total of £60 13s in the inventory drawn up in 1579 with £14 value of crops and £31 in stock. Their links with Pilton and Paviland continued throughout the centuries and the family appears in census returns at the end of the nineteenth century.

The abstract of wills of the Taylor family shows links with the Curtis family: Jenkin Taylor's will of 14 January 1620/21 shows Jenkin Austen, Nicholas Austen and Ann Austen. The modern name Austin or Austen comes from the Old French Aoustin. They were followed by Jenkin Taylor, Rowland Taylor, Margaret Taylor, his wife, John Taylor his son and Philip Taylor, brother-in-law. Edward Curtes, debtor, William Rogers, John Ace, butcher, and John Grove are others mentioned. In similar fashion, Richard Bidder's will (date of probate/grant 1674) gives the names of his sons and daughters – Ann, Jane, Mary, Grace, Richard and Daniel – with his grandsons' names – John Stote and Simon Stote. Together with Beynon, Button, Bevan, Thomas, Griffith or Griffiths, Richard or Richards, Tucker, the Stote, Taylor, Curtis and Bydder families are among the farming families which, with the clergy of the Austin or Austen family, make up a good part of the community of Rhossili over a period of many years between the sixteenth and nineteenth centuries. The Owen Beynon who was born in Oxwich in 1769 appears to have spent some time in Rhossili, then at Horton, where he is shown as a blacksmith leasing a house and smithshop in 1792. Members of the Button family appear in Porteynon Rent Rolls before they appear in Pitton. In considering the farming families of Rhossili we will find a tendency for later generations to farm land in parts of the village which was tenanted by their ancestors, but it is equally true that many of the smaller farmers of Rhossili, Middleton, Pitton and Pilton have now disappeared. However, when Owen Beynon of Oxwich took out a lease in 1796 of land formerly tenanted by John Thomas, the various fields were to be cultivated for the next two centuries by his descendants, who still live in Middleton. The Thomas family have continued their family farming tradition until recent times.

In examples of the transition to patronymics and matronymics we have the examples of the inventory of Owen Davies dated October 1721; his will was dated 22 August 1719 and Probate was granted on 31 March 1722. Among the persons mentioned are his son Thomas Bowen, his daughter Anne Davies, his sister Elinor Davies and his grandson Owen Davies. This last complication was due to the fact that Owen Davies' son-in-law was called Thomas Davies! We have already noted a lease dated 2 March 1664 which related to land in the manor of Pilton *alias* Pitton: Elizabeth Hill is mentioned as the wife of Rees ap Hugh, her children are named as Nathaniel Pugh and Lydia Pugh.

The Stote family arrived in Rhossili with their family name fairly fixed: Stott, Stote, Stotte, Stoat and Stoate appear in variations shown in the 1992 edition of the International Genealogical Index in Devon. The entries include a nucleus of 100 Stote names, as has already been mentioned, just a few miles directly across the Bristol Channel from Rhossili. Early forms of the name include John Stott, 1296, Elena la Stott, 1312 and, in a Military Survey of 1522, John Stote apprentice to Margaret Buckinham appears. By 1665, when the Rhossili Parish Register of 1641-1797 records the marriage of John Stote to Jane Rees on 9 November, the name appears in a regular form. One gravestone in Rhossili churchyard records the burial of Isaac Stote who, with his wife Mary (Mally), was involved with smuggling activities at Middleton; she was formerly Mary Rogers.

Two features of the farming families' names of Rhossili can be highlighted. One is that only a few of the family names so far mentioned feature in the names of village families in Rhossili today. The second feature is that the names of a number of families reflect their patronymic or matronymic origins: Beynon, Richards, Thomas, Bevan and Griffiths are examples of surnames derived from personal names, others derive from occupational surnames. The turnover in family names is sometimes regarded as a puzzling and rare phenomenon in rural villages – names found in Rhossili in the seventeenth century seem markedly different from those found in the census returns of the nineteenth century. It is often the case, however, that if the history of a parish is traced over a period of several centuries the turnover of the surnames found seems very large so that even over a moderately short time, such as a hundred years, there appears to be very little continuity. The majority of such families were tenants of the Penrice and Margam Estate, as were the majority of tenant farmers in Gower. The acquisition of the Earl of Pembroke's manors in Gower by the Mansel family in 1666 gave this family additional land, wealth and prestige. The Mansel family continued to play a dominant role in the fortunes of Gower and Rhossili for another century when the family name died out. When the Trustees of the Penrice and Margam Estate acquired for Christopher Rice Mansel Talbot much of the land in Gower sold in 1820 from the Popkin estate, the family would have been confirmed as the principal landowners in villages such as Rhossili.

Land Tax Assessments of the late eighteenth century confirm the status and land-holding of the various landowners in Rhossili and the tenancies which were then in place. In 1781, Rhossili's assessment quota was £26 9s 6d and it was the same both eight and seventeen years later. It gives the quota attatched to each holding and confirms the individual tenant. The titles of the assessments are in standard form – the difference being the date of 4th June 1781 on the first, and 20th June 1789 on the second. The initial entry is a column showing the names of proprietors and copyholders – in the return for June 1781, this is headed Landlords. Next come the names of the Tenements and Tenants' Names. The first entries in the assessments for the *Parrish of Rossilly* refer to the Glebe Land, tenanted by Richard Clark; the incumbent was the Revd. Benjamin Hales, who was assessed on the Glebe Land and Tithes. The largest group of tenants were leased land by Thomas Mansel Talbot under the Penrice Estate – in Pilton a shared tenancy by Samuel Clement and John David is held in both assessments, but the tenancy of Matthew Button gives way in 1783 to Daniel Curtis and he appears as the tenant in 1789. The various families at Pitton or Pitton Cross appear as Robert Button, Elizabeth Bynon, widow, and William Taylor in the earlier assessment; but William Cleament and William Richard appear later in Pitton, with William Taylor's land at Kenmoor also being taken over by William Richard. The Mill at Pitton is initially in the hands of John Evan, but then Mary Evan, widow, takes over. The contrast in this early section is between the high assessment of £1 3s 2d for Samuel Clement and John David at Pilton and the 9d for land tenanted at Kenmoor by William Taylor and William Richard, and also Matthew Morris of Middletown. Similarly the assessment of 9d at Pitton Cross for Robert Button in 1789 would be for poorer land on or near Pitton Cross Common. George Harries at Middletown gives way to William Tucker, Griffith William Senior's two tenancies at Middletown and Mount appear to be tenanted by David Thomas Junior and David Thomas Senior from 1783, and by David Thomas from 1789. Of the two tenancies of Sarah Stote, widow, in 1781 and 1789, one has been transferred to Isaac Stote in 1798. By this time, too, it has been explained the earlier tenancy of John Thomas at Middletown was now held by Owen Beynon. We know from an estate map of 1780 that the holding of John Thomas was 15 acres; in 1789 it was held by Owen Beynon, but by Will. Bowen in 1791. We can account for this change by a Lease which shows Owen Beynon at Horton in 1792: a freehold Lease by Thomas Mansel Talbot of Margam to Owen Beynon of Oxwich, blacksmith, of a house and smithshop in the Manor of Horton – dated 22nd May 1792 – shows where Owen Beynon had gone. A later lease of 1796 shows Owen Beynon as tenant of the 15 acres of John Thomas – the field names on the map of 1780 can be confirmed by the Tithe Map and Apportionment Schedule of 1845-47 for Rhossili as being the same field names in the holding of Edward Beynon and William Beynon, whose descendant still farms them as part of Ship Farm, Middleton, two hundred years later. The one further farmer at Middletown was David Griffith, whose family were connected with Riverside Farm.

The clear-cut entries for Rhossili show George Thomas, Matthew Bynon, followed by George Bynon with William Taylor who follows Mary Taylor, widow. Part of their tenancy – Sorry Bargain – has one of the lowest assessments at 8d. One of the higher assessments is £1 1s 9d for one tenancy of the Bynon family. John Griffith and John Roger, of Ashtree Farm, were two other farmers at Rhossili – the list then reverts to Pitton where Thomas Bynon, Mary Gammon, widow, Griffith William Junior, Avis Bowen, widow, Robert Bydder and Mary William, widow, hold small amounts of land in 1781. William Lewis held Griffith Williams' Farm at Pitton in 1789. The next entries deal with the land of John Bennet Popkins, who is shown as being the owner of land in Rhossili on the map of the Manor of Rhossili completed by John Williams for the Penrice and Margam Estate: just under 50 acres is noted – identified by the letter 'A' on various parts of the map. The Land Tax Assessment of 1781 indicates there were five properties which he leased to tenants or held himself – two of these were quite substantial, judging by the amount of Land Tax payable. Three were held by members of the Bydder family: Middletown – Richard Bydder (£1 4s 7d Land Tax payable); Pilton – Robert Bydder (£1 1s 9d) and Fernhill – Robert Bydder (5s 8d). In 1782, the properties at Pilton and Pernhill were held by Mr Popkins himself. One other property at Fernhill was held by Matthew Bynon in 1781 (9s 2d Land Tax payable), and a property at Kingshall by William Bynon, who also held it in 1789. At this time, Middletown (Matthew Morris), Pilton (Morgan Bynon) and Fernhill (Morgan Bynon) had moved from the Bydder family to new tenants. The property tenanted at Fernhill by Matthew Bynon in 1781 was now held by George Bynon. The land at Hillend of John Morris – which was adjacent to the Glebe Land – was tenanted by Richard Clark Senior in 1781; his son, Richard Clark Junior tenanted the Glebe Land of the Rev. Benjamin Hales. Mr Thomas Lott had acquired this property by 1789 and it was now leased to Thomas Bevan. The largest single holding was that of John Bynon at Pitton, held from the Honourable George Venables Vernon Esquire: the Land Tax Assessment was £2 3s 6d in 1781. By 1789, it was held by Ann Bynon, widow. Philip Taylor held Flodders from the Reverend William Butler, Richard Bydder held Sluxton from Mary Price, widow, and Richard Clark Senior held another small property at Hillend from Daniel Button in 1781. The only change by 1789 was that Thomas Matthew held Sluxton. One very interestingly-named piece of land, Freeland, was held by Sarah Stote, widow, from William Richard in 1781 and John Hoskin in 1789. By 1814, it appears that this piece of land was the only land in Rhossili not held by C.R.M. Talbot or John Bennet Popkins – it is shown as belonging to William Richard. Matthew Button, who was both Assessor and Collector in 1781, received £1; Morgan Bynon was Assessor and Collector in later years – Collector in 1782 and Assessor in 1783 when William Taylor was the Collector. George Bynon's salary was £1 in 1789 – other Assessors and Collectors were Matthew Morris, George Thomas, Morgan Bynon, William Bowen, with Isaac Stote being the Collector in 1800.

The families of Rhossili are clearly shown two hundred years ago – at a time when leases show individual family names and parish registers reveal relationships, but well before the census returns give better detail every decade from 1841 to 1901.

Land Tax Assessments: Glamorgan – Parrish of Rossilly June 1781

Assessments at four shillings in the pound based on the annual value of land

Landlords	Tenements	Tenants' Names	£	s	d
The Rev. Benjamin Halls [Hales]	Glebe	Richard Clark Junr.		18	4
Ditto	Tithes	Mr Benjamin Halls [Hales]	2	12	1
Thomas Mansel Talbot Esqr.	Pilton	Saml. Clemt. & John Davies? [John David]	1	3	2
Ditto	Pilton	Matthew Button	1	2	3
Do	Pitton	Robert Button		8	9
Do	Do	Elizabeth Bynon wid.		13	9
Do	Do	Do		12	2
Do	Do	William Taylor		12	6
Do	Kenmoor	Do			9
Do	Mill	John Evan		6	–
Do	Middletown	Matthew Morris		12	11
Do	Kenmoor	Do			9
Do	Middletown	George Harries		10	8
Do	Do	Griffith William Sen.		7	7
Do	Mount	Do		1	1
Do	Middletown	Sarah Stote wd.		9	11
Do	Do	Do		10	8
Do	Do	John Thomas		7	3
Do	Do	David Griffith		8	–
Do	Rossilly	George Thomas		10	10
Do	Do	Matthew Bynon	1	1	9
Do	Wormshead	Do		2	3
Do	Rossilly	John Richard		5	5
Do	Do	Mary Taylor wd.		8	8
Do	Sorry Bargain	Do			8
Do	Rossilly	John Griffith		8	8
Do	Do	John Roger		11	7
Do	Pitton	Thomas Bynon		1	–
Do	Do	Mary Gammon wd.		1	1
Do	Do	Griffith William Junr.			8

Landlords	Tenements	Tenants' Names	£	s	d
Do	Do	Avis Bowen wd.			6
Do	Do	Robert Bydder			6
Do	Do	Mary William wd.			9
John Bennet Popkins Esqr.	Middletown	Richard Bydder	1	4	7
Do	Pilton	Robert Bydder	1	1	9
Do	Fernhill	Do		5	8
Do	Do	Matthew Bynon		9	2
Do	Kingshall	William Bynon		2	3
John Morris Esqr.	Highlend [Hillend]	Richard Clark Senr.	1	2	11
The Hon George Venables Vernon	Pitton	John Bynon	2	3	6
The Revnd. William Butler	Flodders	Phillip Taylor			4
Mary Price widdow	Sluxton	Richard Bydder		9	2
Daniel Button	Hillend	Richard Clark Senr.		2	3
William Richard	Freeland	Sarah Stote Wd.		1	3
Matthew Bynon for his Salary			1	–	–

Matthew Button Assessor   Matthew Button Collector   £26 9 6

The crops grown by the farmers of Rhossili are given in the Crop Returns of 1801. During the Napoleonic Wars, the Board of Agriculture, which had been informally established in 1797, decided to collect accurate statistical information concerning crops raised in the harvest of 1801. The incumbents of each parish were required to make returns of the acreage in 1801 given to the cultivation of wheat, barley, rye, oats, potatoes, peas, beans and turnips or rape. A space was provided for General Remarks.

A sample of the returns is given below showing acreage:

	Wheat	Barley	Oats	Potatoes	Peas	Beans	Rye	Turnips or rape
Penrice	101	163	105	11	–	–	–	–
Porteynon	49	108	42	10	½	½	–	–
Reynoldston	40	65	32	4	–	–	–	–
Rhossili	48	76	39	5	6	2	–	7

The proportions of wheat, barley and oats for Rhossili are comparable to Reynoldston. It grew the second highest acreage of peas in the eight parishes which grew the crop (out of sixteen shown in the full table for Gower). Rhossili was one of three parishes growing beans and – with four other parishes – grew acreages of turnips or rape.

Exceptionally, the parish of Llanmadoc has a return which states: *There are no field potatoes, peas, beans or turnips in this parish, but a sufficiency of potatoes in the gardens for the consumption of the inhabitants*. In every village in Gower, *tater hays* or potato gardens would be found and Rhossili was no exception. Every cottager, it is suggested, cultivated his tater hay or potato patch and, near the coast, many tater hays were sited on the shore's edge where quantities of seaweed were available for manure. One at Rhossili was a small encroachment on the cliff common and was tenanted by Sarah Stote: it overlooks Mewslade Bay and would have originally been formed by encroachment at a time when Sarah Stote had a holding of 20 acres in Rhossili. By 1845 it had been joined by another enclosure tenanted by William Bevan in 1814, which he himself fenced off from the cliffland. In 1814 it only had a fence as a boundary but by 1845 it had a proper stone wall and was officially tenanted. It is easy to identify where a straight stone wall has been built across former cliffland to create the new enclosure, as it butts on to the previous curving walls. David Wilfred Beynon had this garden in more recent times under rent from the Penrice and Margam Estate; he sub-rented it to Johnny Beynon, Middleton. In a later exchange of land it went to the Button family of Pitton Cross who grew daffodils and herbs on the ground. Recently, in new ownership, it formed part of a holding where vines were cultivated to produce Mewslade Bay wine.

A closer focus on the individual farming families of Rhossili relies heavily on the key maps of John Williams for the Penrice and Margam Estate between 1780 and 1786: *A Map of the Estate of Thomas M. Talbot Esquire in the Parish of Rossilly* was completed in 1780 and a similar one in 1783 is described as *A Map of Pilton Hamlet in the Parish of Penrice*. The farmers of Rhossili in 1780 included Matthew Beynon, John Griffith, John Rogers, George Thomas, William Taylor's widow and John Beynon, who together held nearly 142 acres in the open-fields in the Vile. Seven farmers of Middleton held nearly 130 acres in the Vile and, to a greater degree than those of Rhossili, in enclosed fields sloping up to Rhossili Down and gently down towards Mewslade Bay, according to Margaret Davies writing in 1956 in *The Agricultural History Review*. They were William Griffith, George Harry, David Griffith, Sarah Stote, late John Stote, John Thomas and Matthew Morris. The neighbouring farms in Rhossili included those of John Rogers at Ashtree Farm, George Thomas and John Griffith – their families continued to farm the fields shown on the estate map of 1780 in succeeding years but only one of these families, the Thomas family, continues to farm in Rhossili at the present day. Ashtree Farm in 1814 was tenanted by William Rogers; his wife, Elizabeth was some thirteen years younger than he was, but died first in July 1844. Three of their children – John, William and Ann – appear in successive Census Enumerators' Returns for Rhossili. Ann married David Williams of Swansea, but died in 1861 aged 46. The census entries which feature the family in 1861 show William Rogers, widower, 74, Farmer of 18 acres; John Rogers, 41, and William Rogers, 39, his two sons; their house servant was Eleanor Lewis, 27. She was born in Llanmadoc, and by 1871 appears to have become William Rogers' daughter-in-law as there is an Eleanor Rogers who had married John the elder son. The son of the marriage of John and Eleanor Rogers was called John, the daughter was Elizabeth – their father died on Christmas Day 1857, aged 47, so does not feature in the census of 1861. Shortly after the census of 7 April 1861, William Rogers, widower and farmer of 20 acres, died aged 85. The surviving son William remained unmarried, his sister-in-law Eleanor acted as housekeeper, and her family (John, 16, and Elizabeth, 14) are shown as nephew and niece respectively of William Rogers, unmarried, 57, farmer of 19 acres, in the census of 1871. By 1881, John Rogers is shown as son of William Rogers farming at Rhossili, but the correct relationship is restored in 1891 where John is the nephew who is *Assisting on the Farm.* The tenancy of the farm passed to John who was living at Ashtree – next to the farm – when he died on 16 February 1917 at the age of 62. His housekeeper at this time was my grandmother on my mother's side, Florence Beynon. Harry Richards had tenanted the land when John Rogers retired, and it was later tenanted by his two sons, Bowen and Harold Richards. Ashtree Farm, adjacent to the Rhossili Parish Church, enjoyed the distinction of having an ash tree growing horizontally in the farmyard. The former house and farm buildings have been very sympathetically converted into a modern dwelling, with an exterior whose appearance retains the stone clad walls of the original farmhouse and buildings. The map of 1780 clearly identifies the landholdings connected with Ashtree Farm – the long, narrow strips of arable land running up towards the farm and house, making up 19 acres.

The Griffith or Griffiths family are shown at Rhossilly Farm in a Rent-Roll of 1831 from the Penrice and Margam Estate: two names shown on the same gravestone in Rhossili churchyard which are those of John Griffiths and his son, Isaac Griffith confirm the variation in the surname. Another family gravestone unfolds the tragedies which befell John Griffiths and his wife after 1780: at this time the family farmed 32 acres in Rhossili according to John Williams' map. Shortly after this time, Mary – daughter of John and Ann Griffith – died on 29 August 1784, aged 15; their daughter Jennet died on 31 August 1784, aged 12. The two deaths in two days in 1784 were followed by the death of Ann Griffiths on 31 March 1789, aged 45. John Griffith, we assume, continued to farm with his eldest son John, and his younger sons, Thomas, Joseph and Isaac. The deaths of two of the younger sons are shown by an inscription; *'Two sons of John and Ann Griffith, who were driven by a storm to sea out of this bay 17 May 1800, and perished.'* These were Thomas, aged 23, and Joseph, 14. Eleven years later the eldest son John died – his death is recorded in these words:

> *Here lieth the body of John the son of the above John and Ann Griffith whose death was occasioned by a violent blow with a stone at Langennith on the 5th day of July 1811 and died the 7th Aged 38.*

My tomb you see, remember me Who now is laid in clay
Man with a stone my blood did spill And took my life away.
Tho' man could do no more to me Than take my life away
God will rise me from the dust, At the Great riseing day

When John Griffiths died on 13 September 1824, aged 84, his son Isaac Griffiths farmed the land tenanted by the family – in 1831 it amounted to 42/43 acres. Isaac died in July 1835 aged 47, and Robert Thomas – who already tenanted another farm – took over the property. Later tenants of the land included John Thomas, son of Robert Thomas, and his sister Elizabeth who was married to John Button. A son of John Thomas called George Thomas followed in the family footsteps and then two brothers – sons of this George Thomas – farmed two separate holdings. George Thomas in 1941 farmed Rhossili Farm, his bailiff was Sid James who lived in Rhossili Farmhouse. His brother Sidney Thomas farmed fields linked with the Pound, near the Green, and the farm buildings nearby, now converted to Little Hill House, but he lived at the Old Coastguard Station. The son of Sidney and May Thomas – Gordon Thomas – continued with the family holdings and his sons, until recently, kept up the centuries-old farming tradition of their ancestors.

The Stote family occupy a fascinating niche in the annals of Rhossili life: the family appears to have been established in Rhossili by the time of the Restoration of Charles II in I660. In a *valuation of tithe and gliebe*, noted earlier as having been carried out in I662 John Stote had a tenancy of 15 acres and a John Stote features in a lease of 1664 when Anne Austin of Rossilly, Jane Rees her daughter and John Stote for £12 secured the tenancy of messuage and lands of 7½ acres at a yearly rent of 35 shillings from the Rt Hon. Philip [Herbert], Earl of Pembroke. John Stote married Jane Rees in 1665 and appears as a Churchwarden in this period. The will of John Stote of Rhossili – dated 4 April 1704 – with probate granted on 18 April 1706 mentions Jane his wife and Simon Stote his son, who is the executor. At an earlier date, *Simon Stote of Rossilley* received a freehold lease from the Hon. Edward Mansel, of Margam, Bart. of a mansion house, messuage, and lands – 19½ acres – at Middletowne, for life after the decease of present tenants. The lease, dated 28 January 1680, involved payment of £8 and a yearly rent of £1 15s. Simon Stote also appears as a signatory of the Glebe Terrier for the parish of Rhossili in October 1720. The names John Stote and Simon Stote crop up in later generations of this prolific family: John, son of John Stote, was christened in September 1730; Simon Stote was buried at Rhossili in August the year before. Simon, son of John Stote, was christened in October 1740; in a later entry another Simon Stote, son of John and Sarah Stote was christened in January 1761! A further son, Isaac, christened in January 1763, features in the smuggling stories of the later eighteenth century.

The centre of the stories is usually given as the Ship Inn at Middleton as Horatio Tucker describes in *Gower Gleanings*: Mally Rogers (Isaac Stote's wife) and two

Customs officers accompanied by a servant feature in the tale. At the time of the arrival of the Customs officers at Mally's cottage in Middleton, a cargo of brandy was lying in a secret cellar nearby. The officers were persuaded to imbibe a little brandy which was diluted with hot water from a kettle on the hob which was actually best Hollands (gin). After further helpings the officers fell asleep – the servant had also enjoyed his share. By the time the Customs men had recovered from their nap, the cellar was empty and the kegs were distributed far and wide. On another occasion, a kinsman of Mally's husband called William Stote spent three months in Carmarthen Jail for being concerned in the release of impounded horses from a farmyard in Pitton, the animals having been seized in a raid by Revenue men on smugglers on Rhossili sands. Reports in *The Cambrian* in the year of the Battle of Trafalgar, 1805, record some success for George Beynon, the Riding Officer at Rhossili in tandem with the Sea Fencibles. They have been described as a kind of Home Guard or Dad's Army – they were recruited for the defence of the coast at the height of the Napoleonic Wars.

THE CAMBRIAN:

Saturday February 23, 1805: On Saturday night and Sunday last, Mr George Beynon Officer of the customs, with the assistance of Lieut. Sawyer and the Sea Fencibles, seized on Roscilly Sands 101 casks, containing about 8 gallons each of brandy, rum, geneva and wine which had been landed by a smuggler. The whole has since been deposited in the custom house in this town [Swansea].

Saturday 8 June 1805: Monday last 115 casks of spirits seized by Mr Beynon at Rossilly were lodged in our Custom-House [Swansea].

Friday March 6 1807: a seizure of nearly fifty ankers of smuggled spirits was made at Roscilly on Wednesday night last by the excise officers of Swansea.

Another report suggests that an affray on Rhossili sands in March 1805 led to injuries to two Customs Officers, William Webb and William Seward from Llanmadoc, who were severely manhandled by a smuggling gang. Webb, suffering from wounds, was locked up for the night in Stote's cottage in Middleton, but Seward was allowed to limp home.

The Bevan family of Middleton would have enjoyed three separate tenancies in Middleton when Thomas Bevan divided the 75 acres shown in the Tithe Survey and Apportionment Schedule of 1845 between his three sons, Samuel, John and George: the three farms centred on Ivy Dene, Middleton Hall and what would be called now the Old Farmhouse. Thomas Bevan seems to have divided his tenanted farm land equally between his three sons with the youngest son's portion first; two houses were built so that each son might live entirely separately. An extended family tree, coupled with material from the Tithe Survey and the Census Enumerators' Returns for Rhossili from 1841 to 1891, helps to describe the various branches of the Bevan family of Middleton and the relationship between the Bevan, Chalk and Jones families. Thomas Bevan in the Census Enumerator's Returns for Rhossili in 1841 is shown as having three sons: Samuel, 30, John, 23, George, 22. Thomas Bevan held some 75 acres in the Tithe Survey of 1845. It is worth pointing out that Pilton – in the parish of Penrice until 1879 – might have been the family base before they moved to Middleton. Thomas Bevan, in 1851, is shown as being born in Penrice, together with Samuel and John; George is shown as born in Porteynon, together with a daughter, Jane. At this time – 1851 – George is shown as married, and is a farmer of 20 acres; his father is now shown as farming 47 acres. By 1861, George Gibbs Bevan, as he is referred to now, has six children, but by 1871 he is a widower of 51 and farmer of 27 acres. Samuel, 50, and John Gibbs Bevan, 44, are now shown separately for the first time: Samuel was still living with his father and mother, who were 84 and 79 respectively. John Gibbs Bevan had married and had two children – Mary, 2, and John Gibbs Bevan, 3 months. This is the census of 1861 but, by 1871, the three families and farms are distinct and separate. John Gibbs Bevan, with his wife, Ruth, 43, farmed 18 acres. She is shown as being born in Llandewi; Mary, 12, John Gibbs Bevan, 10, Thomas, 8, Rowland, 6 and Silvanus, 3 are their family. Samuel Bevan, marrying late, was now 60; his wife Elizabeth (Betty), was much younger than he was. Their son, Samuel, was 1-year-old; his father died in August 1871 when he fell off a load. George Bevan, we have already noted, was a widower by 1871, aged 51 and farming 27 acres: his children Frances, Jane, William and Eliza, had a younger sister Harriet, 6. George Gibbs Bevan, 62, was in 1881 a retired farmer, living with his son, George Bevan, 32, who was a shoemaker. His son-in-law, William Chalk, farmed 20 acres. John Gibbs Bevan was still a farmer – his eldest son John Gibbs Bevan was a blacksmith. The widow of Samuel Bevan – Elizabeth or Betty Bevan – had remarried by 1881: she was now the wife of William Jones, formerly a widower with a family of his own. He had been a sailor but his father was a farmer of 12 acres. In the 1881 census, William Jones and his family farm property at Middleton adjacent to the farm of John Gibbs Bevan, Senior: at home on census night we have William Jones, 38, farmer of 50 acres; Elizabeth, his wife, 44; Francis Jones, 7, born Oystermouth; Elizabeth Jones, 6, born Oystermouth: and Margaret Jones, born Rhossilly. The stepsons – Samuel Bevan, 11, and William Bevan, 8 – had both been born in Rhossili. In 1891, William Chalk, 35, farmer, has living with him his wife Mary Ann, four of his children, his father-in-law George Gibbs Bevan, and his brother-in-law, also George Gibbs Bevan. John Gibbs Bevan (Senior) had died so the John Gibbs Bevan, who is the son, has his wife Jane, and his mother Ruth, living with him: his first child, Anne (Annie) had been born in October 1890. William Jones and Elizabeth managed the adjacent farm – William Bevan was now 19; Francis Jones, 17, is classed as *Seaman Seas*. Unfortunately, John Gibbs Bevan died in June 1904 at the age of 43, leaving his wife, Jane, to bring up their six children. It was the eldest daughter, Annie, who was her mother's principal help; Jane Bevan lived to the ripe old age of 96 and died in 1958. Her daughter Annie died in 1993 at the age of 103. A photographic portrait of Auntie Annie, taken on the occasion of her 100th birthday, shows a remarkable lady whose memory spanned the time from Queen Victoria's later years to the present day. It was a source of delight to talk to her about the old days and to tape record some of her memories: it put into a clearer perspective many of the families of Rhossili, Middleton and Pitton, together with events in the village at a time when she was growing up before the First World War. She married Tom Jenkins who died in 1942 at the age of 63 so Mrs Annie Jenkins – Auntie Annie – was a widow for 50 years. In an interview recorded on 9 November 1988, when she was only 98 years old, she shared her memories.

The two adjacent farms of the Jones and Bevan family shared the barn and the machinery – using the barn for storing corn. According to Auntie Annie, they always left the corn in the barn. The Joneses would have the highest side, the Bevanses the lower side from them. There was never any trouble. She also recalls that Miss Matty was the school mistress at Rhossili School – Annie Bevan and Bertha Beynon were the two youngest girls and Sid Beynon and William Beynon were the two youngest boys. The family had three carts carrying corn: *'We'd have three carts carrying corn, and I was always the middle one, one in the field, and one in the rickyard and one in between.'* Once the corn was safely stored the work did not finish – at some point the corn would be threshed and the threshed corn taken to the nearest mill for grinding into flour. As Pitton Mill was no longer in use, this meant a trip to Middle Mill, Burry. *'I stayed so late once that when I was coming through Burry it was getting dark and [I] didn't have lights you see and had grandfather on Pitton Cross coming to look for me.'*

A map of 1780 of the manor of Rhossili shows the respective tenancies of John Griffith and David Griffith, members of a family whose early association with Rhossili can be traced back to a lease of 10 acres of land in 1656. The tenancy of John Griffith in 1780 was 32 acres in Rhossili, it was to pass to Robert Thomas in later years through family connections. A John Griffiths is shown as marrying Jane Thomas on 12 March 1794. Robert Thomas is shown as marrying Elizabeth Griffith on 8 December 1813. The holding of David Griffith of Middleton in 1780 was 19 acres but was 16 acres in later years. This tenancy of 16 acres was centred at Riverside Farm and was shared by a David Griffith and John Griffith in 1845. It is significant that in both families nearly all the children died before their fathers, which will explain the later change in the tenancy of land farmed by the Griffith/Griffiths family. In the Tithe Map for Rhossili in 1845, John Griffith is shown as the co-tenant with David Griffith of Tithe No.166 (1r 8p) *'House & premises'*, which would be Riverside Farm. They each have separate hold-ings of land: David Griffiths holds 8 acres 1 rood 5 perches. John Griffiths holds 7a 3r 13p. The death of George Griffiths, a son of David Griffiths, in 1895, brought about the division of the holding, with David Richards becoming tenant of *'Land late George Griffiths'* at a rent of £7 3s 4d and Edward Beynon becoming the tenant of *'House &*

Land' at a rent of £8 5s 4d. Riverside Farm/Riverside Cottage was later occupied by a son of Edward Beynon, Stanley Beynon, whose daughter Belinda inherited the property.

Riverside Farm is an early dated house of 1749, situated at the bottom of what is now called School Lane. It would undergo significant modifications in recent years but would have included features not fully revealed elsewhere in the settlement of Rhossili. The use of a joint-beam ceiling, consisting of parallel beams (that is, a single ceiling not double) which carry the floor boards without the use of joists is a common Glamorgan feature and was particularly popular in the eighteenth century. It had a central stair passage as did Rhossili Farm, Pilton Green Farm, High Priest and Paviland. The placing of the main stairway, usually a dog-leg, in the middle of the house was regarded as the breakthrough which revolutionised the whole design of the house. It also had a bed-outshut feature which is described as being characteristic of Gower, where it occurs as early as the sixteenth century. This is also noted at Paviland and Pilton Green Farm, as well as being a feature of Great Pitton Farm today.

The early entries in the Rhossili Parish Registers confirm members of the Guy and Richards families were to be found in Rhossili in the seventeenth century. Three documents at the National Library of Wales, Aberystwyth, confirm the start of the link between the Guy family and 'Chimley-Moore' nearly three centuries ago. A chattel Lease by John Thomas of Merlais, co. Glamorgan, to Richard Guy of Rossilly, refers to the lease of a messuage and lands called Pilton, Parish of Penrice, for 21 years, at a yearly rent of £23, with royalties reserved and specified services. This is dated 10 October 1712. Two years later, the counterpart of chattel Lease by Edward, Lord Mansel, Baron of Margam, to Richard Guy of Penrice, of lands called Chimley-Moore, also gives power to build a house thereon, in the Parish of Penrice, manor of Pilton *alias* Pitton. It is for three lives at a yearly rent of 40 shillings and is dated 25 December 1714. Richard Guy is shown as the tenant of Chimney Moor in 1751 at a rent of £2 2s, but by 1768 an entry in an 'Old Life Book' of the Penrice and Margam estate shows Chimney Moor in the tenancy of William Guy with himself only 61, suggesting that others of the lives in a lease had died. The counterpart of a lease in reversion by Thomas Mansel Talbot (by Revd William Davenport LLD, Rector of Bredon, co. Worcester, his attorney) to *'John Richard of Rossilly, of a messuage and lands called Chimley Moors in Penrice parish, and Manor of Pilton or Pitton, for two lives after decease of William Guy in November 1771'* shows the eventual intention for the homestead to pass to another family. The marriage of George Richards to Catherine Guy on 27 December 1771 confirms the union of the families, with the land formerly tenanted by the Guy family now being placed in the name of John Richard. Among the monumental inscriptions in the church-yard of the Parish Church of St. Cattwg in Porteynon is one *'Sacred to The Memory of William Guy of this parish who died July the 16th 1813 aged 63 years Elizabeth his wife died Sept.12th 1834 aged 81 years.'*

We can judge the size of the holding by reference to a Map of Pilton Hamlet in the Parish of Penrice in 1783 which was completed by John Williams. It shows Greyland

Green and Kimley Moor with all the fields on the left of the road as far as Pilton Green. The total acreage of 27 acres 3 roods 10 perches is almost exactly the figure shown in the Tithe Map and Apportionment Schedule in November 1844, which shows 18 perches instead of 10. By this time, Thomas Richards was the tenant. He had married Jane Edwards of Pilton in 1841 – on the marriage certificate he is shown as the son of George Richards. This George Richards was a son of George Richards and Catherine Guy, and had married Eleanor Thomas in 1796. Thomas Richards was baptised in October 1814, so by the time of the census of 1841 which gives names and ages he is shown at Pylewell at the age of 25 with the possible occupation of Chandler. His father, George Richard, 70, with his wife, Eleanor, 70 are the tenants of Chimney Moor. By 1851, as we have noted from the Tithe Map and Apportionment Schedule, he would have been the occupier of Kimley Moor as a farmer of 27 acres. In an intriguing series of entries in the later census material we find Thomas Richard still farming Kimley Moor in 1861, with the help of a ploughman named George Richard and a house servant, Thomas Richard, 9, who is shown as being born in Tredegar. He was the son of William Richard, 30, farming at Pilton Green, who also had a daughter who was born in Tredegar – Mary, aged 4. The marriage of William Richard and Ann Richard (Thomas) may be one shown as taking place at Trelleck in Monmouthshire in 1850. The speculation centres on what William Richard was doing in Monmouthshire at this time: it seems he was a fireman working in a colliery before he returned to Rhossili where his family is shown as one of two families at Kimley Moor: Thomas Richards and Jane Richards are shown – he is a retired farmer. The other family is William Richards, Ann Richards, and three of their younger children. By this time he is farming 30 acres. The family farming continues with the name of Joseph Richards, who lived to the age of 93; his son, Joseph Norman Richards carried on the farm until his death in 1977. The daughter of Norman Richards and Mary Ann Morris who had married at St Mary's Church, Swansea on 25 February 1931, later married Terence Beynon, with John and Christopher Beynon being the two sons of the marriage.

The manor of Pilton *alias* Pitton was distinct from the manor of Landimore and Rhossili as it was held by the Mansel family. Another landowner here in the same area was a member of the Popkin family. Here we can look at two families occupying different tenancies: the Beynon family – in a tenancy referred to in a will as being Lower Pitton – were to be found initially at West Pilton. The Thomas family holding was from the Mansel Estate. The two tenancies were eventually combined in what today is known as Great Pitton Farm. John Beynon Sr, in a will proved in 1717, is described as Yeoman; his children were all minors at the time of his death. Caleb Thomas, gentleman, was designated as tutor, which suggests close links between the two families which were cemented further when John Beynon, eldest son of John Beynon Sr, married Anne Thomas. David Thomas, youngest son of Caleb Thomas, is shown as the tenant at Pitton until the time of his death in 1796, at the age of 80, but in fact he was only the technical tenant. Land Tax Assessments show the tenancy of John

Beynon and, after his death, Anne Beynon his widow is shown in 1789 as the tenant. David Thomas had secured a Lease while he was alive but named as two of the three lives in 1776 his two grand-children John Beynon and David Beynon. When he died in 1796 the phrase 'in reversion' meant that the tenancy reverted to any of the lives named earlier – in this case John Beynon, his grandchild, now 31. He in turn named in the lives for the tenancy in 1796 his son George Beynon, who had been born in 1792. The two tenancies were held separately: the Popkin family eventually disposed of property in Pitton in 1820.

The central farm at Pitton is shown in the list of landowners in the Land Tax Assessments as being in the ownership of George Venables Vernon. The last Baron Mansel of Margam, Bussy Mansel, who died in 1750, left as his heir his daughter Louisa Barbara Mansel. She married George Venables Vernon in 1757, who became the second Lord Vernon on the death of his father. He is shown as the landowner of Pitton Farm in the Land Tax Assessments in the right of his wife, even after her death in 1776. She bequeathed the Briton Ferry Estate which she had inherited from her father, subject to the life of her husband, to the fourth Earl of Jersey. This was how the Earls of Jersey assumed control of the Briton Ferry Estate of which Pitton Farm was part. When the second George Venables Vernon died in 1813, the third Lord Vernon was a step-brother – a son of his father's third marriage. In the next six or seven years, faced with the necessity to redeem a mortgage, a massive sale of the Briton Ferry Estate took place. The sales catalogue must weigh around half a hundredweight. The document describing Pitton Farm indicates it was to be auctioned in 1818, unless previously sold. It covers two pages, giving a sketch map of the layout of the fields around the farm, naming them all and confirming that the tenant (and original lessee) was David Thomas. The leases of the farm were claimed on the lives of John Benyon [Beynon] aged about 52, David Benyon aged about 46 and in reversion John Benyon aged about 25. The latter two names appear to be John's brother and son.

The property was acquired by Lord Crawshay, but the Tithe Map and Apportionment Schedule for Rhossili in the 1840s shows the landlords to be Sir Josiah Guest and William Meyrick. In the Return of Owners of Land of 1873, Sir Ivor Guest and Mrs Meyrick hold 181 acres at Rhossilly, which is the acreage of Pitton Farm. Great Pitton Farm has been noted as having a traditional Gower feature in the form of an outshut seen in an illustration of the feature. It features in the category of houses with a Hall and Outer and Inner Rooms: it would have been described as a three-unit, chimney-backing-on-the-entry house with hall between the outer and twin inner rooms. The mention of its thatched roof and a lateral entry stone stairs built within an outshut is accompanied by a note of a five-bay barn. The present building is noted as displaying the typical Gower features of a fireside bench and bed-outshut although now heavily modernised.

Pilton Green Farm facing out on to Pilton Green Common has a special niche in the catalogue of Rhossili buildings. It is apparently of late eighteenth century build and provides an example of the bed recess, but is best described in the category of what might be termed a longhouse, although the cross passage was a separate entity between the house and the cow-house. It has a distinctive attribution as being in the Hearth-passage Group (B): Long-houses with hall, cowhouse and heated inner. It had a six-bay barn.

The Counterpart of a Chattel Lease by Jane Talbot and John Ivory Talbot, trustees, to John Phillip of Rossilly dated 9 January 1764, is of a ruinous messuage and garden, with liberty of enclosing part of the Sound and crabbing-ground near Worm's Head in the parish of Rossilly manor of Landymore, for 99 years determinable on three lives. The amount of £5 5s was to be paid, and a yearly rent of 4 shillings. The modest rent of four shillings for the ruinous messuage and garden suggests that the new tenant was taking over a semi-derelict property with power to enclose part of the cliff land. It would not have been physically possible to enclose part of the rocks which make up the crabbing-ground of Crabart near Worm's Head! A fuller examination of the document confirms what had happened: the Indenture was between Jane Talbot, widow, of Margam, and John Ivory Talbot of Margam, who were acting Trustees of the Last will and testament of the Reverend Thomas Talbot late of Margam . . . Clerk Deceased . . . and John Phillip of the Parish of Rossilly. The sum of £5 5s is the consideration money, but there is also *'Consideration of the Expence Costs and Charges which he is to be at in Repairing the Cottage or Dwelling House herein after mentioned.'* This, then is a typical example of the practice described by Bernard Morris, where the incoming tenant is given favourable terms for his lease, in return for undertaking to repair the ruinous messuage. This ruinous messuage or dwelling house had been previously occupied by the now deceased John Thomas, labourer, who had also had the garden there; the new tenant was given *Liberty of Inclosing part of the Waste or Common Clift Called the Sound with the Crabbing Ground near Worms-Head thereunto belonging.* The three lives were those of John Phillip, Elizabeth Phillip and Anne Phillip – the last two being referred to as the daughters of John Phillip. The yearly rent of Four shillings, *'Together with One Pair of Fatt Pullets on every the first day of January yearly or the Sum of One Shilling at the Election and Choice of the said Jane Talbot and John Talbot'* was also mentioned, together with the sum of *'Five shillings in lieu of an Heriot and Five shillings upon every Assignment, Forefeiture, etc.'* A similar document is a lease for three lives by Thomas Mansel Talbot of Margam to Thomas Clark of Rossilly, dated 22 May 1792: this time, though, the lease is of a newly erected cottage and garden at Sheep's Green near Rossilly Down in the parish of Rossilly. This property would have been the building on one side of Sheep Green, at the top of what is now called School Lane. The consideration money of 5 shillings, and a yearly rent of 5 shillings, suggests that the newly-erected cottage could have been built by the incoming tenant, as these appear to be favourable terms similar to those granted nearly thirty years earlier to John Phillip. Rowland Rees in 1794 leased a house and field and Harpits near Rossilly Cliff; this latter name as Harepits became a house name later.

The properties mentioned here – such as Thomas Clark's newly-erected cottage in 1792 in Middleton at Sheep Green – were contemporaneous with one of the eighteenth century dated buildings in School Lane. This was High Priest, which was built in 1797 according to its dated inscription, and had a central stair passage as already described. When John Beynon occupied it in the last century, the reference to him as Johnny Beynon, High Priest may have led people to think he was a preacher of some kind, or that Rhossili had acquired a temple among its rural dwellings! Ship Farm is a dated building where there is a discrepancy between the date given in the Glamorgan Inventory, 1763, and the date of 1749 noted on one of the two stone plaques above the modern porch. This cannot be clearly explained; the other date of 1893 represents a phase of additional building. It was called a single-unit direct entry house such as that at Pynnon-newydd, Wick, dating from around 1700 and represents a restored concept of a type of dwelling like those found in Gower. The direct-entry house with a chimney on the end gable might also feature adjoining farm buildings – some direct-entry houses were free standing, others were in the same range as their farm buildings, which in some cases could have been built at the same time as the house. The end-chimney direct-entry house has a wide distribution nationally, its numbers inflated by the popularity of this form of plan for the cottages of the poor. The two in Rhossili which appear as direct-entry houses with chimneys in the end gable are Ship Farm and Talgarth, the latter also having a bed cupboard. The chimney at Ship Farm is on the side where the house joins on to the farm buildings – this is the original house, the second stepped part, with a second chimney on the end gable, being a later extension. The cupboard-bed mentioned for Talgarth would have been in a wide, internal recess similar to the bed-outshut – it was sited at the side of the fireplace but did not require an outshut. Ship Farm and Talgarth, with Pilton Green Farm, would have featured a thatched roof, which was once a common sight in the Vale of Glamorgan and Gower; now the hazard of fire has led to their replacement, as happened at Talgarth. A further factor which led estates, and other owners, to replace the thatched roof would have been the lack of suitable long wheat straw, the traditional Glamorgan thatching material. Bundles of helm, reeds, rushes, ferns and broom might also serve, besides the traditional straw. The use of the building as the Ship Inn would have altered its original character to some degree, even before the building phase marked by the stone plaque dated 1893. It is the setting used for smuggling stories involving members of the Stote family; when it ceased to be used as an inn in the present century it became the base for the farming family of Beynons. One branch of the family moved down from Sheep Green to take over the use of the farmhouse, with its associated farm buildings.

The mill at Pitton was one of the last to be built in Gower according to Horatio Tucker in *Gower Gleanings*. It was never a custom mill, but provided most of the barley and oat meal for the villagers of Rhossili. The mill used as its source of energy the small stream that flowed from Rhossili Down; the springs from this source were harnessed at Pitton during the Second World War to provide the first mains water supply for

Rhossili. The earliest reference to the families who looked after the mill mentions Philip Tailour, a witness at the Survey of Penrice in 1632, who is mentioned as having a lease for a grist mill, dated 1631. The sequence of entries in the Penrice and Margam Manuscripts which relate to the mills of Gower include one in a tabulated Rent-Roll or Survey of the Manor of Pitton *alias* Pilton by John Button in 1710, giving dates of leases and names of tenements and tenants as well as rents and fines; John Button is shown as the Bayliffe. The date of a lease given as January 1669 is some forty years after the earlier lease to Philip Tailour, and refers to Marie Hugh; A water grist mill called Pitton mill with the *'Suite & Customs'* is leased to *'the said Mary'* only.

By the early eighteenth century (1720), the contribution of Pitton Mill to the Rhossili Parish Church is defined – together with dues from other sources – in a glebe terrier.

> *There is due at Easter yearly for offerings, from every Man and Wife, Three Pence, from every Widower or Widow, a Penny and a half penny, and from every person never Married, and past ye age of sixteen years, a halfpenny. There is also due that time yearly from ye Parish jointly, Three shillings and four pence for looking to the Parish Register Book. And from the Mill, commonly called Pitton Mill, Three Shillings and Four Pence, and also from every Tradesman Fourpence.*

The repair of Pitton Mill, through the provision of timber, is mentioned in the document of June 1725 which refers to Pilton mill, the two names invariably appear as Pitton *alias* Pilton when the manor of Pitton is described in manorial court rolls. The counterpart of a chattel lease to John Evan dated 9 July 1759 deals with the water corn-grist mill called Pilton Mill, a house called Pant, and lands in the Manor of Pilton *alias* Pitton; it is for three lives at a yearly rent of £1 1s 0d. On the same date – 9 July 1759 – there is a similar lease to George Evan of a water corn-grist mill called Middle Mill and lands for 99 years determinable on three lives, at a yearly rent of £6 19s 0d.

Amongst the Land Tax Assessments of the later eighteenth century, an *Assessment of the Parrish of Rossilly made the 4th Day of June 1781*, has John Evan as the tenant of the Mill with an assessment of six shillings. Mary Evan, his widow, shows the same amount of six shillings in the Land Tax Assessment of June 1789. Rent rolls show John Ace, 1796, William Evan in the early nineteenth century, and William Taylor in the later nineteenth century, having responsibility for the Pitton Mill. The Taylor family worked it to its close in the late nineteenth century – in the last decade William Taylor left the milling to his wife while he took up teaching in Rhossili village school. It is suggested that William Taylor was appointed master at Rhossili School on 1 April 1878 and was replaced by Miss M. Johnson from 9 January 1882, although she did not open the school until the 23rd January 1882 and began the school log book on that day. A William Taylor is shown as a widower of 71 years of age in the Census Enumerators' Returns for Rhossili in 1891, where he is described as a Retired Miller. It seems from this evidence that his career as a teacher ended in 1882 and, as there is no mention of another Miller in the Census Enumerator's Return for Rhossili of 1891, it seems likely that it ceased operation in 1890.

Bryan Taylor in 'The Water Mills of Gower: an historical perspective', *Gower XLII* (1991), describes the Pitton Mill site as an overgrown ruin, but the remains of the mill-pond some twenty feet above the mill (probably feeding an overshot wheel) can be identified, also a worn millstone. The mill house in the lane above – Higher Pitton – is now part of a larger dwelling; the new extensions behind the original structure do not hide the character of the original building, although they tend to dominate it.

Rhossili's heritage in the form of farmhouses, cottages and farm buildings is not easily identified in the modern village: in 1801 it would have comprised 36 houses and 158 people but the renovation and alteration of older properties, together with the infill of modern properties on what were once farm fields has disguised the appearance of the old village. To recapture the flavour of the older settlement requires the mental removal of many of the properties seen today. Looking out from the churchyard you would need to remove the old coastguard houses which came in the later nineteenth century, also the new coastguard houses and the new Rectory which was built in the 1920s at a cost of £2,000. The Worm's Head Hotel was the site of Worm's Head Cottage, so that from the churchyard there was an unimpeded view to Worm's Head.

Nineteenth Century Rhossili

When Nicholas Carlisle published *A Topographical Dictionary of the Dominion of Wales* in 1811, he respectfully dedicated it to the Reverend Thomas Beynon: from it we gain a glimpse of the parish of Rhossili at the beginning of the nineteenth century. RHOS-SILI, as Carlisle called it, had at this time 36 houses, with a population in 1801 of 158 people. This would compare with a theoretical figure for Rhossili of 143 which was described in Stuart days: at that time it was calculated on the basis of 38 names and the number of hearths per household. The 38 names compares with the 36 houses of 1801: the final total of 158 persons in 1801 allows for a slow period of growth in the eighteenth century. The money raised by the Parish Rates in 1803 was £31 16s 4d, at 2s 11d in the pound. Carlisle goes on to tell us: *'It is situate upon a Bay, to which it gives name, on the Bristol Channel; and where there are great Eddies and Counter-tides, so as to render it dangerous to anchor there, except in good weather.'*

The limestone trade had to be carried out in the summer months, as the ships anchored at Kitchen Corner up against the floating quarries faced the prospect of destruction if gale force winds and heavy seas sprang up: the wide expanse of water from the Outer Head to Burry Holms gave no protection from the north-west or west. The Diocesan Report of 1809 gave the yearly value of the Benefice arising from Tythes, Glebe Land and Surplice Fees as £102 15s 0d, a useful figure to compare with that given in the Tithe Survey and Award in 1845. Carlisle concludes by giving one of the many explanations of the origin of the name of the village: *'In the division of Glamorgan by the Norman adventurers this Lordship was given to Reginald Sili.'*

At the time of Samuel Lewis' *Topographical Dictionary of Wales* published in 1833, the parish of Rhossili had 61 inhabited houses, and its population had grown to 302 people, nearly double the earlier population figure. Worm's Head had grown, too! It was now seen as *'stretching two miles into the sea.'* We are told that *'the sands, which extend for three miles to the north west of the church, are firm and smooth, affording a pleasant marine walk.'* The account goes on to explain the growth of the village from 158 people in 1801 to 302 in 1831: *'Several of the inhabitants are employed in quarrying limestone of which great quantities are shipped from the bay to different parts of the principality.'* This is an echo of the official explanation given in the Abstract of Answers and Returns in the Census of 1831: *'In the Parishes of Pen-nard, Penrice, Port-eynon and Ros-cily, the Labourers not Agricultural are employed in the Summer season in Limestone Quarries, and in the Winter season in the Oyster Fishery.'* It was a welcome diversification – the villagers who engaged in the trade were able to gain good wages, although the work was hard. There are visible relics of the industry to be seen at Kitchen Corner near the small building called Coonans; by walking along the base of the cliffs on Rhossili Bay at very low tide you reach the flat ledges which mark the loading places. Here there is a sequence of rusting bolt-holes in the rocks, marking the anchorage points where the ships tied up.

Horatio Tucker, in *Gower Gleanings*, and Robert Lucas in *Rhossili: A Village Background* both described the work which went on at the main quarries under the cliffs between Kitchen Corner and Hawkin Hole. The back-breaking work involved both men and women who laboured on the series of shelves, known as *flot quars* or *vlotquars* (floating quarries), which served as working platforms. The stone was quarried at a higher level in the cliffs, then moved down by *shifters* who stacked it at the edge of the platforms; a very hard, dangerous and dirty job which was usually done by women, often relatives of the quarrymen. The men quarried the stone and loaded it on the ships – the sequence of high tides meant that there was enough stone ready for two or three ships, when there was opportunity for them to safely anchor at the flat ledges. *Heavers* were paid two shillings a tide – the equivalent of a day's work on a farm. The trade had quite a long life – the Penrice and Margam Manuscripts include a record of the payment of 4s 4d (4d each), to the thirteen people who helped unload a ship laden with limestone which was driven ashore in 1672. The last export of limestone in the 1890s brought this valuable adjunct to the agricultural economy of the village to an end.

The census material – available in the form of Census Enumerators' Returns from 1841 – can be used to illustrate the role played by the *Labourer Lime Stone Quarry* or *Labourer Lime Stone Quay*. This is how the occupation was described from the census of 1851: the earlier returns for 1841 did not require such a precise statement of occupation to be made. There were no Limestone Quarrymen shown in 1841 according to the returns – they were given a designation, one assumes, of Agricultural Labourers. There is a Lead Miner shown, James Richard, aged 30, and only one *foreigner* who was Robert Perry, Clockmaker, shown as being born in Scotland. The next two returns of 1851 and 1861 are more illuminating: William Richards and Ahijah Tucker, together with Henery Howell from Cheriton are workers on the Quay. Silvanus Williams, Thomas Richards and George Bowen from *Furland Top* worked in the Limestone Quarry. By 1861, William Bevan, Samuel Richards, William Thomas, Richard Bevan and George Richards appear to be new – under their occupation is shown 'Quarries of Limestone'. Matilda Richards is shown as Quarryman's Wife. Caleb Richards, a labourer in 1851, now became a 'Worker in the Lime Stone Quarries', and his wife, Catherine also worked there. She collapsed and died on the *flotquars* on January 7th 1865, aged 50; her gravestone in Rhossili churchyard has added to it the name of her husband Caleb Richards *'who was killed by a fall in a Limestone Quarry at Rhosilly April 30th 1881'* aged 72 years. It was a hard life.

The techniques required to blast the limestone cliffs and dislodge the raw material were obviously known but nevertheless hazardous – it may have been inexperience in the use of explosives which led to an early fatality at Rhossili in 1826. A report in *The Cambrian* on the inquests conducted by Charles Collins, Coroner, included one on a young Rhossili man:

On Monday se'night at the parish of Rhoscilly, on view of the body of Thomas Bevan. The deceased was employed in the limestone quarries near the Wormshead, and in firing the rock, it exploded before he could get out of the way, and a large portion of the rock rolled against him, and forced him over the cliff into the sea below. The body was taken up in about an hour, much bruised. The deceased was a young man about 32 years of age and left a widow and four small children.

The verdict was accidental death.

The population figures for Rhossili in the nineteenth century are based on a prescribed village or parish area set out in the return of 1851 in terms of the boundaries established for Poor Law purposes under the *Swansea Union Gower.* The returns refer to *'The whole of the Parish of Rhossilly including Hillsend the Rectory Rhoscilly Middleton Pitton Pitton Cross, and Pilton, Farms, Rhossilly Down, Wormshead, Sluxton and Fernhill and the Villages of Pitton, Middleton and Rhossilly.'* But, it has to be noted, Paviland and part of Pilton were attached to Penmaen and Penrice parishes respectively until 1880. These two detached hamlets have separate returns within the census although they are part of the community of Rhossili today. The inclusion of the figures for these two hamlets with those of Rhossili, Middleton, Pitton and the other areas of the village gave an artificial boost to the population. Apart from this distorted figure the peak of Rhossili's population came in 1851 when 367 people lived in 65 houses; it was at this time, too, that the percentage of the population engaged in agriculture was at its peak. There was confirmation, too, in a footnote that *The increase of population in Rhoscilly is attributed to the extension of the limestone trade.* If we take the figures for Rhossili in the Census Return of 1841 of 339 persons and add in the figures for Paviland (41) and Pilton (31) we can artificially increase the size of the village community as it is today to 411! This is an impressive, if artificial, figure for the village community of Rhossili at a time when there were no major roads and this rural village was isolated at the end of the Gower peninsula.

The Census Enumerators' Returns 1841-1901 give detailed impressions of the range of size of landholdings in Rhossili. George Williams, joiner, occupied 3 acres and seems typical of craftsmen who carried on a trade while pursuing subsistence farming, or at least a form of it. He might have used his limited acres to grow food for his family's use, with a small number of livestock on the common grazing. Francis Jones, who was mentioned earlier, was a farmer of 12 acres and labourer; George Thomas was a farmer with 2 acres, and a tailor. David Bevan was farming 26 acres but is neverthless shown as grocer. Two brothers – Edward and William Beynon – shared the family holding originally leased by their father Owen Beynon. William Beynon, a farmer and labourer, had 7 acres; Edward Beynon, blacksmith and farmer had 8 acres. A few more examples will suffice: David Williams of Pitton was a joiner occupying 2 acres, his wife is shown as a 'School Mistress', so not suprisingly their 17-year-old son David is shown as *Schoolar*. This description, and spelling, recurs in the Census Enumerator's Return for Rhossili for 1851 and we quickly learn that it was applied indiscriminately – the word S*choolar* being often used for children not yet at work, some of who might be as young as two years old! The large farmers employed one or two labourers but the general pattern, as for Wales as a whole in the nineteenth century, was reliance on family labour. Spare members of the family could become domestic or farm servants with neighbouring families, and this arrangement crops up frequently in the returns for Rhossili. George Beynon, a farmer of 300 acres at Pitton, employed two outdoor labourers; Jane Beynon, widow, of Sluxton, who owned her own farm of nearly 27 acres in 1845 which was farmed by her family, employed one labourer to help with the 77 acres she farmed in 1851.

A random glance at the remaining occupations shown in the 1851 returns gives a convincing picture of an isolated Gower village attaining some measure of self-sufficiency in providing the services it required. Margaret Bevan, aged 79, was a cooper's widow; David Williams, 85, was a carpenter, his wife Sarah was 84. In contrast to these older citizens, Robert Button in Pitton was shown as a Boot and Shoe Maker at the age of 17! Samuel Phillips in Pitton and William Powell in Pitton were blacksmiths, as was David Thomas of Middleton – a good indication of the large numbers of horses to be shod in the days before mechanisation. Dressmakers such as Mary Richards in Pitton, who was already a widow aged 25, perhaps supported her three young children of 6, 4 and 2 years old in this way. William Taylor was the miller, the only mill in the parish being Pitton Mill; other mills such as Lower and Middle Mill in Burry Green were some miles distant.

Towards the end of the nineteenth century an evocative survey of Rhossili appears. When Robert Lucas wrote an invaluable article called 'A Few Little Plans . . . Some Sidelights on Rhossili in the 1880s and 90s' in *Gower XLIV* (1993), he based it on a booklet containing five hand-drawn plans of Rhossili, Middleton, Lower Pitton, Upper Pitton and Halfpenny Street. The booklet was completed by Tottenham Lucas and presented to his brother Loftus Lucas, '*to remind him on his voyages of our old home.*' Loftus was embarking on the clipper ship *Middlesex* on her maiden voyage to Sydney in February 1885; he was an apprentice cadet. The booklet has survived to the present day and enabled Robert Lucas to repopulate the community of Rhossili, showing many of the characters who lived there through photographs taken by Tottenham using an early Kodak hand camera in the 1890s. This fascinating snapshot cannot be emulated but a similar survey can be attempted for 1901, sixteen years later. The death of Queen Victoria in this year, after sixty-four years as monarch, marked the end of an era in every sense. As with many rural areas it is tempting to see the Edwardian era, just before the First World War, as witnessing the final glories of the rural community. Rising at dawn to cut the corn with their sickles and scythes, the men lead the way, the women and children follow to tie up the corn in sheaves and put them in stooks. Meals are taken in the stubble as the corn is gradually cut. This idyllic visual scene is complemented by the imagined sound of the ruddy-faced farm workers talking to each other using words and dialect which could also be found in West Country villages on the other side of the Bristol Channel.

The villagers of Rhossili, mainly tenants of the Penrice and Margam Estate, however, faced a reality of self-sufficiency and survival on their small farms and the need to earn sufficient money to pay the rent of their *Cottage and Garden* or the few acres which they tenanted. *Butcher and Farmer of 6 acres* might be one entry in the census; *Farmer and Joiner* might be another. As we have seen, it was quite usual for women as well as men to be engaged in work at the limestone quarries – usually at times when ships were to be loaded. Their part-time work would supplement the income from the husband's trade or occupation at a time when there were few full-time farmers.

A Rent Roll of the Penrice and Margam Estate for Rhossili in 1901 provides an informative focus, together with the census of 1901. The fifty-six inhabited houses in the community of Rhossili show a reduction from the sixty-one inhabited houses in 1891, the 285 inhabitants of the year had been reduced to 256 by 1901. By this time the village appears to be shrinking, with references to *ruinous* houses at locations on the fringes of the village. The five residences in *Kidmoor* or *Kidmoor Lane* which were beyond the the last house at the very top of what is today called School Lane had dwindled in number. William Beynon, Sarah Beynon, John Beynon and William Beynon (who was my grandfather on my mother's side), still lived in *Kenmoor Lane* before moving to Prospect Cottage nearby. Some sixty properties are shown in the Rent Roll of 1901 with the rent of a *Cottage and Garden* mingling with the houses, land and farm-houses of the larger farmers. In addition to the rents paid by tenants the Rent Roll shows other transactions: the setting up of a Rocket Life-Saving Company in Rhossili near the end of the nineteenth century is reflected in a payment of *1/- a year* by the Board of Trade for the *Life-Saving Apparatus House*, whereas *£2 a year* was paid with regard to the *Lookout House, Semaphore and Flagstaff.* The School Board Officer was responsible for payment of *£1 10s* for *Cottage & Garden, Middleton, late J. Chalk*, a site related to the school, with a similar payment per John Beynon, Clerk of the School Board of *£1 for School House*. The Board of Admiralty paid *£56 a year for Coastguard Houses* and Thomas Davies, one of the larger farmers at Pilton appears in connection with a payment relating to the *Wesleyan Chapel* there. The first entry on the Rent Roll for Rhossili refers to Rhossili Farm. John Thomas, who was the largest farmer in the Rhossili part of the community, died on 8 March 1901 aged 81; his 'representatives' were negotiating new terms for the lease of the properties the family tenanted, including 75 acres of land. The rent of Rhossili Farm at £68 7s 6d was the main tenancy. George Thomas would pay an increased rent which would be £45, and his brother would have his rent increased by £32, both changes to be implemented from Lady Day 1902. The other holdings mentioned included *Harepits Hay and two cottages* – Morgan Beynon would rent Harepits Hay and one cottage at £5 and George Thomas at £3 would have tenancy of the other cottage and garden.

The neighbours of Rhossili Farm included Sam Bevan who rented two properties and John Rogers who farmed Ashtree. The 19 acres shown as being farmed by a John Rogers in the John Williams' map of 1780 were still the basis of the family's holding over a century later. William Rogers' nephew John had taken over the tenancy when William died in 1894 and continued to farm it until his own death in 1917. The rent was £20 6s. Samuel Bevan was, as described by Robert Lucas, one of the most versatile members of the community: a cooper by trade, he was a farmer of twenty-six acres, also making wills, dealing with probates and acting as census enumerator in his spare time! *Bay Cottage* at £24 6s 10d would have included the payment of rent for his land, the rent of £2 for the *House Garden & Croft "Creeks"* was for a second property shown at the sharp corner at Rhossili which had the name Devon View and is now Creek House. The property is still referred to as *'Creekes'* by some village inhabitants.

The tenants at Middleton in the late nineteenth century included the Bevan, Beynon and Richards families. Thomas Bevan held 75 acres in the Tithe Survey of 1845 and the Rent Roll of 1901 reflects how he had divided it between members of his family in three farms centred on Ivy Dene, Middleton Hall and what is now called the Old Farmhouse: *Middleton Hall Lands at Pilton at £28 18s* is the entry here. William Chalk had married the daughter of George Gibbs Bevan: *House and Land Middleton at £19 4s* is shown. John Gibbs Bevan tenanted *Cottage & Garden, Garden, Land at rent of around £28.* George Richards, Junior, also in Middleton, was required to pay rent for *Cott & Garden Post Office & Shop 10s.*

The Post Office opened with the appointment of George Richards on 29 June 1885. He is described in the directories as a grocer of Middleton and the office was known originally as Middleton. This accounts for a postmark of 20.11.1886 showing MIDDLETON GLAMORGAN. The designation was changed to 'Rhossilly' in 1901. The Ship Public House and land at Middleton were tenanted by William Beynon at £25 17s 10d. Two farmers – Edward Beynon and William Beynon – had similar holdings: William Beynon had *House and Land at Sheeps Green* at £11 11s 6d. Edward Beynon had *House & Land at £8 5s 4d.* Among the large farmers in the community of Rhossili were the Beynon family at Pitton who farmed some 300 acres; Thomas Davies at Pilton was the son of William Davies who had farmed 135 acres at Pilton; his neighbours included Charles Morgan at Pylewell. The Curtis family of Paviland who farmed 425 acres were tenants of Thomas Penrice.

It is from the section of the Rent Roll headed 'Pilton' that we can draw our final sequences, starting with the Lucas family at Talgarth's Well: Phillip Lucas in 1901 at *Talgarth's Well £2 10s* was the tenant. Negotiations were proceeding further up School Lane over re-allocation of land at Kenmoor Lane: the *Cottage & Garden (in ruins) Kenmoor Lane* had been formerly leased to George Richards who had died, so the lease had expired on 18 December. William Beynon is now shown as the tenant at 5s. Mrs George Bowen, mother-in-law of William Beynon, Vernals, had also died in April 1901 so a *Cott and Garden at 10s and a Croft at 10s* are taken up per William Beynon

Vernals Representatives. William Beynon also had further tenancies of a *Cott & Garden & Croft at £3* and his own tenancy at Vernals had a rent of *£22*. Cimla Moor, in the tenancy of William Richards, was farmed by a family which acquired the use of the land in 1771 when George Richards married Catherine Guy. In 1901 it was William Richards who paid *£12 as rent* plus *part of Leaden Mears at £5*. In the middle of the Rent Roll is one intriguing entry: Postmaster G.P.O. Swansea paid *2/-* (2 years at 1/- a year) for *Shelter for Postman at Rhossilly at 1/- a year*. It is not clear where the shelter was and whether it was just a hut! The final entry offers a glimpse of the first holiday home in Rhossili a century ago: *House & Garden Middleton at £10 a year* was tenanted by Mrs F. Worsley Benison of Newbrick Chepstow!

The population of Rhossili in the twentieth century went down: the 1891 figure of 285 persons became 256 in 1901 and 246 in 1911. In later years the number of inhabited houses dropped to 57 in 1921 but the population rose to 304. It is indicative of smaller families that when Rhossili had 65 inhabited houses in 1931 it had only 267 people; in 1851, 367 people had lived in the 65 inhabited houses. The face of the community has changed: houses in Rhossili now appear in fields where there were no buildings before. Farmhouses and farm buildings have now been combined into modern homes, ruins appear on the fringes of the village where there were houses formerly as at Kenmoor Lane. Ribbon development has brought the hamlet of Middleton closer to Rhossili, although these two parts of the village have not yet been completely joined up. In completing a survey of the village a hundred years ago and comparing it with the village today one of the significant questions to be asked later is whether the character of Rhossili as a community has altered. Is it a working farming village? Were most of the present inhabitants born and brought up in the village? Are there fewer farmers actively engaged in agriculture? It is unlikely that all the answers will be Yes.

The picture of the villagers of Rhossili obtained from the census material can be complemented by profiles of the major landowners in the nineteenth century whose tenants many of them were. Three need to be mentioned: Thomas Mansel Talbot, Thomas Penrice and Christopher Rice Mansel Talbot, whose death in 1890 ended the male line of descent in this family, as the death of Bussy, Lord Mansel, Baron of Margam Park had ended the male descent in the Mansel family in the mid-eighteenth century. When Bussy, Lord Mansel died on 29th November 1751 a note in a memorandum contained in a survey of the Mansel estate in parishes in Gower confirms that he was *the last of that honourable family, whereby the name is become extinct*. By the will of Christopher, 3rd Lord Mansel, the estates in this event would pass to the Reverend Thomas Talbot, Rector of Collingbourn Ducis, Dorset, who was associated with Bussy, Lord Mansel in the granting of leases in the 1740s, such as the one to John Stote of Rossilly in 1746. The vast family estates of Penrice and Margam were inherited by the Reverend Thomas Talbot whose son, Thomas Mansel Talbot, was to bear the family names of his father and his illustrious ancestors the Mansel family. It was Thomas Mansel Talbot whose reconstruction of Penrice included a *'most elegant mansion'*, which was four storeys high and erected *'in the shadow of the romantic ruins of the old Mansel stronghold.'* One literary traveller, Henry Skrine, expressed his astonishment *'that its owner should desert the noble seat of Margam, in the midst of a populous and plentiful country, to form a fairy palace in a dreary and desolate wild, far from the usual haunts of men, and near the extremity of a bleak peninsula.'* But Thomas also had plans for Margam which included the superb structure of Margam Orangery.

The eight children of the marriage of Thomas Mansel Talbot to Lady Mary Lucy Fox-Strangeways included one son, Christopher Rice Mansel Talbot (1803-90), who was to become a greater local and national figure than his father. His life has been described under the apt title, *The Wealthiest Commoner: C.R.M. Talbot. M.P., F.R.S.*, by John Vivian Hughes, whose account conveys a vivid picture of one of the major figures of Wales in the nineteenth century.

He was born in 1803 at Penrice Castle and his life, with that of his father who died in May 1813, spanned a century and a half from the mid-eighteenth to the end of the nineteenth century. It was with these two figures – principally through their agents such as Hopkin Llewellyn – that the villagers of Gower parishes such as Rhossili were involved. When Thomas Mansel Talbot died and his widow, who was twenty-nine years his junior, later re-married, her second husband, Sir Christopher Cole, became a Member of Parliament for Glamorgan and as Christopher Rice Mansel Talbot's step-father he was regarded as a seat-warmer for his step-son. When C.R.M. Talbot became a Member of Parliament for Glamorgan he was to continue in the House of Commons for an uninterrupted period of fifty-nine years. His concern with affairs did not prevent him taking a detailed part in the management of estate affairs, as is seen in a sequence of correspondence concerned with sheep-stealing on Worm's Head.

He was the largest landowner and tithe-payer in the County of Glamorgan, owning more land than either the Marquess of Bute, the Earl of Dunraven or any other land-owner. In the Returns of Owners of Land completed in 1873, his holdings in Glamorgan alone were 34,000 acres which brought in a gross rental estimated as being over £44,000 a year. In 1847, in Rhossili, over 35 persons are listed as tenants of C.R.M. Talbot on the Schedule of Apportionment of Rent-charge. They held between them some 860 acres of land, so it is obvious that the estate management carried out by his stewards and land agents in Gower generally, and in Rhossili in particular, affected many lives. We can see C.R.M. Talbot in actions which affected people in Rhossili in two examples; in the first he appears as the Plaintiff in a case in the Proceedings of the Summer Assizes for Glamorganshire in 1834. *Lewis and others* were alleged to have been involved in trespass and had infringed his rights of *wrack de mer*. The issue of ownership of wreck in Landimore manor was raised – Rhossili was still part of this manor at this time. The rights involved *'royalty on vessels wrecked on the Rossilly Sands in the said Manor; payments for laying nets and digging lime stones there,'* the assertion being that *'when fragments of wreck . . . were thrown up, they were hauled to Penrice Castle, where they were kept, if not claimed by the owners in a year and a day.'* The Judge addressed the Jury and advised them *'that even if there had been no documents to prove Mr Talbot's rights, inference and long usage would have established.'*

The second example, taking place in 1868, was by coincidence lodged between two events which might have been expected to occupy C.R.M. Talbot's attention more fully than happenings in Rhossili. In 1867, the passing of the Second Reform Act, which extended the power to vote to many more people, could have been expected to considerably influence the composition of the House of Commons, of which C.R.M. Talbot was a member: Lord Derby called it a *'leap in the dark.'* In 1869 C.R.M. Talbot was present in his yacht *Lynx* for the opening of the Suez Canal, which was to transform world communications. In between these events we see him initiating a series of letters to his brother-in-law John Dillwyn Llewelyn relating to sheep stealing on Worm's Head:

Penrice Castle   March 21 1868

Dear Llewelyn,

As you were on the bench when the Worm's Head sheep stealing case was heard, I write a line to ask you whether I am correct in understanding that Mr Strick withdrew the prosecution in consequence of a hint from the bench?

The case appeared to hinge on whether the sheep was alive or dead or dying at the time it was taken. The implications of this argument were evident to Talbot who wrote that it appeared to divide the consideration of a felony. A dead sheep may be taken without felonious intent, but *'stealing a mangy one is not felony.'* Dillwyn Llewelyn confirmed he was on the bench: *'We thought that the taking of a diseased . . . carcase did not amount to felonious intention which was necessary to support the indictment.'* He offered to forward the depositions for Talbot to see, which Talbot did not seem to think was totally necessary, arguing that prisoners could by this precedent be let off *'the stealing of clothes on account of the raggedness & unhealthyness of the article.'* He continued by pointing out that the skin of the sheep was *'worth say 6d at least'* and the mutton would have been good if it had been killed by bleeding by a butcher. He concluded this letter: *'I do not believe one word about it being dead. I have lost nearly 30 sheep from Wormshead in 4 years.'*

The third letter is written in ironic fashion and reads:

Penrice Castle   March 31 1868

Of course, when the magistrates, and their clerk, and the solicitor for the prosecution, are all agreed that the state of health of a sheep is a material part of the issue when it is stolen and that to steal a weak or dying or dead sheep is no crime, I suppose my ignorance of the law must be admitted who think otherwise.

As for Mr Strick, he seems to have cross-examined his own witnesses, ridiculed them, & complimented the accused on leaving the bar without a slur on their character. In fact it would appear that it is I who have done wrong in taking any notice of an act which I erroneously supposed to be an illegal one.

Yours most truly,
C.R.M. Talbot.

Very polite, but you can tell he was annoyed!

The Returns of Owners of Land in 1873 show only one other substantial landowner in Gower, Thomas Penrice of Kilvrough. With 5,411 acres, including land at Paviland and Rhossili, and a gross rental estimated at over £5,000 a year, he was a man of substance and a descendant of the Penres or Penrice family of earlier centuries. Major Thomas Penrice purchased Kilvrough Manor in 1820 and added to his Gower estates by an exchange of lands with the College of All Souls, Oxford, by an Act of Parliament which received the Royal Assent on 27 July 1838. In exchange for land and other property at Newton Bromshold and Higham Perrers in Northamptonshire, he received the Rectories or Parsonages of Pennard and Llangennith in Gower; the Glebe and Manor of Priorstown (otherwise East Town, Llangennith); *'the Advowsons of the Vicarages and Parish Churches of the said Parishes of Pennard and Llangennith.'* His nephew, also called Thomas Penrice, took over the properties at the time of the Tithe Survey and Award, and it was his daughter, later known as Lady Lyons after her marriage to Rear Admiral Algernon MacLennan Lyons, who was involved in some sales of land in Gower in the early twentieth century. These major landowners, with others such as Sir Josiah Guest and William Meyrick, feature in the Tithe Survey and Award of 1845-1847. The holdings of John Bennet Popkins had made him an important figure in the eighteenth century, but the extensive lands he held in Rhossili according to the map of John Williams in 1780 had been acquired in the early nineteenth century for the Penrice Estate of C.R.M. Talbot.

Shipwrecks at Rhossili

The author of *The False Signals of Rhossili* alleged that the wreckers of Rhossili used a young servant girl from the local inn to carry a lantern on the Worm's Head. The use of a lantern – tied to the head of a horse or donkey – would simulate the impression of a light from another ship as it bobbed along a rocky headland. This created the illusion of a safe passage but lured unwary mariners to their doom. The death of the servant girl when she defied the wreckers is followed many years later by the repentance on his death-bed of her murderer in this imaginative tale which has no substance in fact. Gower coasts were commended by J. Clark in 1843 in *A South Wales Itinerary* as being free from wrecking, *'so detestable a practice with the marauders of the neighbouring coasts'* even if they were prepared to take part in other illegal activities such as smuggling.

Intermingled with other folk-lore, however, is a reality: tragic tales of ships blown off course and ashore on Gower beaches and cliffs. The local villagers, in the darkness of the storm, often had to listen agonisingly to the cries of wrecked mariners and their families who had tied themselves to the masts or rigging in the hope that the ship would still be intact at dawn and they might be saved. Those who forsook the ship's masts or rigging to seek safety by launching a ship's boat might meet the same fate when the boat overturned. Even in these final agonies, there is the basis of a later tale: the choir practice in a Gower church is interrupted by a cry of horror from a villager who had seen in the churchyard, or peering through the window of the church, the ghostly manifestation of a sailor. His pale face was entwined in seaweed and he had seawater running out of his hair. He appeared at the very time a shipwreck was taking place on nearby Llangennith beach.

Beached on Gower sands or hurled on to the base of Gower cliffs, the wrecked ships form a graveyard along the Gower coast. The evidence of parish registers provides the cold ring of truth: nine successive entries in the Burials Register of Rhossili Church between 3 August 1844 and 26 August 1844 show *'A stranger washed ashore'* or *'A female washed on shore'*. The churchyards of Gower, such as that at Rhossili, have their 'Sailors' Corner' where drowned crew as well as passengers were laid to rest – unidentified in many instances. The inscription at Rhossili reads: *'Dedicated to those who perished at sea and reside here. Known only to God'*. The timber skeletons of sailing ships such as the *Helvetia* and the paddle-wheel of steamers such as the *City of Bristol* are to be found on Rhossili Beach; a barnacle-covered anchor is still seen on the causeway as you cross to Worm's Head. These are some of the shipwrecks of the nineteenth century which brought about the formation of lifeboat companies and the establishment of the Rhossili Rocket Life Saving Apparatus Company, which provided over a century of service from 1876.

The wreck of the *Shepton Mallet* on Pilton Cliffs at Rhossili around 1732/3 brought an investigation into the whereabouts of the wreck from the ship and also prompted another investigation as to the disposal of wreck from an earlier shipwreck in 1677. Depositions were made by John Creek, yeoman, Edward Tucker, mason, and Thomas Griffiths, yeoman, concerning their involvement in the disposal of wreck from the *Shepton Mallet*. Moses Thomas, gentleman, in evidence cleared up what had happened to the *'Head or Lyon of a Shipp'* found under Pilton Cliff over fifty years earlier. Francis Bevan, tenant at this time to Mr George Lucas of Hills in the parish of Reynoldston, carried this figurehead to the house he lived in at Pilton. It was *'Noised in the Countrey'* that Francis Bevan had acquired this item and William Richard of Pilton, *'then Bayliffe to Sir Edward Mansell of Margam'* searched the house of Francis Bevan and the item was carried away for the use of Sir Edward Mansel as Lord of the Manor of Pilton. This deposition, confirming past legal practice, showed the procedures for dealing with wreck which should have been followed in the case of the *Shepton Mallet*. When *'several things on board the said shipp and Great parte of the said Shipp as alsoe of her Taibles, Furniture and apparell came on shore'*, the *'Mast, Cables, Sayles and other things belonging to the said Shipp'* were taken and placed in the custody of John Harry. These depositions accounted for some of the ship's masts, sails and cables but, as soon as the news of the wreck spread through the coastal community of Rhossili, these *'country people'*, as they were referred to, had removed much of the cargo before the authorities had got wind of the wreck.

Tom Bennett, in *Shipwrecks around Wales*, described the *Shepton Mallet* as a square-rigged sailing ship, assumed to be about 180 tons: she was wrecked on 12 February 1731 at Pilton on her way home to Bristol. A valuable cargo from the West Indies included cotton and sugar from Barbados, packed tightly over a cargo of ivory tusks taken on board on the Ivory Coast as a form of stabilising cargo before the final leg of the voyage. When she hit the Gower cliff at Pilton, the contents of her cargo were quickly discovered and severely plundered by the local *country people*. In March 1731 this led to the posting of notices in over 20 parishes from Carmarthen in the west to Briton Ferry in the east, as George Edmunds describes in his book *The Gower Coast*:

> *This is to give notice to all persons concerned in taking away, concealing or receiving any of the elephant' teeth, cotton or other goods salved out of ye Shepton Mallett of Bristol, lately stranded near Porteinon, and if they do not bring forthwith the goods to ye Custom House, Warehouse, or Mr Caleb Thomas' at Pitton, they will be prosecuted as ye law directs.*

Some fifty one tusks were recovered, but the fate of the remainder remains a mystery to this day. As George Edmunds comments, one wonders *'what would a fisherman or farm labourer do with a 6 foot elephant's tusk?'*

In between the wreck of the *Shepton Mallet* in February 1731 and the more well-known rescue by the Rhossili Rocket Life Saving Apparatus Company of the crew from the wreck of the *Roche Castle* in January 1937 on Paviland Cliffs there are countless incidents of wreck and rescue at Rhossili. On 19 January 1796, the Collector of Customs at Swansea wrote to the Board in London reporting the loss of the brigantine *Priscilla* of Dartmouth, a few days previously. The vessel, bound from Bristol to Alderney with barrel staves, bottles, candles, soap and tar, had also been driven ashore under Pilton Cliffs like the *Shepton Mallett* and went to pieces. A part of the cargo had been recovered and was held by the customs and by Thomas Mansel Talbot as lord of the manor. The Collector of Customs finished his report: *'It is feared that the crew has perished; a cat was the only living thing on board'*. The *Sisters*, bound from St Ives to Neath, went down with all hands off the Worm's Head in November 1797; a similarly-named ship, the *Sisters*, again of St Ives, was bound for Swansea when a south-west gale drove her ashore at Rhossili on the evening of 27 November 1838. The crew got ashore, but the vessel broke up within a week. The Chester sloop, *Grace*, with a cargo of oak from Bridgwater to Liverpool, was swamped by heavy seas and forced ashore at Rhossili at the beginning of February 1839. She became a wreck on the exposed beach, and was sold by auction on 22nd February 1839. Local ships, too, came to grief: the Swansea brig, *Nancy*, foundered off Worm's Head with the loss of all hands in April 1811. The wreck of other ships on other parts of the coast of Glamorgan was reported regularly in *The Cambrian*; it reported on Saturday 25 January 1806 on the wreck of two ships – the *Thomas* and the *Harriot*:

> *Monday morning, two brigs, the* Thomas *. . . and the* Harriott *. . . both from Lisbon, bound to Bristol, laden with wine, fruit and buffalo hides, were wrecked. They were wrecked, it seems, on the Glamorganshire coast on the Nash Sands. The* Thomas *sank immediately, and the* Harriott *was expected to go to pieces every moment when our advices came away.*

The crews were saved but, the report continues:

> *The country people, much to their disgrace, and as is too frequently practised, began to commit depredations on the property, but the neighbouring volunteers having assembled soon after the accident, were of infinite use in protecting the cargoes from the ravages of these unfeeling despoilers.*

The Chester sloop, *Grace*, with a cargo of oak from Bridgwater to Liverpool, was swamped by heavy seas and forced ashore at Rhossili at the beginning of February 1839. She became a wreck on the exposed beach, and was sold by auction on 22nd February 1839. The frequent shipwrecks, such as those described, reflect the busy trade of the nineteenth century and also the fact that the steep southern coasts and western face, which includes Worm's Head, Rhossili Bay and Burry Holms, made the Gower peninsula a dangerous shore for the unwary or unlucky navigator.

The scale of shipwrecks can be judged by a report in 1815 by the Customs Collector of Swansea that in his first district – lying between Worm's Head and Pwlldu – there had been more than twenty wrecks in the past eighteen years. It was his opinion that a lifeboat was wanted at Oxwich – a suggestion which was not taken up. When the Royal National Institution for the Preservation of Life from Shipwreck was formed in 1824 there were no lifeboats on the coast of Wales. The first stations were at Laugharne and Swansea but the former station only lasted a few years. The Northumberland Report of 1851, recorded that *'on the south coast of Wales from Cardiff to Fishguard, a distance of 200 miles, there is one life boat at Swansea and that unserviceable.'* It was to be at Mumbles and Porteynon that a lifeboat service was eventually established with Rocket Life Saving Apparatus Companies at Oxwich and Rhossili complementing the efforts of the lifeboat crews.

The placing of a lightship by Trinity House on the western end of the Helwick Sand Bank on 1 October 1846 was probably due to the loss of the paddle steamer *City of Bristol* at the Llangennith end of Rhossili Bay some six years earlier. The Helwick lightvessel was to be part of the scene near Rhossili for the next one hundred and forty years, its powerful beam lighting up bedrooms in Middleton and Rhossili at night, carrying its warnings over a considerable distance.

In 1844, the pages of *The Cambrian* described scenes which were reminiscent of similar occurences in the month of August in recent years when horrendous gales and stormy seas brought the loss of ships in the Fastnet yacht race. Such a violent storm – described as a *'complete hurricane'* – was reported in the edition of 10 August 1844 under the headline *The Late Terrific Gale*:

> *On Friday night last [2 August] and Saturday, the Welsh coast was visited with a storm more appaling [sic] in its aspects and disastrous in its consequences than any which had visited this part of the country for years past. The wind, which blew nearly due south, was somewhat strong during the whole of Friday . . . until it was nearly midnight, when the wind changed to the south-west, and indeed afterwards veered to all points of the compass. It blew a complete hurricane, and though the raging of the storm was terrific on land, its consequences were infintely more disastrous at sea.*

> *So great was the fury of the storm that houses in Cambrian and Gloucester Place [Swansea] vibrated from their very foundations. Apple and other trees, which might have been observed on Friday studded with fruit, were to be seen on the following morning entirely stripped and torn up, while many were rendered useless.*

> *The storm was very limited in its extent, its effects having been almost exclusively confined to the Welsh coast, along the line of which, from Mon-*

mouthshire to Pembrokeshire, especially in Swansea Bay to the vicinity of Worm's Head and Carmarthen Bay, its results have been disastrous to the shipping, and melancholy as far as loss of life is concerned.

The *Margaret*, Philip Thomas, master, *'laden with a valuable cargo of oil cakes, cheese and other provisions'*, was driven ashore on the Broughton sands, shortly after leaving Porteynon. The crew saved themselves, *'but the vessel has gone to pieces'*. The *Mary* of Bridgwater was driven ashore near the same place: she had been bound from Chepstow to Swansea with a cargo of bricks, hay, seed, etc. and must have been blown down channel beyond Swansea during the hurricane. A passenger who was on board perished. Late on Friday night, or early the following morning, the schooner *Thetis*, during the height of the gale, sank in six fathoms of water while riding at anchor in Oxwich Bay. The crew of four took to the rigging and survived, being rescued by a *Captain Marshall with his smack.*

The total loss of the *Triton*, laden with copper, came when she was *'driven by the violence of the wind ashore near Porteynon point, in the vicinity of the Worm's Head, Gower.'* The crew, consisting of three persons, were washed overboard and met a watery grave: only the master was saved. The loss of the *Julia*, which was *'driven ashore near the Worm's head'*, brought the death of one of the crew. *'One of the most melancholy losses'* was that of the *Friends* of Ilfracombe, which was lost in Carmarthen Bay. The master, the crew, the master's wife and children were all lost – it was reported that *'some of the bodies have been found.'* The list of ships damaged runs to several column inches in *The Cambrian*.

The fate of the schooner rigged paddle steamer *City of Bristol* is graphically described in the press reports of its wreck and in the harrowing tales given in evidence at the inquests on the deaths of nearly all the passengers and crew. These inquests – reported in *The Cambrian* – appear in the days and weeks which followed her tragic loss in November 1840. She was 209 tons and was built at Bristol in 1827, 144 feet in length, 35 feet (including the paddle wheels) in breadth. All that remains today, just beyond Diles Lake, Llangennith, are parts of her twelve foot diameter paddle-wheel mechanism, still lying among the waves and visible on a fairly low tide. Under the title *'The Late Hurricane'*, *The Cambrian* described *'the high winds of Thursday, Friday and Saturday last'* which had *'occasioned the loss of much life and property among the shipping of the country. The melancholy task of recording the entire loss on our shores on Wednesday evening last of the fine steam-vessel the* City of Bristol*, Stacey commander'* is followed by details of what happened on her voyage from Waterford, as described by the only two human survivors. The vessel foundered about six o'clock in the afternoon on the sands at Llangennith, *'in consequence, it is thought, of the commander mistaking the Worm's Head for those dangerous sands, the Helwicks, from the appearance of the breakers.'* Steaming through the darkness, white water was suddenly observed on her larboard side, and with a sickening thud she grounded on the beach. Engines were reversed, but the powerful steam paddles failed to refloat her and she turned broadside on to the pounding seas. Accounts suggest that there were twenty-nine persons on board – twenty-three crew members and six passengers: only two survived, William Poole and Thomas Hamlin (also referred to as Thomas Anstice). William Poole was knocked overboard by a piece of mast which fell on him, breaking some of his ribs, but he swam and floated ashore on a piece of plank. Thomas Hamlin, the ship's carpenter, lashed himself to the wheel until the ship broke up, then jumped into the water and swam ashore. A few cattle and some pigs also got ashore – the livestock cargo originally being 15 bullocks and 280 pigs; barrels of oats and barley, together with flitches of bacon, were also in her cargo. *'The cries of the unfortunate persons were heard distinctly on shore, but it was utterly impossible to render any assistance without a life-boat, but unfortunately there is not one stationed in the district.'*

By the following morning the terrible reality was apparent – the desperate cries for help in the darkness as the seas ran high could not be answered by the villagers of Llangennith who crowded the beach in the very dark night. The Coroner's Inquest on the body of Captain Stacey, *'her lamented Commander'*, was held at *'the dwelling-house of William Tucker, called the King's Head'*, before Charles Collins, Coroner. William Taylor was the foreman of the jury of twelve villagers which heard the evidence of William Poole: he described the grounding of the vessel and confirmed that, *'the sea was running too high to use the boats'*, so they stayed by the vessel hoping *'that she would hold together until the tide left her.'* The cook, James Cromwell, was the first person washed away, and the stewardess soon after. In about an hour and a half, or two hours, after this, the vessel separated into three parts. Thomas Hamlin, the other survivor described the final moments at high water as the vessel began to break up: *'A sea also came and washed most of the persons from the quarter deck, and the following sea swept the quarter deck of everything.'* The villagers, though unable to rescue any of the crew or passengers, were commended for their assistance in every other way: *'In connexion with this lamentable occurrence, it is due to the inhabitants of the lower district of Gower to state, that their conduct, both as respect the property and two survivors, has been most praiseworthy. For several days property to a considerable amount, and some of which might easily have been taken away, lay on the beach, and yet not an article of the slightest value to the owners was removed.'*

It was in 1876 that the Board of Trade decided to establish a Life Saving Apparatus Company at Rhossili and, there being no Coastguard at this time, the task of enrolling volunteers was entrusted to Sam Bevan. The inaugural launch of the Porteynon life-boat came on 10 May 1884; the wreck which was a decisive factor in the formation of the new station was that of the *Agnes Jack* on the night of 27 January 1883. The inauguration of the Life Saving Apparatus Companies at Oxwich and Rhossili was a welcome and necessary reinforcement in the battle to save lives from wrecked ships, raising the chances of survival even if not all passengers and crew could be saved by these means. The techniques used in practice sessions by the Rhossili Rocket Life Saving Apparatus Company took place above a little cove on the east side of the Oldcastle headland. Just above the cove were the remains of a rocket post used by the Rhossili Rocket Crew, whose full complement was eighteen. A rocket was fired out towards the rocket post from a point close to the former Coastguard Station at Rhossili; this had a fine line attached to it. Three or four men followed the line out – which they could not do in a real rescue of course – and played the part of the crew of the wrecked ship, the rocket post simulating the vessel's mast. The fine line had a hawser attached to it which was hauled out to the rocket post mast and made fast. Then a breeches-buoy would be used bring one or more of the men ashore. The first test of the new Company at Rhossili came in 1879 with the wreck of the *Mary Stenhouse* on Rhossili sands. My great-uncle John Beynon described the event in *An Eye-Witness Account of Shipwrecks on the Gower Coast*:

> There had been only one practice drill when the company in 1879 attended its first wreck on Rhossili sands. Mr W.H. Betts had been sent as Coast-guard to Rhossili. He was stationed at Hoarstone.
>
> On a very dark night the Mary Stenhouse, *on tow from Liverpool to Swansea, ran ashore near the Old Rectory. Whether the towing tug slipped her cable or parted it when she found herself in the breakers was never discovered, but the vessel ran aground in very heavy seas.*
>
> With Coastguard Betts in charge, the Rhossili Life-Saving Apparatus Company were soon on the scene. The first rocket missed and after the smoke had cleared, the rocket tube was missing over the cliff, and members of the company were sent to look for it. It was recovered from the surf and brought back on shore. The second shot found its target, landing on board.
>
> Quickly, the gear was rigged up and a man brought ashore asked if any boats had been found. It was learned that when the ship struck, some of the crew launched a boat and ten men with a woman – the captain's wife – went aboard. But the boat swamped and broke up, all the occupants being drowned. The other ten members of the crew, with the carpenter's wife, had stayed aboard, all being saved.

The vessel was eventually taken off the beach with a tow line from a Llanelly tug: 'Safely taken to Swansea by the Llanelly tug, all that was left were the remains of the small boat and some bodies. The Llanelly folk claimed a substantial sum for salvage.'

The most prominent wreck remains on Rhossili Bay – outlined against the background of Worm's Head in countless photographs and paintings – are those of the *Helvetia*: a *Sailing Vessel Barque Rigged*. She was carrying a cargo of 500 tons of timber from New Brunswick to Swansea. The *Helvetia* was driven on to the southern end of Rhossili beach on 1 November 1887 – her bow section has been part of the seascape and landscape of Rhossili for over a century. *The Cambrian*, Swansea, Friday 4 November 1887, described a *serious gale* which had affected shipping, causing several shipwrecks, including that of the *Helvetia*, and consequent loss of life in some cases:

> *The Norwegian barque* Helvetia *drifted on shore near the Worm's Head on Tuesday and became a total wreck. One man (the carpenter), got ashore in a breeches buoy and the others were found to be safe when the tide served. The* Helvetia *hails from Horten [Norway], Captain Stevenson, from Campbeltown. . . . The captain reported that he was off the Mumbles on Monday night, burning flare-up lights and other signals, in hopes of getting a pilot, but, failing to do so, and a fresh breeze springing up from the S.E., he was obliged to stand down channel. The vessel was seen at about eight o'clock on Tuesday morning standing down channel, abreast of the Helwick Buoy at which time the wind was blowing a strong gale, and backing to S.W. She was labouring very heavily, and drifting to leeward, and appeared to be unmanageable. She drifted across the Helwick Shoal, where she lost part of her deck load, and then ran round the Worm's Head into Rhosilly Bay and let go her anchors, but when in close proximity to the Worm's Head struck the rocks while at anchor. The coastguard and the rocket brigade stationed at Rhosilly got their apparatus across the sound on to the Worm's Head, obtained communication with the vessel, and brought one man ashore, the rest refusing to leave their vessel, but subsequently, as the tide rose, they came ashore, together with effects, in their boats, leaving their vessel riding at anchor under the shelter of the Head, but at 5.30 p.m. she parted from her anchor and drove on the sands, where she lies a total wreck, and her cargo washing upon the beach.*

This *'fine old oak ship'*, as she was described by John Beynon, remained on the beach but her cargo was auctioned and taken away in ships which were anchored and beached near the remains. The timber was transferred to the *Cambria* and another ship but some Canadian deals washed out of her hull – no doubt to the delight of the local populace! During the operations, the anchor of the *Cambria* stuck firmly in the sand and several men were were employed to carry it across the sands at low water, leaving it attached to a buoy at Kitchen Corner. The boat sent to recover it later capsized, spilling her crew into the sea: five of the six occupants were drowned, the only survivor, a fireman, swam ashore. What remained of the *Helvetia* was bought by John Gibbs Bevan who made use of the deck timbers for flooring.

Left at her last resting place for well over a century now, the *Helvetia* is now much better known than she was in her lifetime for the sparse remains which show up prominently on the vast expanse of Rhossili beach. The ship was wrecked on 1 November 1887. Just over three years later, in the Census Enumerator's Returns for Rhossili in 1891, a marine artist is shown occupying two rooms at West Pilton. James Harris, single, was at this time 44 years old; he is referred to as an *Artist, Marine Coast, and Sculptor*. He used his talents to portray in a fine drawing the dramatic events at Rhossili which culminated in the eventual wreck of the *Helvetia*. Its dramatic evocation of the stormy conditions off the Worm's Head is realistic; its portrayal of the events is accurate, showing that coastguard Darch and the Rhossili Rocket Crew had got the Life Saving Apparatus across the causeway and set it up on the Inner Head. A line had been fired across the ship and one man brought ashore by breeches buoy.

Another notable rescue was that of the remaining crew members of the *Cresswell* which was a *Barque Rigged Sailing Ship* of 464 tons. At the time of her wreck, the ship was severely off-course, sailing over the Helwick Shoal and striking the rocks under Paviland Cliffs at 9.30 a.m. on 27 January 1881. The Captain, with his wife and three crew members, launched one of the ship's boats and rowed ashore. Six Porteynon men – at a time shortly before the setting up of the lifeboat station – launched a boat and rowed out to her, taking off four men who accepted their help. It was then reported to the Coastguard that a boat had left the ship with survivors – what had not been appreciated was that five other men still remained on board, having refused the offer of help from the Porteynon men because they could not take their chests of belongings with them. When the Coastguard investigated, he found some men still aboard and summoned the Rhossili Rocket Crew. The rocket apparatus was set up on the cliffs at Paviland about two hours after the Porteynon men had taken their four survivors ashore. The first rocket was accurately fired and the breeches buoy brought quickly into use as the ship was breaking up. Minus their sea chests, the remaining five men came ashore, the last crew man being rescued ten minutes before the *Cresswell* broke up.

Visible remains on Rhossili beach include those of the barque of 376 tons called *Vennern* of Sonderho, Denmark, but known locally as the *Vernani*. She is described in some accounts as a Norwegian iron sailing-ship. The remains of the ship are to be seen at the mouth of a little cove on the east side of Oldcastle headland – just above the cove are the remains of the rocket post, used in practice sessions by the Rhossili Rocket Crew. She had taken shelter from strong easterly winds in Rhossili Bay, along with other vessels. On October 24th 1894, while the vessels lay at anchor, the wind veered north-west and the *Vernani*, which was carrying ballast, began to drag her anchor. Distress rockets were seen coming from her and the coastguards fired a rocket from the cliff top at Old Castle Point. The rocket fell short, as the vessel was too far from the shore. As the tide was at a low ebb, the coastguards manhandled their gear down to the sands and prepared to fire a second rocket to get a line aboard. Whilst the rocket equipment was being set up, a light was seen moving from the vessel, it was lost for a while, then was seen again further from the wreck and nearer the shore. A boat was seen outlined against the heavy running seas and everyone made towards it so that, as the ship's boat beached, it was hauled to dry land. The master of the *Vernani*, holding a lantern, sat at the stern with his wife next to him. He and his crew had used an interesting technique to get his boat and crew to the shore in one piece. A stout rope was attached to the stricken vessel and paid out as the ship's boat, a whaler pointed at both ends, neared the shore, keeping the boat head on into the waves and preventing it from being capsized.

The ship remained at Old Castle Corner – her iron hull was sold for £54. The remains, embedded in the sand at the foot of the cliffs, can be distinctly seen today, a century or more after the *Vernani* sailed into the shelter of Rhossili Bay. It is a permanent reminder of the challenges faced by sailing-ships in adverse weather conditions.

The *Ben Blanche* was driven ashore on Paviland Cliffs in thick fog soon after midnight on 18 December 1933. Her cargo was 150 tons of potatoes for Fred Ley & Sons and she was ever after referred to as the *Potato Boat*. The Rhossili Rocket crew, as usual, were quickly on the scene and soon had a line aboard, but received no response. Having to wait until dawn, they eventually found that the crew had left in their own boat and had been picked up by a vessel in the Bristol Channel. So the attempt at rescue by the Rhossili team was, on this occasion, a back up to the successful efforts of the crew of the *Ben Blanche* to save themselves.

It is evident, from the sample already described, that the cliffs under Paviland and Pilton claimed more than their fair share of wrecks: the *Leonie* was one the few ships to be wrecked at Fall Bay. The storms experienced along the coastline of Gower can reach horrendous levels – during one of them in 1910 the *Leonie*, carrying a cargo of pit props, was wrecked at night. She was driven by the pounding seas against Tears Point at Fall Bay – which is sheltered from westerly gales but on this occasion, presumably, the wind was from a south or easterly direction. Described as a French schooner, the vessel had a seventy-year-old captain who was badly bruised as one of the worst seas in living memory swept the ship mercilessly onto the rocks, smashing her hull. Fortunately no lives were lost – it was a miracle that all the crew survived the dreadful weather and raging seas. By the time the Rhossili L.S.A. reached Tears Point, the *Leonie* had already broken up, and the crew were struggling ashore in a sea of pit props. My great-uncle John Beynon in *An Eye-Witness Account of Shipwrecks on the Gower Coast* later described Fall Bay as a *'moving sea of wreckage, soon reduced to matchwood'*, but it had all washed away within a few hours, from Tears Point and the Bay. For months afterwards, the surrounding nooks and crannies along the coastline were full of the *Leonie*'s pitwood cargo, every cove and corner was jammed with pit props. No trace of the wrecked vessel was ever found – in contrast to the regular pattern, where the sheltered coves and sandy beach of Rhossili reveal skeletal remains of ships which are still visible today. Some ships escaped this indignity, such as the *Mary Stenhouse* which was refloated and towed away. The *Cleveland*, a Second World War destroyer, ran aground at Diles Lake on her final voyage to the breaker's, and had to be cut up on the beach and taken away as scrap from where she lay.

It was in this spirit of not sparing themselves in their efforts to save and aid wrecked mariners that the villagers of Rhossili in the Rhossili Life Saving Apparatus Company made herculean, courageous efforts to get to the wreck of the *Roche Castle* in 1937. Their efforts brought the rescue of all the crew save one and an award from the Board of Trade which signified national recognition of this Company's outstanding achievement. Both my great-uncle, John Beynon, and my father, David Wilfred Beynon, have described the events. My father gave George Edmunds, author of *The Gower Coast*, his version of events when they met in 1977. The steam trawler, *Roche Castle*, was returning home to Swansea with a full hold of fish caught off Ireland – fog in the Bristol Channel became denser as the vessel, with her eleven man crew neared Swansea. They hit the coast only a few miles west of their home port. With an almighty crash, the vessel hit the rocks under Paviland Cliffs on the night of 10 January 1937; Mumbles Coastguard received a message from Burnham Radio Station that an S.O.S. message from the *Roche Castle* had been intercepted, and the Mumbles lifeboat was launched. It was unable to help and it was up to the Rhossili L.S.A. Company to try to get the men off. A search of the coast had located the vessel under Paviland Cliffs but the rescue company had great difficulty in getting to the scene of the wreck. Half a mile away, their lorry and trailer conveying the gear sank axle deep in mud and could not get any further. The equipment had then to be manhandled to a position about 170 yards from the wreck, a task achieved but not without great difficulty. The ship, according to Wilfred Beynon's account, had her own lights on, and a portable searchlight which was a great help on a dark and foggy night. The first rocket went right across her, the crew of the vessel hauled out the *whip* and made it fast to the mast. But the rocks which lay between the L.S.A. and the wreck made it difficult to keep the gear clear owing to the sag in the line. The district coastguard, A.J. Jeffers, who was on the scene, together with a member of the rocket crew, scrambled over the hazardous rocks to a point about midway between the vessel and the firing point; from here they were able to clear any fouls of the gear as they arose. At this time the Captain, James Insole, hoped to get his vessel off the rocks on the flood tide, so he kept the breeches buoy at the mast and waited. On the rising tide a heavy swell got up which caused the stranded vessel to rock violently and the crew, becoming alarmed, wanted to get ashore quickly with the sea breaking over their ship. Great problems were experienced in keeping proper tension on the rescue line – as the first man prepared to come ashore in the breeches buoy another crewman tried to get in and hang on. As they were being hauled in, the vessel gave a lurch which slackened the hawser and then another violent lurch, which made it very taut. This sharp jerk to the line also jerked the breeches buoy and catapulted one of the men in the air. He fell between ship and rocks, to be crushed or drowned. The other man reached the shore

– but not before being completely submerged in the boiling surf or flung in the air. Eventually he was flung out of the breeches buoy, but rescued by the District Officer, even though the surging sea washed both of them off their feet. With the help of a lifebelt the District Officer scrambled back to the rocks and safety with the half-drowned sailor. The hawser was set up as tautly as possible to avoid the same fate for the rest of the crew, who were brought off safely, but singly and speedily, as the vessel rolled and bumped on the rocks on the incoming tide. The remainder of the crew of eleven men were landed safely within 45 minutes.

The official report of the rescue concluded: *'The members of the Rhossili Life Saving Company worked magnificently under most trying conditions'*, and in appreciation of the services rendered on this occasion the owners of the vessel presented a cheque for distribution amongst those concerned. The District Officer was awarded a Silver Bowl by the Board of Trade in recognition of his leadership and courage. The rescue was highly regarded by the Board of Trade, and the Rhossili Life Saving Apparatus Company was awarded the Board's Shield for the company rendering the best service of the year. It was a great honour and the first time it had come to Wales. This shipwreck disaster is the one remembered and recalled most often by the life-saving fraternity at Rhossili, for it was this rescue that won them their laurels. The wreck also brought fame to Mr G.H. Holman, according to George Edmunds: he was a keen amateur photographer and it was his photograph of the wreck which was shown in the London daily papers and subsequently seen all over the world. Those who know Paviland Cliffs will appreciate that it was taken at some considerable risk. Chief Inspector Captain Rashley made the presentation of the Board of Trade's Shield at a public meeting at the Rhossili Parish Hall, in the presence of Lady Blythswood, D.R. Grenfell, MP for Gower, and other guests. Commander Hurst assisted in the holding of a celebration dinner and, later, replicas of the shield were presented to all members of the company. A tablet was fixed to the rocket wagon. The distinction brought to the village by its courageous rocket crew was suitably celebrated. In a photograph of the presentation ceremony Captain Rashley is seen presenting the Board of Trade shield to my great-uncle, John Beynon. The heroic achievement of a small life-saving company on the south-west coast of Gower places the stories of shipwrecks in their true perspective – the tragic tales are matched by ones of courage and humanity, enhancing a tradition of service which still lives on.

In an age of high technology and modern equipment, rescue helicopters, lifeboats and inshore lifeboats provide a swift response to maritime emergencies with support from rescue agencies such as that at Rhossili which rescue persons injured by falling down the cliffs, or search for missing persons lost on the beaches. The last rocket rescue took place some time ago, and it is some years since the last rocket was fired in anger. From 31 March 1988, the breeches-buoy, line-throwing rescue operations ceased: the end of an era came on Sunday 17 April 1988 when the assembled company, with a final photographic record, then relinquished the principal part of its historic role. It had been, for over a century, a vital contributor to coastal rescues in a remote part of rural Gower and forms a proud part of the heritage of the village of Rhossili.

The everlasting presence of the sea pervades the atmosphere of coastal villages such as Rhossili – sometimes literally, when wind-born spray sweeps even to the top of the high cliffs, or when the scent of seaweed reaches inland to Middleton from Mewslade Bay and Fall Bay. In all its moods, the sea is part of the landscape, whether it is softly sweeping in along Rhossili Bay in summer, with the sun catching the wave tops or grinding and clashing the pebbles along the shingle beach below the former Lookout Station. The vigorous crash of the waves is followed by an immense rattle as the tide withdraws – rolling and sucking up the loose shingle and pebbles. The sound evoked is reminiscent of the scenes conjured up by J. Meade Falkner in *Moonfleet*. The closing description of the novel reads:

> *We never leave this our happy Moonfleet, being well content to see the dawn tipping the long cliff-line with gold, and the night walking in dew across the meadows; to watch the spring clothe the beech boughs with green, or the figs ripen on the southern wall; while behind all is spread, as a curtain, the eternal sea, ever the same and ever changing. Yet I love to see it best when it is lashed to madness in the autumn gale, and to hear the grinding roar and churn of the pebbles like a great organ playing all the night. 'Tis then I turn in bed and thank God, more from the heart, perhaps, than any other living man, and that I am not fighting for my life on Moonfleet Beach.*

Edgar Evans: a Gower Hero

The celebration of the designation of Gower as the first Area of Outstanding Natural Beauty in Britain in 1956 was also marked by a visit on 5 July 2006 by Prince Charles and the Duchess of Cornwall. Their visit included an ancient little village church, where they viewed a memorial plaque to 1st Class Petty Officer RN Edgar Evans.

Edgar Evans had completed an epic journey of Antarctic exploration under the command of Captain Robert Falcon Scott, CVO, RN, which reached the South Pole in January 1912. He, together with Dr Edward Adrian Wilson, Lieutenant Henry R. Bowers, Captain Lawrence E.G. Oates and Captain Scott himself, perished on the return journey. The memorial plaque was placed in St. Mary's Church, Rhossili by Edgar Evans' widow, Lois Evans (*née* Beynon). It confirmed the roots of Edgar Evans, who was born in Gower and was a native of Middleton, and as such he was always claimed to be a Gower hero. On the eighty-second anniversary of his death – 17 February 1994 – a belated but entirely fitting tribute was paid to him at Swansea: a civic ceremony in honour of Petty Officer Edgar Evans was held at the Brangwyn Hall, Swansea. It was held in the presence of his daughter, Mrs Muriel Evans, with civic dignitaries and guests such as the famous explorer Robert Swan and officers and members of The Captain Scott Society, under whose auspices the occasion was held. Following the unveiling of a bust of Edgar Evans, which was commisioned from the Gower sculptor Philip Chatfield, the film of the final fateful expedition by Herbert G. Ponting was shown, *90 Degrees South*. The photograph used by Philip Chatfield to complete the bust was of Edgar Evans as a member of the five-man team, taken at the South Pole on 18 January 1912; where they had just reached their goal in the snowbound, desolate wastes of Antarctica. It was a moving occasion for villagers of Rhossili who were among the audience in recognition of a local hero – the contribution made by a native of Gower who was born in Rhossili and who took part in two expeditions with Captain Scott to the southernmost regions of the world.

Edgar Evans – in life and in death – was inextricably linked with his leader, first in the Royal Navy and then as a loyal and invaluable member of the final expedition. It was the unstinting loyalty and unswerving courage of Edgar Evans which led to his inclusion as one of the five-man team which made the last daunting dash on the final leg of their journey to the South Pole. '*In life, Petty Officer Evans realised his one ambition – to stand beside his beloved Chief at the South Pole. In death, the once mortal home of his indomitable soul lies deep in the eternal ice – his, the uttermost sepulchre on earth*' (Herbert G. Ponting).

The roots of Edgar Evans and his family lie in the villages of Oxwich and Rhossili in Gower: later his family moved to Swansea. His father was Charles Evans, son of Thomas Evans of Oxwich, his mother was Sarah Beynon, daughter of William Beynon of Middleton, Rhossili. She is shown as 22 years of age when she married Charles Evans in 1862: her father at this time was shown as a publican. The wedding at Rhossili Church, by Licence, was conducted by the Rector of Rhossili, the Reverend J. Ponsonby Lucas. Charles Evans, 23, was shown as a *Mariner* – he had, according to some accounts, rounded the Horn (Cape Horn) a number of times, and had sailed from Swansea on the Glasgow trade. He later worked at Weaver's Mill when the family moved to Swansea but does not always feature in the census returns for the earlier period, suggesting he was away on voyages until later in his life. The marriage of Charles Evans, mariner, Oxwich and Sarah Beynon, Rhossili, had produced four children according to the census of 1871, which also shows that Charles Evans was away from the family home on census day. Sarah Evans, now 30, was shown as a *Sailor's Wife* living at Furland Top (Fernhill Top). William Charles Evans, 7, scholar, had acquired the name of his father and also his mother's father. John Austin Evans, 4, Mary Ann Evans, 2, and Jane Ann Evans, 1, were the other three children. All these children are shown as having being born in the parish of Rhossili. By 1881, when the family are shown as living at Pitton, Sarah Evans, *Mariner's Wife*, has four further children who were the only ones shown as living with her at the time. Arthur, 7, Edgar, 5, George, 3, Eliza Jane Evans were the family by now – by this reckoning Edgar Evans, born on 7 March 1876, would have been one of at least eight children, not seven as shown in some sources. He was baptised at Rhossili Parish Church on 30 April 1876. So Edgar Evans was born at Middleton, Rhossili and is confirmed as living with his mother in a cottage in Higher Pitton at the time of the census in 1881.

Early the next year the family moved to Swansea, as we see from an entry in the Rhossili School Log Book: '*31 March 1882 Annie, Edgar and Arthur Evans left the school this week, gone to Swansea to live.*' The family moved to live in Hoskins Place, off Oxford Street, and Edgar Evans attended the St. Helen's Boys' School in Vincent Street from 1883 to 1889. Two years later, in 1891, the Census Enumerator's Returns show the whole family at 4 Pilton Place, Swansea with the head of the family, Charles Evans, appearing as *Mariner Seas* at the age of 52. After leaving school, Edgar Evans worked briefly in the Telegraph Department of the old Post Office in Castle Bailey Street. He joined the Royal Navy as a *Boy 2nd Class* in 1891 and as a six foot tall, strongly-built boy he eventually became a physical training instructor at HMS *Excellent*, Whale Island, Portsmouth.

He served for two years from 27 June 1899 on HMS *Majestic* the flagship of the Channel Squadron, becoming first a Leading Seaman and then a Petty Officer, Second Class. It was here that he met Robert Falcon Scott and, when Scott was chosen to lead the first Antarctic expedition, Edgar Evans was among the Royal Navy personnel who had served on the *Majestic* to be selected to serve. The *Discovery* expedition was to last three years from 1901 to 1903, although not all the forty-seven men on board remained in the Antarctic throughout the period of the expedition. The voyage reached Lyttelton, New Zealand, which was the last port of call before the Antarctic; here further stores, coal, equipment and livestock were added including forty-five sheep. From Quail Island in Lyttelton Harbour, where they had been placed in quarantine, the dogs for two dog teams were collected and the ship left New Zealand on 21 December 1901. It was too late in the year for long-distance sledging but, before the sun vanished over the horizon for the long Antarctic winter in April 1902, there was an opportunity for testing equipment and men for the task to come. Edgar Evans now had his first taste of the perils of Antarctic adventure.

The type of clothing and footwear suited to Antarctic conditions, which ranged from blizzards to dangerous ice slopes, was not fully appreciated by the party which set out under the command of Charles Royds. They did not know how to load the sledges or use the cookers. The dog teams went lame. By the fourth day the men were exhausted – Royds decided to press on with two men, sending the rest back to the ship; this party under Michael Barne pitched tents in a blizzard, but could not get the cookers to work. Frostbite affected all but two of the men – the majority of the men had ski boots on but two of the party were wearing reindeer-hide boots called *finniskoes*.

Elspeth Huxley in *Scott of the Antarctic* provides a dramatic account of the outcome:

> *Experienced men would have stayed where they were whatever the discomforts, but they were not experienced and had to learn at a price. The wrong decision was made, they left their tents and gear to make their way on foot to the ship, and soon found themselves on a steep slippery slope where to keep a foothold was almost impossible. Petty Officer Evans stepped on to a patch of bare ice, fell, and hurtled out of sight. Barne sat down and slid after him, vainly trying to check his speed with a clasp knife. Quartley followed. All three men, as by a miracle, were arrested by a patch of soft snow on the edge of a precipice at whose foot the sea pounded. A yelping dog flashed past and disappeared into a swirling storm. One of the seamen, Frank Wild, took charge of the party left at the head of the slope and led them in the direction in which he thought the ship must lie. Suddenly he saw the cliff at his feet and the dark sea far below; another step would have taken him over. His cry of warning halted all but [George] Vince, one of those wearing finniskoes which had no grip on the slippery ice. Like the dog, he vanished into the abyss.*

The search party found Barne and Evans rather badly frost bitten, but with Quartley they eventually found the ship. It was a lesson to all the party to carry forward to the sledging season.

In the principal journey Captain Scott, with Dr. Edward Wilson and Second Lieutenant Ernest Shackleton RNR, reached a point which was 300 miles nearer the South Pole than any previous expedition. Shackleton, who had contracted scurvy, had to be hauled on one of the sledges in the later stages of the journey and was invalided home on the relief ship, the *Discovery* still being trapped in the ice. The long, cold Antarctic night awaited those who remained.

Edgar Evans' adventures were not yet over, as he was one of the party included in the Western Journey where, in the later stages of the expedition, he and Captain Scott fell down a crevasse. William Lashly, the third member of the three man team, saved their lives by using his immense strength to hold the sledge while he fitted a ski beneath it and then hauled them both up. *'My word, but it was a close call'* was the summing up by Edgar Evans. They reached the ship on Christmas Eve, 1903. The two relief ships *Terra Nova* and *Morning* were able to reach the anchorage at Hut Point in February 1904 and the three-year expedition was over as *Discovery* was freed from the ice. A number of the party were singled out for special mention, including William Lashly, who was promoted to Chief Stoker, and Edgar Evans, who was promoted to Petty Officer 1st Class. Scott summarised their qualities:

> *These are both men of magnificent physique. They accompanied me on my sledge journey to the interior of Victoria Land. I would remark that I think that journey reached the limit of performance possible under the conditions, in order to point out that it could not have been accomplished had either of these men failed in the smallest degree. Their determination, courage and patience were often taxed to the utmost, yet I never knew them other than cheerful and respectful. On one occasion Lashly undoubtedly saved our lives by his presence of mind when Evans and I had fallen into a crevasse.*

After his return to Britain, Edgar Evans went to the gunnery school at HMS *Excellent* at Portsmouth to qualify as a gunnery instructor, then became a torpedo instructor at HMS *Vernon* Torpedo School at Portsmouth. He is shown in a photograph with one of his gun crews at the Royal Navy Tattoo competition for field gunnery at the White City in London: the competition was won in both 1906 and 1907 by one of his gun crews. In the meantime, he had returned to Rhossili to get married.

Edgar Evans was now 28 years of age and at Rhossili Parish Church on 13 December 1904 he married his first cousin Lois Beynon who was 25 years of age. They were married by the Rector of Rhossili, Lewis Hughes, by Licence – both Edgar Evans and his father, Charles Evans, showing their rank or profession as *Mariner*. William Beynon, publican, was Lois Beynon's father and the Ship Inn at Middleton was the venue for the wedding breakfast, two sittings being held in the picnic rooms there. *The Gower Church Magazine* for January 1905 reported the event:

> *On Dec. 13 a very interesting and pretty wedding took place in Rhossili Church. The contracting parties were Miss Lois Beynon, daughter of Mr and*

*Mrs Beynon, of the Ship Inn, Rhossili, and Mr Edgar Evans, of Swansea –
one of the popular crew of the* Discovery, *the vessel that recently returned
from the expedition to the South Pole . . . The church was full of interested
friends and outside also were the usual tokens of rejoicing, several being
actively engaged in firing large guns.*

The marriage bore three children – Norman, Ralph and a daughter, Muriel, who
became Mrs Muriel Hawkins. She was one of the family present at the civic ceremony
at the Brangwyn Hall, Swansea, on the 82nd anniversary of her father's death.

Captain Scott announced his plans on 13 September 1909 to lead another expedition to follow that of Ernest Shackleton, whose epic journey had reached a point which
put them 97 geographical miles and 113 statute miles from the South Pole. Scott said:
*'The main object of the expedition is to reach the South Pole and secure for the British
Empire the honour of that achievement.'* Petty Officer Edgar Evans and Chief Stoker
William Lashly were among the thirty-eight men chosen as the main party, with 27
officers and men to crew the ship, which was the *Terra Nova.* Petty Officer Evans, the
Expedition's equipment officer, who had joined the *Terra Nova* at Cardiff from his home
in Rhossili, took the opportunity to say goodbye to his wife Lois and their family,
together with some of his relations in the Cardiff area. On the evening of 12 October
1910, the *Terra Nova* reached Melbourne via Cape Town: Scott received a telegram
here which had been sent by Roald Amundsen from Madeira on 9 September 1910. It
read: *'Beg leave inform you proceeding Antarctica. Amundsen'.* Scott's reaction was to
announce that he was not going to change his plans in any way or compete in a race
to the Pole, which would interfere with the scientific research planned. The lavish
hospitality in New Zealand brought serious concerns and jeopardised Edgar Evans'
place on the expedition, as in an intoxicated state he fell into the water while going
aboard the *Terra Nova.* Scott told Edgar Evans to pack his gear and leave the ship –
he was discharged from the expedition. The next morning Scott, who had stayed
behind in Lyttleton to finish off some business, was waylaid by Edgar Evans who
pleaded with him for a second chance. Scott eventually relented and they travelled by
train to rejoin the *Terra Nova* at Port Chalmers. Edgar Evans now had to ensure his
contribution to the expedition equalled or exceeded that of others in Scott's team if he
was to redeem himself.

The ship left for Antarctica on 29 November 1910 with its company of sixty-five men
whose average age was twenty-six: Edgar Evans, aged 34, was among them. The
Terra Nova survived a tremendous storm with mountainous seas and battled through
a belt of pack-ice. In Antarctica, a depot-laying party with all the dogs and eight ponies
was intended to set up depots as far south as 80 degrees. Victor Campbell and five
companions were landed on King Edward VII Land and a similar party led by T. Griffith
Taylor was to carry out geological work in the mountains of Victoria Land where Scott,
Lashly and Edgar Evans had been on their Western Journey several years earlier. Griff

Taylor was appreciative of Scott's decision to attach Edgar Evans to the expedition, as his previous experience was very valuable. The depot-laying party reached a point 142 miles from Hut Point – not quite at the 80th parallel as Scott had hoped. Here, on 17 February 1911, they built a cairn and laid a ton of stores at *One Ton Depot*. On their return they were given news by Victor Campbell's party of their encounter with another ship in the Bay of Whales; this was Amundsen's team in the *Fram*. On 23 April 1911, the sun vanished beneath the horizon and would not reappear until August. The long Antarctic night was spent in preparations for the bid to reach the South Pole. Scott's journal reveals the work carried out by members of the team: *'P.O. Evans and Crean have been preparing sledges; Evans shows himself wonderfully capable, and I haven't a doubt as to the working of the sledges he has fitted up.'* The men occupied themselves repairing sleeping bags, making better ski-boots and a prototype of a snow-shoe for the ponies and trying out an improved lining for one of the tents.

The return of the sun on 23 August brought with it a programme for exercising ponies, dogs and men to get them to a peak of fitness – the journey to the South Pole with motorised sledges, ponies and dog teams would be rounded off by a team man-hauling their sledges with supplies on the final leg. Captain Scott had set 1 November 1911 as the date for departure; Amundsen made a premature start on 8 September but, with temperatures down to –69°F, the party had to return. On 15 September, Scott set out with 'Birdie' Bowers, George Simpson and Edgar Evans to the Ferrar Glacier – in ten days they covered 175 miles dragging 180lbs per man without dogs or ponies. Scott noted in his journal: *'The objects of our little journey were satisfactorily accomplished, but the greatest source of pleasure to me is to realise that I have such men as Bowers and P.O. Evans for the Southern journey. I do not think that harder men or better sledge travellers ever took the trail.'* The two motorised sledges left Cape Evans ahead of the main party but only reached Safety Camp and Corner Camp, leaving the four-man party to resort to man-hauling the supplies. The ten-man party which followed on 1 November 1911 was accompanied by two dog teams. Each of the ten men led a pony, as Scott records: *'Bones ambled off with Crean, and I led Snippets in his wake. Ten minutes after, P.O. Evans and Snatcher passed at the usual full speed.'* From Hut Point to the South Pole and back was 1,532 geographical miles, 1,766 statute miles. Every step of the way was to be undertaken on foot, with or without skis; depots were laid every seventy miles with fuel and food for a week for the returning parties.

When they reached the foot of the Beardmore Glacier (which Ernest Shackleton on his earlier expedition had named after his patron) the party began to man-haul the sledges up to the plateau, which was over 10,000 feet higher than the Great Ice Barrier. The three four-man teams were made up of the ten members of the original pony party, together with Lieutenant 'Teddy' Evans and William Lashly. Scott's team consisted of himself, Edward Wilson, Lawrence Oates and Edgar Evans – it seemed likely that this would be the team which would make the final bid to reach the South Pole. The ascent of the Beardmore Glacier – which was over 100 miles long and in places forty miles wide – required energy, brute strength and perseverance. On 13 December 1911, in nine hours, the party covered less than four miles. However, at the 85th parallel at an altitude of 6,500 feet, they were back on course compared with Shackleton's expedition. The first returning party, after helping to establish the Upper Glacier Depot, set off back to Hut Point, leaving the two remaining sledge teams with twelve weeks' supply of food and fuel to be pulled by eight men. At an altitude of 10,570 feet, which they reached after sixteen days, they had reached the highest point of their journey. The polar plateau route which brought the final party towards the South Pole found them going slightly downhill. William Lashly, on his forty-fourth birthday on 25 December 1911, fell down a fifty foot deep crevasse and had to be hauled out by his team mates – Bowers, Evans and Crean. The sledges were shortened to ten feet on 31 December 1911 – it was during this operation, carried out by Edgar Evans and Thomas Crean that Edgar Evans cut his hand rather badly, but Scott was not made aware of the accident. Camp 56 in early January 1912 was, Scott records: *'Within 150 miles of our goal. Last night I decided to reorganise, and this morning told Teddy Evans, Lashly and Crean to return. They are disappointed, but take it well. Bowers is to come into our tent and we proceed as a five-man unit tomorrow.'*

This decision has been criticised from several standpoints: *'Cooking for five takes a seriously longer time than cooking for four, perhaps half an hour on the whole day'* was noted by Scott. Re-packing of food units was necessary as five men were embarking on the last lap and only three now returning. Five men would have to sleep in a tent designed for four. The extra man would be an asset – particularly someone as tough and hardy as Bowers.

The returning party of 'Teddy' Evans, Lashly and Crean ran into serious difficulties on the return journey of 800 miles to Hut Point for, after three weeks, Evans developed symptoms of scurvy. His companions dragged their leader on a sledge in a semi-conscious state to within thirty-five miles of their goal. Thomas Crean left Lashly to nurse Evans and set off without skis, sleeping bag or tent to reach Hut Point, where he arrived in eighteen hours. A dog team set out to successfully rescue the sick man. Crean and Lashly were later awarded the Albert Medal.

The Polar party faced the prospect of reaching the South Pole after eleven or twelve days. On 6 January 1912, they crossed the line of latitude where Shackleton's expedition had turned back. On Monday 8 January, a blizzard interrupted their march and it was at this time, on the verge of reaching the South Pole, that Scott made a lengthy entry in his journal setting down his appreciation of the all the good work done by Petty Officer Edgar Evans:

A giant worker with a really remarkable headpiece. It is only now I realise how much has been due to him. Our ski shoes and crampons have been absolutely indispensable, and if the original ideas were not his, the details of manufacture and design and the good workmanship are his alone. He is responsible for every sledge, every sledge fitting, tents, sleeping bags, harness, and when one cannot record a single expression of dissatisfaction with any of these items, it shows what an invaluable assistant he has been. Now, besides superintending the putting up of the tent, he thinks out and arranges the packing of the sledge; It is extraordinary how neatly and handily everything is stowed, and how much study has been given to preserving the suppleness and good running qualities of the machine. On the barrier before the ponies were killed, he was ever roaming round, correcting faults of stowage.

They were nearing their goal on 16 January 1912 when Bowers spotted something which looked like a cairn, and half an hour later they identified a black flag tied to a sledge. *'The Norwegians have forestalled us and are first at the Pole,'* wrote Scott: they could see the tracks of sledges and skis in the snow. *'We camped on the Pole itself at 6.30 p.m. this evening,'* wrote Wilson, and added: *'Oates, Evans and Bowers all have pretty severe frost-bitten noses and cheeks, and we had to camp early for lunch on account of Evans' hands.'* A photograph taken at the South Pole shows Oates, Scott with a Union Jack, and Evans standing: Bowers and Wilson, who are seated, have a flag on either side of them. Scott had a final word: *'Great God! This is an awful place and terrible enough for us to have laboured to it without the reward of priority. Well, it is something to have got here, and the wind may be our friend tomorrow.'* He also wrote: *'Now for the run home and a desperate struggle. I wonder if we can do it.'* The homeward journey was marked by worries: Wilson suffered from snow blindness and strained a tendon in his leg; Scott records further anxieties as Oates was suffering from a very cold foot and Evans' fingers and nose were in a bad state. By Sunday 28 January, their limited rations of food were beginning to have an effect – it may have been their growing weakness which contributed to the falls which Scott, Wilson and Evans suffered. Scott wrote: *'We are pretty thin, especially Evans, but none of us is feeling worked out.'* On Sunday 4 February 1912 Scott recorded a further setback: *'Just before lunch unexpectedly fell into crevasses, Evans and I together – a second fall for Evans, and I camped . . . the party is not improving in condition, especially Evans, who is becoming rather dull and incapable.'* This was considered to be the result of concussion from the morning's fall but in fact it was a symptom of his declining condition due almost certainly to scurvy. Roland Huntford in *Scott and Amundsen* has given detailed study to the physical complications which had almost totally undermined the health of Edgar Evans by the middle of February 1912:

Biggest and heaviest of the party, Evans nonetheless had to make do with the same rations as the others. He was, therefore, starving more, deficiencies were accelerated, and his condition grew proportionately worse. Everyone was thinning, but Evans most of all. The injury to his hand, received while shortening the sledges, refused to heal and by the end of January he was unable to help with the camp work. Alone in being so incapacitated, he was on that account oppressed by a sense of failure. . . . The wound that refused to heal, also suppurating cuts and continual nose bleeds, all suggest that, after leaving the Pole, Evans was suffering from advanced Vitamin C deficiency, and may have been in the early stages of scurvy. One of the effects of the disease is to make the blood vessels fragile. In that condition the normally insignificant shock of falling waist-deep into a crevasse as Evans did, could be enough to injure a blood vessel and cause a slow brain haemorrhage. That would explain what was happening to him.

The crisis of 16 February 1912 was described by Wilson, Oates and Scott: *'All the afternoon the weather became thicker and thicker and after 3¼ hours Evans collapsed – sick and giddy and unable to walk even by the sledge on ski . . . Evans' collapse has much to do with the fact that he has never been sick in his life and is now helpless with his hands frostbitten.'* (Wilson). Oates, in his account, faced up to the possiblity that Evans would not be able to continue: *'Evans . . . first had to get out of his harness and hold on to the sledge and later said he could not get on. . . . God knows how we're going to get him home. We cannot possibly take him on the sledge.'*

The next day – 17 February 1912 – Edgar Evans seemed better and started in harness, but then, for the first time, was unable to pull. Wilson wrote his version of the events of this sombre, tragic day: *'The weather cleared and we got away for a clear run to the depot, and had gone a good part of the way when Evans found his ski shoes coming off. He was allowed to readjust and continue to pull, but it happened again and then again, so he was told to unhitch, get them right and follow on and catch up. He lagged far behind till lunch and when we camped we had lunch and then went back for him.'* Wilson mentions that Evans *'had fallen and had his hands frost-bitten and we then returned for the sledge and brought it and skid him on it, as he was rapidly losing the use of his legs. He was comatose when we got him into the tent and he died without recovering consciousness that night about about 10 pm.'* Scott, in lengthy entry in his journal describes the *'very terrible day'.* Later Scott read the funeral service over Edgar Evans, who was buried in his sleeping bag under a cairn of ice blocks. The party struggled to achieve pitiful marches of six or seven miles: the next four weeks were focused on new worries as the atrocious surfaces and intense cold undermined their efforts. *'Wish we had more fuel'* and *'the fuel shortage is still an anxiety'* were Scott's entries. In addition, Lawrence Oates' feet were in a terrible state: his toes were black and gangrene was setting in. On a date which was recorded by Scott as *'Friday, March 16 or Saturday 17 Lost track of dates but think the last correct',* the entry reads:

Tragedy all along the line. At lunch the day before yesterday, poor Titus Oates said he couldn't go on; he proposed we should leave him in his sleeping bag. This we could not do, and we induced him to come on, on the afternoon march. In spite of its awful nature for him he struggled on and we made a few miles. At night he was worse and we knew the end had come . . . He slept through the night before last hoping not to wake; but he woke in the morning – yesterday. It was blowing a blizzard. He said "I am just going outside and may be some time." He went out into the blizzard and we have not seen him since.

On 21 March 1912, they were within eleven miles of One Ton Depot with its store of food and fuel which might have revived their fading efforts to survive. A blizzard defeated them as for ten days it raged. In that time, Wilson and Bowers wrote letters while Scott wrote business letters and made detailed notes in his journal. Some of these final letters to his family have been given to the Cambridge University's Scott Polar Institute. The last entry is dated 29 March 1912:

We are weak, writing is difficult, but for my own sake I do not regret this journey, which has shown that Englishmen can endure hardship, help one another and meet death with as great a fortitude as ever in the past. We took risks, we knew we took them; things have come out against us, and therefore we have no cause for complaint, but bow to the will of Providence, determined still to do our best to the last. Had we lived, I should have had a tale to tell of the hardihood, endurance and courage of my companions which would have stirred the heart of every Englishman. These rough notes and our dead bodies must tell the tale, but surely, surely a great rich country like ours will see that those who are dependent on us are properly provided for.

Surgeon Atkinson was the leader of the search party, including William Lashly and Charles Wright, which discovered, eight months later, the tent which was the final resting place of the remaining members of the party. After the recovery of the letters and diaries, the bamboo supports of the tent were removed and the tent collapsed over the bodies: a mighty cairn was built which was finished the next morning. Atkinson led the party back to Hut Point. The *Terra Nova* arrived in McMurdo Sound on 18 January 1913 to take the expedition home. Before leaving the Antarctic, the expedition erected a great cross of Australian jarrah wood on the top of Observation Hill, overlooking the Great Ice Barrier. On it were the names of the five comrades – Scott, Wilson, Oates, Bowers and Evans; a line from Tennyson's poem *Ulysses* was placed underneath the names. *'To strive, to seek, to find, and not to yield'.*

Thousands of miles away from Antarctica and its great cross of jarrah wood on Observation Hill, the birthplace of Edgar Evans provides in its ancient church a fitting memorial to a Gower hero:

TO THE GLORY OF GOD
AND IN MEMORY OF
EDGAR EVANS
1st CLASS PETTY OFFICER, R.N. AND A NATIVE OF THIS
PARISH, WHO PERISHED ON THE 17th FEBRUARY 1912
WHEN RETURNING FROM THE SOUTH POLE WITH THE
SOUTHERN PARTY OF THE BRITISH ANTARCTIC EXPEDITION
UNDER THE COMMAND OF
CAPTAIN ROBERT FALCON SCOTT, C.V.O., R.N.

"To strive, to seek, to find, and not to yield"

ERECTED BY LOIS EVANS

Rhossili School

The death in April 1998 of Miss Jeannette Maund, the last headmistress of Rhossili School before it closed in 1969, triggered memories of *The School on the Hill*. This is how Miss Maund referred to the school in an article which she wrote in the year of the closure of the school and which appeared in *Gower*, the Journal of the Gower Society. The building which came to be used as Rhossili School was originally the almshouse or poor-house of the parish of Rhossili and its adaptation and use provided a settled location for the education of Rhossili village children. Few who attended will have forgotten the trek up what is now School Lane – the steep slopes proving particularly challenging for the limbs of those who attended the Infants' Class. Those with memories of Jeannette Maund would come from a younger generation, those who remember Miss Ada Thomas and Miss Lily Button need longer memories. One former pupil – Mrs Annie Jenkins (Auntie Annie) – could clearly recall her days at Rhossili School around her hundredth birthday! She suggested: *'Bertha [Beynon] and I were the two youngest there and then Sid and William Beynon . . . they were the two youngest boys and we were the two youngest girls.'* Some of the youngest boys such as Sid Beynon and William Beynon did not always wear short trousers: *'they were in petticoats'*, according to Mrs Annie Jenkins.

The growth of nonconformity in Wales in the seventeenth and eighteenth centuries and the efforts of the established church members contributed to the emergence and growth of denominational and non-denominational schools. The strands of the educational developments in Wales include Thomas Gouge's Welsh Trust. By the time of Thomas Gouge's death in 1681, some 300 schools had been founded in Wales.

E.T. Davies in the *Glamorgan County History*, Volume IV, suggests that unendowed schools were to be found in every parish in Gower in the early eighteenth century, with the exception of Llandewi and Reynoldston. There were schools in Bishopston, Cheriton, Ilston, Llangennith, Llanmadoc, Llanrhidian, Nicholaston, Oxwich, Pennard, Penmaen, Penrice, Porteynon and Rhossili. These were schools which sometimes depended on the goodwill of the clergy of the parish, who taught the children of the village as part of their duties as parish priests, or else they helped a man or woman to eke out a living by making a small charge for the children who attended the school in the person's home. The children were taught to read in English, drilled in the Catechism of the Established Church and possibly taught *account* or arithmetic.

The Society for the Promotion of Christian Knowledge helped with the education of poor people in Wales, but it was the Reverend Griffith Jones who adapted its ideas in the Circulating Schools he established after 1731. These schools brought fleeting opportunities to children and adults in places as remote as 'Pilton in Rossilly', 'Fernhill in Rossilly', and Middleton Village some two hundred and fifty years ago. Itinerant masters arrived in villages and held classes for two or three months – usually in winter, when children and adults could best be spared from their work on the land. They taught poor people to read and the Catechism. Most Gower schools were taught in English – denoted by E.S. in the records of the Circulating Schools published in *Welsh Piety*. In 1744-45 the numbers at *Pilton, Rosilly* were 58; in 1746-47 at *Fernhill, Rosilly* there were 52. These early visits to the remotest part of Gower were followed by others: in 1766-77 at *Middleton Village, Roshilly (E.S.)* there were 39 and 34 attending on the two occasions the school was held. Among the testimonials printed in *Welsh Piety* was one from *Rosilly in Glamorganshire* dated 11 July 1747 from David Owen, Curate of *Rossilly*. The itinerant *'Master of the Charity School at Rosilly'* was praised in that he *'behaved very soberly, carefully and industriously in the said Office'*. It was also certified that: *'he taught and instructed the Children under his care and Tuition to Read and particularly to say by Heart, the Church Catechism, they having been examined therein several Times by me.'*

The end of Circulating Schools which made an important, though fleeting, contribution to the education of old and young in Gower villages, left a gap which the Sunday School movement attempted to fill. Farmhouse kitchens, barns and inns were used, but it was the local church or chapel which was the normal venue. The chapel building established at Pitton in 1833 remained in use as a school room even after the building of the new chapel there later in the century. The Church Sunday Schools in Gower included one at Middleton and a Wesleyan Methodist Sunday School at Pitton in 1845. At Pilton, a school preceded the building of a chapel – William Griffiths enrolled 37 pupils at Pilton Green in March 1821 and the building of Immanuel Chapel at Pylewell near Pilton Green followed in the same year. From 1848 the chapel at Pitton was used for two hours every week for Sunday School which within two years had an average attendance of around 60. The chapel at Pitton remained in use as a school-room following the building of a new chapel at Pitton; it was later used as a granary before being converted into a private building called, appropriately, *The Old Chapel*.

The setting up of a Departmental Commission of Inquiry into the state of education in Wales led to the appointment of Commissioners and Assistant Commissioners to visit all the schools and present individual assessments of their facilities and standards: *The Reports of the Commissioners of Inquiry into the State of Education in Wales* (London, 1847) followed their inspections. By this time there were two day-schools and two Sunday schools in the parish of Rhossili: the figures for scholars attending Sunday schools would, of course, include a good number of those who attended day-schools during the week. Nevertheless, the total of scholars attending schools in Rhossili was 179, a favourable figure to compare with that for Llangennith which had 190 – the highest total for south-west Gower. At Rhossili, the Church School at Middleton (1833), was housed in premises 15 feet by 9 feet, with a state of repair described as *Good*. The private School at Pitton had premises 16 feet by 10 feet: both schools enjoyed *Tenancies at Will*. There was insufficient furniture and apparatus at both schools – but while the furniture at Pitton was deemed to be in good repair, that at Middleton was in bad repair. The attendance of the thirty children on the books of the Church School had an even spread in age: ten had been there for less than a year, ten from one to two years and ten from two to three years. The private school at Pitton had eighteen pupils: fourteen boys of varying ages and four girls. At the time of the Assistant Commissioner's visit to Middleton he found the thirty children involved initially in Religious Instruction and then in various groups: letters and monosyllables involved 4 pupils, 6 were reading simple narratives, 16 pupils were writing on slates, 2 on paper, 2 were learning first rules of Arithmetic. No details were forthcoming from the private school: *'I merely filled a schedule, the master not being much disposed for me to examine his school,'* reported the Assistant Commissioner, David Williams. The income from school pence at Pitton was £20, as you would expect in a private school – at Middleton it was £2, with the 39-year-old lady teacher's salary being £12. At Pitton the master was an ex-farmer aged 33.

It was a move to what was then the parish almshouse or poor-house that placed Rhossili School in its familiar location as the *School on the Hill*. The poor-house was a thatched cottage with partition walls – the first floor was removed and what was left was one big room with an earth floor. In the census of 1861, Margaret Williams is shown as *Schoolmistress*; her wages were nine shillings a week, paid by Mr C.R.M. Talbot. The Elementary Education Act was passed in 1870 and provided for the setting up of schools where there were none. Its intention was to *fill the gaps* where the two national societies which provided schools- the National Society of the Church of England and the British and Foreign School Society – had not established one. The Act also provided for School Boards to run the schools and led in time to the setting up of the Rhossili School Board from 13 February 1875. Its inaugural meeting was held on 4 March 1875 at the Ship Inn. The Reverend John Ponsonby Lucas became Chairman, with Samuel Bevan as Vice-Chairman and also *'Clerk without Remuneration.'* The Chairman later was William Powell, who was shown as a blacksmith and Wesleyan local preacher in the census of 1871. The founding of School Boards did not necessarily bring the end of voluntary support for schools in Gower: the extent to which the Rhossili School Board relied on members of the Talbot family who had been the benefactors of education in the village in previous years is shown in their deliberations. On 24 May 1875, they agreed to ask Mr C.R.M. Talbot for a site for the school house: five years later, on 5 January 1880, it was resolved *'that application be made to C.R.M. Talbot to kindly repair the Schoool Room, and make it adequate to the requirements of the Education Act.'* At a meeting of the School Board held on 1 April 1878, it was resolved *'that William Taylor shall be the Schoolmaster and shall take Charge of the School under this Board, from the present date at a Salary of £30 per year.'* For nearly a century the educational needs of the children of Rhossili were to be catered for in their own village.

The powers of the School Boards were clearly defined. They were elected bodies, empowered to levy a rate to establish and maintain schools in districts where voluntary provision was inadequate, and they were able to frame bye-laws for the compulsory attendance of children aged between 5 and 12 years old and for setting the school leaving age. They also had discretionary power to waive the payment of *school pence* for poor families. The Rhossili School Board took vigorous action with regard to attendance: on 7 October 1878. They had already decided to put up notices throughout the parish in an attempt to enforce attendance at school. Evidently there were a number of parents who continued to keep their children away from school too frequently – on 4 August 1879 the Clerk was authorised *'to give those parents who neglect to send their children to school final notice that legal proceedings will be taken against them if they still further neglect to send them.'* The principal efforts of the School Board from 1875 to 1882 were focused on upgrading the school building and accommodation to the required standard, and even a teacher's residence was mooted. A General Report of 1877 by HM Inspector Mr Binns stated that *'Nothing as far I am able to ascertain has been done towards providing efficient schools at Oxwich and Rhossilly.'* After pleas for support had been made to C.R.M Talbot to *'kindly repair the School Room and make it adequate to the requirements of the Education Act'* it was resolved at the School Board meeting on 1 November 1880 that an *'advertisement to be put in "The Cambrian" newspaper to invite tenders for rebuilding and enlarging the old school.'* The subsequent tender was awarded to George Morgan, who had submitted one for £151: it was £8 below the tender of Henry Rosser. However, in October 1881 there were grumbles about delays in the completion of the work.

Mrs Annie Jenkins attended Rhossili School in the 1890s: *'Well there was a lot in school in those days . . . there were about fifty five, or something like that.'* A Directory entry for Rhossili in 1895 refers to a Board School (Mixed and Infants) created in 1876 for 63 pupils. In one year the Rhossili School Log Book records 62 pupils – double the figure who attended in the 1930s – the average attendance of the 62 pupils was, however, 30. The School Log Book shows the comings and goings of pupils. As noted in the previous chapter, *'Annie, Edgar and Arthur Evans left school this week, gone to Swansea to live',* is the entry for 31 March 1882. In the same year, 1882, we find an entry which is similar to those often found in the Log Books of rural village schools:

'School very thinly attended. The elder children away haymaking'.

8 June 1883: *'Was obliged to close the school the whole of the day on Monday owing to most of the children being wanted at the sheepwashing'.*

There were other distractions recorded by Miss Lucy Boutelle in 1883:

8 February: *'Low attendance due to some children being kept home to clean swedes'.*

14 March: *'Children away planting potatoes'.*

15 February 1884: *'Almost all the older boys away as a ship wrecked so they are [at] work on it'.*

This refers to the wreck of the *Samuel*, which went ashore in Sound, near Worm's Head on Tuesday, 12 February 1884. Her cargo of 500 tons of coal was disposed of to the local villagers for a shilling a cartload, or threepence a bag. The older boys were needed to help load and carry the coal away from the wreck to the nearby grass slope. From there, a rough road was cut to the Lookout Station at the top of the cliffs and the coal brought up by horses and carts or donkeys.

The Inspectors' Reports for Rhossili School which were written up in the School Log Book by the Head Teacher or Clerk to the School Board found much which was worthy of comment. On 29 August 1882, the HMI found the school in very good order and commented that the instruction had been *'most efficiently carried out by the mistress'*, Miss M. Johnston. There was, however, a high turnover of staff – seven in the years 1882 to 1891 – and this would have been a source of serious concern to the School Board. The School Log Book also shows the controversies over the staffing and disciplinary problems which led later to irregular and improper entries being made in the Log Book by the Head Teacher.

There was still much to be done, as an Inspector's report of 1893 makes clear:

The arrangement of the school desks is not satisfactory. They should stand in parallel blocks of three deep along the length of the room, and the stove should be moved aside to allow of this. A wooden dado around the wall is necessary and this would prevent the draught coming up tween the floor & the walls. Three or four flat-topped desks suitable for infants must be provided without delay – and some new wall maps are required. The boys' porch or cloakroom must be protected from the weather by a door, and that for the girls is also insufficiently protected and is not quite large enough. The gate between the two playgrounds must be replaced. The rough stones removed at the entrance to the boys' porch. The approaches to the girls' offices improved and the stream in the playground diverted.

In September 1894, the report read:

The school does not seem to have passed as satisfactory an examination as usual. The closing of the school for five weeks on account of an epidemic and for repairs would account for the falling off. The staff should be strengthened. The stream which runs through the playground must be diverted or covered in, the wall at the back of the playground made safe, wall maps and pictures provided and a urinal erected without delay (Article 85(a) of the Code).

It had accommodation for 54 children, who ranged from Lower Infants to Standard VII. Both departments were under one roof; a western porch was erected in 1900 and a partition erected in July 1908 which divided the room into two separate classrooms. The 728 square feet of floor space had boarded flooring, with two slow combustion stoves for heating; two coal-houses, one holding 4 tons and one 2 tons were required. Filters were used for obtaining drinking water: for other purposes, water was laid on from a well on the hill to basins in the cloakrooms. For both older scholars and infant scholars, earth closets were provided: a note in the Compendium suggests *'Cleaner's husband digs earth closets out when instructed by the Head Teacher.'*

The appointment of Elizabeth Green as Head Teacher in 1896 was followed by her resignation in 1898. Her successor, Mr Richard Hughes, later made an entry in the School Log Book giving some account of the reasons for her resignation, before he departed in a cloud of controversy at the end of June 1898. After a surprise inspection, which was critical in its report, Mr Hughes outlined in the School Log Book the situation he had inherited: The entry reads:

> *I am sorry to find that the discipline has given me a great deal of trouble since I have been here. There is tremendous strife in this parish on account of Miss Green's (my immediate predecessor) desire to secure Olive Bevan, the Clerk's daughter, as Assistant under Article 68. The School Board split into two sections over the matter – the Reverend Mr Lucas and Mr William Thomas supporting Miss Green and the other members against her. The result was that Miss Green resigned. Some say she was really dismissed – and the Reverend Mr Lucas, Chairman of the Board, and Mr Thomas, resigned in disgust.*

We have the School Board Minute Book for a further twist to the story: *'August 18, 1898: Mr Richard Hughes, Head Master given 3 months to quit his post.'* While working out his notice, Richard Hughes must have made entries in the School Log Book, on pages 256 to 269, setting out the circumstances of his dismissal in terms which were critical of the School Board. These were later removed. The last few months of his headmastership were particularly acrimonious: the School Board resolved on 7 November 1898 that *'the Clerk come to the School on the last evening this Teacher holds School and demand the keys of cupboards and drawers.'*

In 1903, following the Education Act of 1902, School Boards were abolished and their powers and duties were transferred to county and county boroughs. Elementary schools were to have managers appointed solely by the Local Education Authority in the case of provided schools, and jointly for non-provided, that is Church, Schools. Members of the School Board, whose work ended on 30 September 1903, took the opportunity to make a final entry in the School Board Minute Book: *'As a Board we desire to place on Record that this Board has worked together carrying out the duties of the Education of the Children in this district in a most agreeable manner. We have not always seen eye to eye in every "matter" at the commencement but after discussing the question under Consideration we have always agreed as to what was proposed to be done. . . . Our work has now come to a close.'*

William Powell, Chairman; William Beynon, Pilton; William Beynon, Middleton; and the Clerk, John Beynon signed the final entry. A succession of schoolmistresses took Rhossili children into the *School on the Hill* and gave them better opportunities than had been available to their parents and grandparents.

Rhossili School is one of the success stories of Gower's educational advancement, as eventually pupils started to enter colleges and universities, having achieved secured grammar school places through the tuition they had received in their little rural school. The work of Miss Edwards has been described in glowing terms by members of the Bevan family; Miss E.M. Davies was the mistress in 1914 when the average attendance was 43 pupils; Miss D.W. Evans was the mistress in 1920. The two major figures from this time were Miss Ada Thomas and Miss Lily Button, Head Teacher and Infants' Teacher respectively. Miss Ada Thomas of Church Park, Rhossili commenced duties on 1 December 1922 and she, with Miss Lily Button – who had all the pupils up to seven years of age – provided the dedication, expertise and motivation which carried many pupils from Rhossili village into careers and professions beyond the limits of village life. The School Compendium entry completed by Miss Ada Thomas gives details for Rhossili School: *Rhossili Council School Mixed & Infants Dept. Gowerton Group.* It confirms that it was built in 1875 and was formerly a workhouse. It opened as a school under the Education Authority in January 1882.

The human touch is seen in the life of this little village when a pupil – Margaret Bevan – left to go to another school. Her sister Mary Bevan (now Mary Beynon), has the letters written by pupils of Rhossili School to Margaret around 29 September 1942, bringing her up to date with the world-shattering events which had taken place in Rhossili. Two incidents were mentioned in many of the letters: they were incidents in which the Land Workers' van had crashed and another van had caught fire. Further details from pupils such as Ernie Beynon and Teddy Chappell confirm that: *'One day the land-boys lorry crashed into a lamp-post and some of the men were hurt.'* They were all taken to hospital after their vehicle crashed into a telegraph post. Holwell's oil van caught fire near Pylewell, destroying the stock of methylated spirits, oil, plates, saucers and serviettes, according to Valerie Jones. A butcher's van of Mrs W. Tucker was left outside Mr Gammon's house (at the top of what is now School Lane). It ran over the edge of the bank into the gutter some distance below and two tractors were needed to haul it out. More seriously – there was no-one in the van – was the fire at the home of Mr and Mrs Johnny Beynon of High Priest, Middleton. They had only managed to save their money and nothing else.

At Rhossili School the detailed instruction in tables, arithmetic and basic subjects occupied a good part of the day – the careful consistent teaching of handwriting, spelling and mental arithmetic. These were the working moments in the school, leavened by the occasional relaxation in the classroom which might take the form of listening to gramophone records. Two favourites always provided a complete contrast: Charles Penrose sang the *Laughing Policeman* which brought a rising crescendo of laughter until the class were weeping with enjoyment. The pupils laughed and laughed hysterically at times! This record was followed by one whose sadness evoked real tears: the thoughts of Sydney Carton in a *Tale of Two Cities* as he solemnly accepted his fate. *'It is a far, far better thing that I do, than I have ever done. It is a far, far better rest that I go to than I have ever known.'* Memories of the village school include the sharing of its facilities with evacuees during the Second World War – at one time a rota of mornings for evacuees to use the school, with village children in the afternoons, alternated with village children attending in the mornings the next week with evacuees in the afternoons.

Pupils preparing for the 11-plus, however, did not always get a morning or afternoon off, as they were required for extra tuition at Miss Ada Thomas' cottage at Rhossili! The dedication and skill shown by the two teachers – Miss Button and Miss Thomas – did, perhaps, give Rhossili pupils an edge in the examinations to determine entry to the Gowerton Boys or Girls Grammar Schools. Miss Button had all the pupils up to seven years of age: *'you had to handle three different ages and all kinds of ability in one class,'* she recalled in *Yesterdays Gower*. *'At one time, I remember, there were eighteen children going to the grammar school at Gowerton.'*

It is difficult to remain unbiased in an appraisal of a village school in a remote community, which offered its pupils such a high standard of education for the most part that their career prospects widened. The avenue to grammar school and, later, university was trodden by boys and girls from Rhossili School who went on to become teachers, scientists, successful farmers and members of other professions. Unknowingly at the time, their talent had been teased out, coaxed and encouraged by dedicated teachers who taught their pupils well. Thomas Nicholas, writing over a century ago in *The History and Antiquities of Glamorganshire and its families* tried to give a balanced view of the Englishry and Welshry of Gower. His phrase is worthy of inclusion: *'The impression is prevalent among the "Welshry" that in point of religious culture the English-speaking Gowerians are sadly deficient; but it is on all hands admitted that they are industrious, cleanly and orderly, and not behind in intellectual faculty. The mental soil is good if only tilled.'* A native of Rhossili would appreciate and accept this comment.

It is nostalgia and regret which creep in when looking back at the closure of Rhossili's little village shool in 1969. When she became the Head Teacher at Rhossili School, Miss Jeannette Maund built on the traditions of the little village school which she came to know and love. Her time as Headmistress made an imprint on the life of the school and we know the school made an imprint on her. The building of a new school at Knelston which catered for all the children of south-west Gower from the villages of

Penrice, Oxwich, Reynoldston, Llandewi, Knelston, Porteynon and Rhossili brought to an end the individual village schools. Jeannette Maund wrote an epitaph for Rhossili School which appeared in *Gower*, Volume 20, in 1969 and which she called *The School on the Hill*:

> *The small solid building situated in one of the most beautiful spots of Gower, overlooking Mewslade Bay, with a background of sloping hillside, covered with bracken and at this time of the year colourful with gorse, is still standing like a watchful sentinel, but it is now devoid of the sound of voices and the life of movement.*
>
> *Although now quiet and peaceful, the stones seem to speak of all those who have played, studied and worked within its walls. If only walls could speak what tales they would have to tell, over a period of seventy years.*
>
> *The history of the school's activities would fill a book. They have played a vital part in the life of the village and they have probably had their influence felt in areas further afield. The school's log book will contribute to educational history, and there is much to be learned from it. The life of the school through the years has created a heritage, supplying a jumping-off ground for the business of life. It has been the educational home of so many different types and characters, each playing their own part. May Rhossili School never be forgotten, by those fortunate to have benefited from its existence and who, like myself, feel proud to be included in its family.*

As the last Headmistress of Rhossili School, Miss Maund followed in a line of ladies whose talents and dedication helped to shape many young minds. Her contribution to the education of the children of Rhossili village was brought to mind by so many of her former pupils on hearing the sad news of her death in April 1998.

Then and Now

The Census of 1901 continues to illustrate that at the start of the twentieth century Rhossili was still a thriving agricultural community emerging from its isolation at the end of the Gower peninsula. There were some thirty-three farmers, together with a smattering of farm labourers, who had been joined by three Coastguard families at the Coastguard Station. These were a Chief Boatman Coastguard, who was Francis Norie, and two Boatmen, Charles John Sparks and Alfred Stark. At this time three properties at Hillend, Llangennith were still included in the parish of Rhossili, with one farm being under the supervision of Thomas G. Richards, Farm Bailiff. Morgan Beynon was a retired farmer, William Beynon was the Inn Keeper at the Ship Inn and Philip Beynon is shown as a Farmer/Shoemaker. As well as these three Beynons there were seven other Beynon farmers – most with modest acreages, except for George Beynon at Pitton who is shown as farming over 181 acres in the Tithe Apportionment schedule of 1845-47 and 146 acres in other tenancies. The Button, Bevan and Thomas familes each provided three members of the farming community, with the Richards family adding a further five. Most of the smaller farmers are shown as farming on their own account but individual farmers such as Charles Morgan at Pylewell, Thomas Davies at Pilton, Charles Gordon at Paviland and William Richards at Kimley Moor are among those shown as *Employer*. Later we find in the service records of the First World War the sons of these farmers, who served their King and Country during this tragic conflict.

During the First World War, a fascinating record of the service of Gower men and women was completed by G. Baker Hynes – it recorded on a Roll Of Honour the names of those who in 1916 were serving in the Army or Navy. It reveals that Rhossili men – together with those who had been born in Rhossili but had gone to Canada – had enrolled in significant numbers. The document was published as a supplement to *The Gower Church Magazine*:

Parish of Rhossili

Corporal William R. Williams	26	Sea View
Stoker Walter Jenkins	17	Fernhill Top
1st Class Petty Officer Stanley G. Beynon	18	Ship Inn
Private Sidney Beynon	22	Ship Cottage
Gunner Robert G. Beynon	18	Worm's Head Cottage
Private John Beynon	26	Cochrane (Canada)
Driver Philip Richards	21	Upper Pitton
Private William Gibbs	28	Mewslade View
Private Morgan B. Gibbs	20	Mewslade View

Driver Arthur D. Thomas	21	Sydney, N.S.W.
Lance-Corporal Walter Beynon	22	Riverside Farm
Private Samuel Morris	19	Pilton Green
Lance-Corporal George Beynon	19	Swansea
Private John Beynon		Cochrane (Canada)
Driver George Pelfry	21	Pilton Green
George Thomas	29	Neath
Private Sidney Richards	26	Upper Pitton
Ingram Davies	28	Cochrane (Canada)
Edgar Davies	26	Cochrane (Canada)
William Beynon		Ashtree House R.E.

The census of 1921 showed Rhossili to be a community of 57 inhabited houses and 304 people. The living is a rectory, annexed to the vicarage of Llangennith, joint net income £292. By 1925 the village community had acquired a new Rectory, and Rhossili Public Hall and the Old Rectory had been sold. The Rector from 1920 was the Reverend William Scudamore L.Div. of St. David's College, Lampeter, whose indefatigable efforts resulted in the building of a new rectory. The condition of the old rectory led the Reverend Scudamore to lead a drawn out community effort to have a new one built. *A Plan of the Proposed Vicarage at Rhossili, Gower*, dated 1 June 1922, was drawn up by Charles W. Mercer M.S.A., but by January 1923 it was still not completely certain that the plans for a new rectory would succeed. One correspondent suggested: *'If you ask my opinion I should say, yes, it was most probable that a new rectory will be built, but I cannot say more than that.'* Funding was eventually secured and work did begin in June 1924, in the same year as the Rhossili Public Hall scheme was being carried out. One report noted: *'The work of the building of the New Rectory has now begun, it will cost at least with the present price of materials & labour £1,830.'* A review of the funding was carried out in November 1924 and, despite some delay in payment to contractors in March 1925, the work was duly completed.

At the same time as this modest-sized community was taking on the financial implications of the need for a new rectory, it was also taking on the erection of Rhossili Public Hall, which *affords 200 sittings*, also built in 1924. A Lease dated 8 January 1924 of *'a piece or parcel of land situate at Rhossili in the County of Glamorgan'* gave the parishioners of Rhossili the opportunity of building Rhossili Public Hall in the hamlet of Middleton. The grant from Lady Blythswood to Trustees of Rhossili Public Hall of a Lease of land for the term of *'ninety-nine years to be computed from the Twenty-fourth day of June'* 1923, was to be at a yearly rent of *'one shilling if demanded'*.

F. Jones, tenant, is referred to in the sketch showing the location of the 17 perches of land on which the Hall was to be built. A figure of £3 13s 0d written below the date of the lease may refer to the cost of the legal document drawn up by Strick & Bellingham solicitors of Swansea.

Extracts from the Lease show that . . . 'the Lessor doth hereby demise unto the Trustees all that piece or parcel of land situate at Rhossili in the County of Glamorgan having a frontage to the road leading from the Village to "The Voile" of Forty-four feet and a depth of Ninety feet forming part of the enclosure Nd. 307 on the Ordnance Survey Map for the Parish of Rhossili (1914 Edition) and containing Four hundred and forty square feet or thereabouts' . . . The demised premises to 'be used during the continuance of the said term as and for a Public Hall of a purely Undenominational character for persons residing in the Parish of Rhossili.'

The Lease document opens:

> This Indenture made the Eighth day of January One thousand nine hundred and twenty-four between The Right Honourable Evelyn Lady Blythswood of the one part and

> George Beynon of Ship Cottage, Middleton, Farmer
> George Austin Button of Pitton, Rhossili, Farmer
> Samuel Richards of Bay Farm, Rhossili, Farmer
> George Thomas of Worms Head Cottage, Rhossili, Farmer
> Martin Tucker of Pitton Cross Rhossili, Butcher and
> Hopkin Llewellyn Prichard of Penmaen, Estate Agent
> Hereinafter called "the Trustees"
> [One of the Trustees would be a nominee of the Penrice Estate – the remainder would be representatives of the Rhossili community. Hopkin Llewellyn Prichard was therefore the nominee.]

> Signed Sealed and Delivered
> by the Right Honourable Evelyn
> Lady Blythswood in the presence of

> Evelyn Blythswood

> A. Anthony   Enrolled in the Central Office of the Supreme
>   Court of Judicature the twenty-eighth day of
> D. Given   January in the year of Our Lord 1924 . . .

The achievement in securing a new rectory for the Parish of Rhossili, struggled for over a period of four years, was a reflection of the energy and zeal with which the villagers tackled their need. A similar effort had gone into securing Rhossili Public Hall. The new Rectory, alas, has been sold off, like its predecessor in the Warren.

In the same year, 1924, an event took place in the grounds of Penrice Castle, Gower. A Gower Pageant had been organised in aid of the Gower Nursing Association and the General and Musical Director, Lt. Col. E. Helme, D.S.O. had, with the help of Episode Directors, arranged to present eleven *Historical and Traditional Gower Episodes*. The Patrons of the event were:

His Grace the Duke of Beaufort (Baron of the Seignory of Gower)

Her Grace the Duchess of Beaufort

The Right Honourable the Marquess and Marchioness of Worcester

Major the Right Honourable the Lord Blythswood, KCVO

The Right Honourable the Lady Blythswood

The intention, as Ernest Helme describes in a Foreword to the programme of the event *'was to group certain parishes . . . to enact an episode, historical or traditional, which had originally, according to history, tradition or legend, taken place in the area contained in the parish or group of parishes: further, it would greatly enhance the interest if, when possible, the actual descendants should enact the character of their protagonist forebears.'*

The *'unusual interest and enthusiasm evinced at the parochial meetings'* was matched by extensive rehearsal. Oxwich and Penrice combined to present an episode involving Anne Mansel, who was killed by a stone thrown during a confrontation in the sixteenth century between the Herbert family and the Mansels in a dispute over wreck. Llandewi and Knelston portrayed the Escape of Edward Mansel in the eighteenth century. The villagers of Rhossili in the eleventh and final re-enactment of scenes from Gower's past produced a 'Smuggling Episode of the eighteenth century'. It was claimed that among the performers were descendants and relatives of the characters shown in this *True Story*; no fewer than twenty members of the cast out of twenty-three could claim descent from the original characters. They included seven Beynons (not all the same family), six Richards and two Buttons as well as a Thomas. As the scene was set in Morgan Beynon's Kitchen, Middleton, it is to be supposed that this was where at least some of the smuggling took place.

GOWER PAGEANT
Penrice Castle Gower
August 14th 1924
No 11. – Rhossili

Committee: *President* Mrs W.G. Beynon* *Secretary* Ada Thomas*
Samuel Richards, Rhossili*; Geo. Thomas, Rhossili*;
Mrs R.J. Beynon High Priest, Middleton*, Mrs Brockie, Rhossili

Costumiers: Mrs W.G. Beynon, Great Pitton; Mrs Morgan Beynon, Rhossili;
Mrs W. Williams, Post Office; Miss Ada Thomas, Rhossili

Donator   Mrs Morgan Beynon*

CAST

Grandmothers David Richards*, Samuel Richards*, Mrs W.G. Beynon*
Son Gwyn Beynon*

Daughter Miss Sarah Beynon

Villagers Mrs Brockie*, Mrs Beynon*, Mrs R. J. Beynon* Miss Annie Gibbs
Miss Minnie Richards*

Smuggler Morgan Richards*

Smuggler's Nephews Geo. Thomas* and W. Button*

Excise Officer William Williams*

Excise Men William Williams*, Lemuel Richards*, W. Jones
Alfred Beynon*, Wilfred Beynon*, John Richards*

Children Doris Jones, Ingram Button*, Idris Hopkins*

* Descendants and relatives of Characters

The Grand Finale was to be the rendering of the Seignorial Tribute to Her Grace the Duchess of Beaufort by the Mansels. First, the whole of the personnel of the pageant took part in a processsion past the dais where the ceremony was to take place. The Rendering of the Seignorial Dues to her Grace the Duchess of Beaufort (wife of the Baron Seigneur of Gower), was carried out by the Mansel family, represented by their descendant, Lady Blythswood. These payments were made annually in the form of two golden arrows. This poignant reminder of Gower's past was evocative of the *'six swallow tayled arrowes yearly or vjd'*, which formed part of the feudal tribute of the *'Mannor of Vernhill held by heires of Morgan Vaughan, Owen Perkins and Richard Bydder'* centuries before. On this Thursday, 14 August 1924, Gower's and Rhossili's pasts were recaptured.

The recent changes in village life in Rhossili were faithfully recorded by Mansel Thomas in *Yesterday's Gower* before his untimely death. One of the villagers who recorded his memories was my father David Wilfred Beynon. He was born in 1902 and recalls: *'Of course, every farmer in those early days lived very simple. He'd put a few cabbages in the field with the mangels and a few cabbages in the field with the swedes. He'd grow the wheat, get the flour ground and bake the bread. They'd kill a pig and that was about all. They just lived off the land.'* George Beynon, of Ship Farm, had moved down to the Ship Inn in 1906 from Sheep Green, when it was closed as a pub. The family already owned one field, bought from the heiress of the Kilvrough Estate, Lady Louisa Lyons; it was known as Clerk's Land and was used to grow an acre and a half of potatoes. *'Father used to sell potatoes in Swansea, with a horse and cart,'* recalled David Wilfred Beynon, *'but during the First World War he had to stop that, because our horse was commandeered for the Army.'* Later, the market gardeners of Bishopston bought up the surplus potatoes. It was the selling of surplus crops to a wider market which was to transform the semi-subsistence farming of isolated villages in Gower. Carrots and cabbages, together with potatoes were the cash crops, with sheep, beef cattle and dairy cattle being the main livestock. The early potatoes of Gower, competing with those from Pembrokeshire, were later sold as far afield as Manchester and

Bradford, as well as to people in Newport and Cardiff. The sale of sheep and lambs in local markets – with the sale of the fleeces as well to a Wool Marketing Board – added to the resources of Gower farmers and gave them a better standard of living. Growing tourism added welcome additional income to the local economy and helped to raise standards of accommodation in the villages.

Until the time of the Second World War these changes had not altered the way of life of villagers in Rhossili – it was the war-time acceleration in the production of food which brought villages like Rhossili into the twentieth century. The intensified production required the use of marginal land and Rhossili farmers would have brought every acre available into use during these years. Farming made strides in crop productivity: *'In 1940/1 everyone in the village, except one, sold all his sheep.* They returned after the war – *sheep have been a constant'* confirmed David Wilfred Beynon, as he farmed with his family of seven sons and a daughter. The wider markets of the post-war period brought an outflow of livestock and crops like early new potatoes, the better roads also brought an influx of tourists.

Life on the Home Front in rural communities during the Second World War from 1939 to 1945 can be illustrated by reference to the village of Rhossili in many cases. A number of themes can be explored which show how a small rural village reacted to the demands of a World War. The protection of the population by the issuing of gas masks was carried out. Thirty-eight million gas masks had been issued by the end of September 1938, a year before the Second World War actually started.

In cities, Anderson air raid shelters in people's gardens became a feature. Air raid drills, blackout restrictions and Air Raid Precautions (ARP) were introduced. ARP wardens were responsible for seeing the black-out restrictions were observed and for alerting the civilian population to the imminence of an air raid. They had a uniform, a bicycle and a whistle. Production of food had to be maximised by taking in marginal land and securing more people to work to work on the land. *Lend a hand on the land* was the slogan on one poster which urged people to volunteer to help with agriculture. The Women's Land Army was also formed and young women volunteered to become Land Girls. About one million children were evacuated from the big towns and cities to rural communities – they arrived by train or bus at local village halls carrying their gas masks and a few possessions. They were then billeted with people who had very few or no children. The Local Defence Volunteers or Home Guard were a new defence force set up in May 1940 and within a week around 250,000 volunteers had come forward; the numbers doubled by July 1940. Ration books were issued to control sale of basic foods. People were permitted one egg a fortnight, though supplies were not guaranteed as they were with other rationed goods. Ministry of Food recipes included one for making a pudding with raw grated carrot as well as mixed dried fruit, spices and suet. There is also mention of carrot fudge and a dish called *mashed bananas* which might be made up of bread, parsnips and essence of banana.

Evacuees arrived in Rhossili and initially they would have had to share the facilities at Rhossili School. They alternated in the use of the school for mornings or afternoons.

Miss Atkinson was in charge of the pupils. Ann Harding – a former pupil – has memories of the impact on Rhossili School:

Then there was the shock horror of the evacuees. Some had never seen the sea but were able to broaden our education in other ways. They taught us "Truth or Dare" and a horrible game called "Dardy". Someone armed with a knotted rope was "he" and the rest of us had to hide. When found, we would be flogged. I recall cowering under a furze bush for most of playtime and being highly relieved when the newcomers were taken out to Worm's Head for their schooling.

A radar location station was built on Rhossili Down and a rough road was constructed from Fernhill across to the end of Rhossili Down where the remains of the station can be seen today. Personnel could take supplies across the hill on this road by tractor and trailer. The Observer Corps, which was set up in 1925, was expanded in 1937 to cover the whole of the United Kingdom and linked to the RAF fighter groups. The wartime role of the Corps was to identify enemy aircraft and plot their courses, thus enabling the RAF to intercept and engage them. In 1941, King George VI took the unprecedented step of granting the title *Royal* during wartime as a result of valuable services rendered during the Battle of Britain and in the early days of World War II. The first observation post in the village of Rhossili opened in September 1938 and was situated in a field at the rear of Broad Park under the jurisdiction of 25 Group Cardiff, with the call-sign Juliet 1.

William Beynon (my Uncle Bill), was an ARP Warden and cycled around the village – probably mostly in Middleton – blowing a whistle to sound the alarm when notification had been received by telephone that an air raid was imminent. Until recently his gas mask was to be found at our home at Sea View, Rhossili. The most serious raids of the Second World War locally came in February 1941 with the blitz on Swansea: there were many casualties and the centre of the town was badly hit. The red reflection in the sky over Swansea was visible many miles away in Rhossili. Dim memories suggest that a stray bomb was dropped near Rhossili at some time during the war and landed in Jack Gibbs' potato field which ran alongside the footpath to Fall Bay. Large logs were placed vertically on Rhossili Bay to hinder the landing of enemy aircraft or gliders, but many were soon washed away. A careful eye had to be kept for mines which might have got washed up on Gower beaches. A British fighter aircraft landed on Rhossili Bay in an emergency while another one crashed into the top of Rhossili Down in a fatal incident.

Women's Land Army volunteers worked on many farms in Rhossili. Mrs Rhona Richards who was married to Mr Bowen Richards of Ashtree Farm, first came to Rhossili as a Land Girl. Mrs Gwen Beynon who was the second wife of my Uncle George Beynon was one of the first Land Girls to be billeted on a Gower Farm in 1940.

The Home Guard at Rhossili included the postmaster, Mr William Williams, who had served in the army during the First World War. John Beynon recounts a tale of the Home Guard, including Mr William Williams and his grandfather, Norman Richards, being involved in a mock attack on the radar location station on Rhossili Down. They were able to cut a hole in the perimeter fence and get in before being detected.

The introduction of rationing brought shortages: most farmers could keep them-selves supplied with eggs but the extra supplies of seagulls' eggs from the cliffs and Worm's Head gave extra opportunities for frying or making fishy tasting omelettes which were better than the *rubbery* omelettes made with Dried Egg.

The requisition of land at Scurlage – where the South Gower Sports Club is today – gave American troops a base from where they could take their DKWs (landing craft), down to Porteynon Bay to practise landing manoeuvres for the D-Day landings in June 1944. They blocked the roads in the early morning, so the bus going from Rhossili to Swansea via Blackpill was sometimes held up. The pupils who were going to Gowerton Grammar School for Boys or Gowerton Grammar School for Girls might miss the train from Blackpill to Gowerton and would have a good excuse for turning up late at lunch-time when the next train was due. An impromptu game of football on Swansea sands was better than hiking to school!

The farming scene changed radically after the Second World War and the farming life of this part of Gower underwent its most important change. During the Second World War, Evelyn, Lady Blythswood, transferred the Penrice and Margam Estate to her daughter, the Hon. Olive Douglas Methuen-Campbell to avoid paying crippling death duties. Unfortunately, her daughter died before her, which resulted in death duties having to be paid anyway and the sale of parts of the Penrice Estate followed in 1950. A letter was sent to every sitting tenant offering the farm to him at a stated price – this had to be low because in 1947 the Labour government had passed a Security of Tenure Act, which meant rents could not be raised and no farmer could be ejected. The farmers were offered the land at roughly £50 an acre. When the Penrice Estate sold off land to sitting tenant-farmers in 1950, the certainty of freedom and independence gave scope for ambition and with it greater productivity and efficiency. This, taking a nostalgic look backwards, was probably the time when the village of Rhossili had its highest numbers of farming families, making a decent living even from a small acreage farm. Inevitably, later generations did not always want to retain the farming tradition: some farms were not viable in terms of size, and other farmers acquired the spare land as it became available. In one or two cases, there was no son or daughter to continue with the farm; in others the sole son or daughter may have received a good enough education to leave the village to go to university and seek their living in the professions. Prices of farms – when they came on the market – might well be outside the financial limits achievable by a young villager, the result in some villages being the acquisition of farms in Gower by *hobby-farmers*. David Wilfred Beynon could see this trend away from small-scale farming and the impact it would have on village communities: *'But of course, it's getting harder every year now for the small farmer. And where's a young man going to get the cash to start up on his own?'*

In recent years, homes in Rhossili have been regularly acquired by families whose working members commute to Swansea daily – a trend repeated in other villages in Gower such as Reynoldston. Families who retire and come to live in Rhossili are no longer outnumbered by the retired members of existing village families who continue to live here after they retire. The holiday homes are rarely occupied by short-distance weekend families, but by those prepared to travel long distances at holiday times to enjoy the delights of walking, crabbing and fishing in Rhossili. The overall effect appears to have been the creation of a community made up of fewer farming families, with fewer of the houses being occupied by people whose roots go back to the Rhossili of yester-year. Nevertheless the continuing village atmosphere suggests that there has been some assimilation of new families – equally prepared to enjoy the fruits of village life and play their part in preserving some of its better features by tasteful conversions of old, redundant farm houses and farm buildings. The decline of a characteristic rural culture is not recent – the ending of the isolation of Rhossili as a self-contained, rural community made up of inter-related families dates back many years – the enhanced mobility provided by motor transport being an obvious creator of change.

The features evident in other villages are not always seen in Gower, though. Rhossili never had a *squire*, as such, throughout its manorial life. In later times, the traditional influence of the parson was perceived, although not quite as a *squarson*. We have seen how the increasing influence of nonconformity brought new characteristics to the village – the independence and equality resulting from the acquisition of previously tenanted lands has, however, been a comparatively recent phenomenon. There is often, as G.E. Mingay pointed out in his contribution to *The Victorian Countryside*, a change in the social composition and balance of a community: *'The old inhabitants found themselves at odds with the newcomers' manners, habits and ways of thinking, and found themselves unable to compete in living standards, housing and transport.'* This could lead to cases of families whose grown-up children have to move away since they are outbid for local cottages.

Nevertheless, with young families moving into a rural area the number of children in a small village could well grow, maintaining an active vibrant community. The restriction of local bus services which are not viable and the closure of village shops unable to keep their prices competitive in an age of supermarkets and hypermarkets – these create a reverse trend which could stifle village life. The trend could be exacerbated by the inevitable exodus in all villages of young people who in the modern age wish to enjoy life in a less cloistered environment than their parents and grandparents. The encouraging trend noted earlier, however, is for a larger proportion of new families coming into the village to have young children: they are seeking the opportunity of providing a rural upbringing for them. The retreat to rural surroundings by more and more families seeking a better quality of life could offer a reprieve for some village communities, but in the age of the motor car we all tend to travel to nearby towns to buy our week's groceries at a supermarket, top up our petrol supplies and enjoy our entertainment, while bemoaning the absence of village shops, the lack of decent bus services and the sparsity of local entertainment. The unifying influence of a local village school is absent in many communities.

Rhossili has been, but is no longer, a working village, although its land and landscape may still reflect the features of its development as a settlement where agriculture held sway. The farmers and farmworkers, albeit not the blacksmiths, are still part of the backdrop against which village life proceeds. Cows, tractors, bird-scarers, combine harvesters now share the scene with hang gliders, surfers, rock climbers and coastal footpath walkers. In Gower and in Rhossili, in many cases, the National Trust has replaced the former landholder – the Penrice Estate. It has achieved a measure of management through covenants relating to the strips of the open field system and has acquired land as it has been placed on the market, although it has not yet begun to actively farm the land it has acquired, so some land has gone out of use. The principal crop in the strips of the open field system appears to be corn, with only the occasional patch of cabbage. The variegated pattern of strips as viewed from the Lookout House in former years has disapppeared. Coupled with the air of growing disuse is the common land on which some villagers still have rights, but it is the ramblers and hang gliders who share it with the ponies. No Rhossili farmers are currently engaged in dairy farming as returns have lessened, with principal stock being sheep and beef cattle.

Rhossili has now acquired the air of a dormitory village with a seasonal influx of local visitors from Swansea and tourists from other countries. It seems unlikely that the pattern can be reversed to the old days when Rhossili was an active, vibrant farming community – the number of active farmers today is no more than ten, compared with over thirty a century ago. It could have been foreseen that, with growing pressure on the countryside, farming would acquire more of a land management role on behalf of the many thousands who enjoy the landscape of Rhossili. With the growing hobby of horse-riding, the current picture is one of paddocks amongst the occasional oases of farms, farmed in some cases by the original farming families. It is inevitable that changes have occurred from the position just over a century ago, when 60% of the population of Rhossili were shown as being born in Rhossili. Those who mourn the passing of the village farming community are reconciled to the march of progress. Those who enjoy the close-knit fabric of a village community will find a measure of comfort in Rhossili – those willing to join in village activities will find an outlet. If Rhossili is to retain its individuality, sustain its role as the custodian of some of the finest cliffs, beaches and walks in Gower, and survive into the twenty-first century by tackling life as staunchly as its earlier inhabitants overcame their challenges, it will need the collective effort of all its current inhabitants. It has a proud heritage, some features of which have been extinguished, but if we can recall some of its past and build on its present, then the future is assured. If not, then we may suffer the fate of the tiny, now vanished, community of Blasket Island fishermen off the south-west coast of Ireland, which Thomas Crohan wrote about in these words:

I have written minutely of much that we did, for it was my wish that some-where there should be a memorial of it all, and I have done my best to set down the character of the people so that some record of us might live after us, for the like of us will never be again.

Select Bibliography

Unpublished Primary Sources

Census Enumerators' Returns, 1841-1901.
Penrice and Margam Manuscripts, National Library of Wales.
Margam Estate Collection, West Glamorgan Archive Service.
Penrice Estate Collection, West Glamorgan Archive Service.
Rhossili Parish Records, West Glamorgan Archive Service.
Tape recording and oral testimony of Mrs Annie Jenkins, West Glamorgan Archive Service.
Tithe Survey & Apportionment of Rhossili, 1845-47, West Glamorgan Archive Service.

Published Primary Sources

Birch, W. de Gray, *A descriptive catalogue of the Penrice and Margam Abbey Manuscripts in the possession of Miss Talbot of Margam: 1st-4th series* (London: privately printed, 1893-1903).

Secondary Sources

Davies, J.D., *Historical Notices of West Gower: Part III* (Swansea, 1885).
Davies, Margaret F., 'Rhossili open fields and related South Wales field patterns', *Agricultural History Review*, No. 4 (1956).
Davies, Wendy, *The Llandaff Charters* (Aberystwyth, 1979).
Emery, F.V., 'Edward Lhuyd and some of his Glamorgan Correspondents: a view of Gower in the 1690s', *Transactions of the Honourable Society of Cymmrodorion*, Part 1 (1965).
Emery, F.V., 'Open Fields in Gower', *Gower XXV* (1974).
Field, J., *English Field-names: a Dictionary* (Newton Abbot, 1972).
Lucas, Robert, *Rhossili: A Village Background* (Cowbridge, 1989).
Richards, Doreen, *An Agricultural and Social Study of Rhossili,* unpublished dissertation presented at University College of Wales, Aberystwyth, Department of Geography (1942).
Robinson, W.R.B., 'The First Subsidy Assessment of the Hundreds of Swansea and Llangyfelach', *Welsh History Review*, No. 2 (1964-65).
Royal Commission on the Ancient and Historical Monuments of Wales, *An Inventory of Ancient Monuments in Glamorgan: Vol. III – Medieval Secular Movements, Part II: Non-defensive; and Vol. IV, Part II – Farmhouses and Cottages* (London: HMSO, 1988).
Thomas, J. Mansell, *Yesterday's Gower* (Llandysul, 1982).
Tucker, H.M., *Gower Gleanings* (Swansea, 1951).